Advance Praise for
The Generic Closet

"With Alfred Martin's careful curation and astute analysis, *The Generic Closet* gives us a new way to critically view Black-cast situation comedies and how they police the boundaries of Black respectability and heteronormativity while protecting heteronormative Black masculinity. By dwelling on formal elements of television practices, industrial systems, and genre conventions in the production of black gay masculinities and using the rich analytic of the generic closet we see the limits of reaching for the mere visibility of Black gay men in Black-cast situation comedies. [. . .] The book's remarkable achievement is in detailing the industrial practices of containment and weighing the social impact that the cultural labors of the generic closet achieves in regulating Black gay men in Black-cast situation comedies."

—Herman Gray, author of *Watching Race: Television and the Struggle for Blackness*

"*The Generic Closet* brilliantly demonstrates that understanding the industry and cultural forces at play in Black-cast sitcoms and their treatment of Black gay men is essential for our understanding of US television and its role in the intersectional politics of race and sexual identity. Its analysis is refreshingly accessible while also reflecting the best approaches in fields of TV studies and LGBTQ studies."

—Ron Becker, author of *Gay TV and Straight America*

"*The Generic Closet* is an essential work of scholarship that provides perceptive insight into mediated identity and queer aesthetics. Professor Martin crafts a brilliant, lively narrative that takes up key themes at the intersections of identity formation and respectability politics, genre classifications and the economic imperatives of production, and anti-discrimination and the disruption of social control. His is a study that hits the most essential touchpoints facing our society today."

—Robin R. Means Coleman, author of *Horror Noire: Blacks in American Horror Films from the 1890s to Present*

"Martin demonstrates impressive mastery of a range of methods, from industry analysis, textual analysis, and audience analysis, providing a rich explanation of *why* and *how* Black gay visibility has been so limited. In expanding our historical focus to a group of texts less associated with 'quality' by virtue of both the racial makeup of the audience *and* genre and in its specific focus on Black gay representation, *The Generic Closet* is an essential and necessary contribution to television studies, but will also appeal to readers interested in the history of gay visibility, and the complicated relationship between race, sexuality, and media."

—Kathleen Battles, author of *Calling All Cars:
Radio Dragnets and the Technology of Policing*

"*The Generic Closet* is a necessary intervention not only for the Black scholar but for the Black culture in general. Dr. Martin has created a tour de force that gives gravitas to the Black sitcom and elevates Black gayness into visibility. Simply, thank you for this! Never before have Black gay characters been acknowledged in the sitcom genre—and it is past time."

—Ellen Cleghorne, *Saturday Night Live* cast member (1991–1996)

THE GENERIC CLOSET

Black Gayness and
the Black-Cast Sitcom

—ɰ—

ALFRED L. MARTIN, JR.

INDIANA UNIVERSITY PRESS

This book is a publication of

Indiana University Press
Office of Scholarly Publishing
Herman B Wells Library 350
1320 East 10th Street
Bloomington, Indiana 47405 USA

iupress.org

Manufactured in the United States of America

Cataloging information is available from the Library of Congress.

ISBN 978-0-253-05458-6 (hardback)
ISBN 978-0-253-05459-3 (paperback)
ISBN 978-0-253-05460-9 (ebook)

First printing 2021

This book is dedicated to the two most important men in my life:
Al Sr. (1943–2008) and my hubby, Tom.

CONTENTS

ACKNOWLEDGMENTS

WRITING THE ACKNOWLEDGEMENTS FOR THIS book is a bit like the final scene in *The Wiz* (1978, dir. Sidney Lumet), in which Diana Ross's Dorothy is singing "Home" as images of important people in her life and her journey through Oz flash by. Those who know me know that starting these acknowledgements with a reference to *The Wiz* is a fitting way to begin.

I have to start by thanking Mary C. Beltrán, who was my dissertation advisor at the University of Texas Austin. Although this project bears only a passing resemblance to the dissertation, Mary did not balk at my wanting to take on a topic that some folks thought was "too big" for a doctoral project. Mary's support started me on the road to what is now *The Generic Closet*, and for that, I remain incredibly grateful. I also thank the other folks who served on my dissertation committee: Jonathan Gray, Alisa Perren, Eric Pritchard, Janet Staiger, and Karin Wilkins.

So many people talked to me about this book and gave me the opportunity to "talk it out" while giving a research talk at their institutions. Gabriel Dor is truly the midwife for this book baby. Gabriel was kind and generous and provided an ear whenever I needed it. And more than that, Gabriel read drafts of chapters as I was revising and offered critical feedback that helped make the book better. Noah Tsika read a draft of the full manuscript and asked questions that made me really think through what the heck I was doing and why I was doing it. Racquel Gates (and her adorable family) helped me figure out the introduction while having a lovely brunch at her apartment in New York. Ben Aslinger invited me to deliver a presentation at Bentley University early in the process of writing this book, and that talk set the wheels in motion to rethink its overarching goals. Mia Fischer, my old University of Colorado Denver office neighbor, helped me think more sharply about the book and was the best starting-the-tenure-clock buddy I ever could have asked for. These wonderful humans have my eternal gratitude.

Equally critical to this process were folks who "simply" provided support through laughter and being a supportive ear. Kristen Warner, my academic "big sister," has been such a gift since I first met her in 2011, and I continue to be awed by her brilliance. Mike Rennett, Taylor Cole Miller, Nora Patterson, and Andy Owens (a.k.a. Nora and the Homosexuals, managed by our Svengali Mike) are grad school friends who have been the most amazing cheerleaders an academic could ask for. My cohort homie Keara Goin remains someone I can always talk to when I need to figure out an academic problem. Her clearheadedness came in handy as I was trying to see the forest through the trees while writing. The work of Kathy Battles, Jerry Butters, Herman Gray, Jonathan Gray, Bambi Haggins, Lisa Henderson, Robin Means Coleman, and Beretta Smith-Shomade has been integral to my scholarly and intellectual growth, and they are folks who I've felt have always had my best interests at heart and made me feel that my work mattered. I also thank my University of Iowa colleagues Joy Hayes and Kate Magsamen-Conrad for helping me to navigate finishing the book.

Several senior scholars championed my work early on and encouraged me that I was onto something. Janet Staiger was an early cheerleader whose questions stuck with me long after she asked them. (Janet, you were right—the *Moesha* episode is about gossip.) Jonathan Gray listened to me, a(n overly chatty) grad student, drone on about my "very important" work and yet still mentored me. Herman Gray was extraordinarily generous with his time and mentorship, even as I fanboyed to be in his presence. And Janice Frisch, formerly an acquisitions editor at Indiana University Press, believed in this project and its potential from the start. I am grateful for that vote of confidence.

My family has been an enormous source of support and inspiration. First and foremost, my love, my husband, Tom, was a master at both pushing me to finish when I needed it and backing off and taking me out for dinner or a movie or on a trip so I could decompress. Tom is a partner in every sense of the word and has been for more than twenty years. My sisters, Annette, Lejoan, Trena, and Yolanda, provided enormous emotional support. My dearly departed mother-in-law, Janice, supported me in ways any mother would and insisted that I always call her Mama. My best friends in the universe (and my surrogate family), the Potluck Crew, Erica Lott, Cory Lott, Ayanna McConnell, Rhea Norwood, and Roy Rogers; my Interlochen crew, Heather Dominey, Libby Harris, Janelle Hinkley, Stephanie Holloway, Kevin Hyatt, Jessica Peterson, and Julie

Smith; my Chicago homies, Camille DeBose, Joe Graham, Krystal Villanosa, and Drew Williams; and my former dancer besties, Pat Gold and Elizabeth Zuba—your support has really gotten me through writing this book, and your love means more to me than you will ever know. Dee Blackmon and Omari Gardner kept me in stitches with their unique brand of foolishness, proving that laughter really is the best medicine for a frazzled media scholar trying to finish a book. Angelica Lindsey-Ali, Kenneth Williams, and T. Tara Turk-Haynes gave me new music that provided the soundtrack as I wrote, and for that, I am eternally grateful. My aca-homies, Andre Cavalcante, Scott Poulson Bryant, Matt Sienkiewicz, and Anjali Vats, offered support—through laughter and otherwise—as I worked through drafting this book. A special thanks to Pat Gold, who provided her talents as a retired high school English teacher to make sure my grammar was as good as it should be. Last, but certainly not least, my dearly departed father showed me what it meant to be a person who loves fiercely, takes no prisoners, and cusses like a sailor. I miss him every day and am grateful for all the love he showed me and showered on me.

This book—for *real* real—could not have happened without the interviews I conducted in chapters 2 and 4. The Writers Guild West's Tery Lopez was integral in helping me make contact with several of the writers I interviewed in chapter 2. Some of those writers also helped me reach other writers and showrunners, and I thank them for their generosity and candidness in speaking with me. I especially thank Demetrius Bady, who not only reached out to several writers and showrunners on my behalf but who has also become a friend through this process. I thank each of the twenty Black gay men who provided the interviews for chapter 4 for generously engaging with the series in this book and talking to me so I could write a chapter on media reception.

I am indebted to Ron Becker, Steven Capsuto, and Stephen Tropiano. Their willingness to provide me with copies of television series that I would have been unable to view otherwise helped me make this project stronger, both in my analysis and my methodology.

I also thank several of my dance teachers who instilled in me not only a love of the art of dance but the art of discipline. Without that discipline, I do not think I would have ever finished this book. Leslie and her late husband Gerald O'Day showed me, at a young age, that anything was possible and that I could rise to any occasion if I put my mind to it. I have come a long way from O'Day School of Dance in Detroit, but I take your lessons with me always. Andrea Haynes Johnson (Mama J) taught me to always follow my dreams and that if you shoot for the moon and miss, at least you will hit the stars. Sharon Kay Randolph instilled in me a drive to work as hard and as precisely as I can because life is not a dress rehearsal. Both Mama J and Sharon were proponents of leaving it all out on the dance floor. Sharee Lane taught me that all the flourishes in the world could not hide bad technique—a skill that has served me well as I have worked through writing *The Generic Closet*.

I am indebted to Lisa Keränen, chair of the Department of Communication at the University of Colorado Denver, for her support of my work and this book while I was starting my academic career there. Last but not least, I thank my current chairs of Communication Studies, Tim Havens, and African American Studies, Venise Berry, for their support. In particular, Tim has been one of my loudest cheerleaders since we met at the International Communication Association annual conference in Phoenix in 2012 and I rambled on about my work.

I am not sure *The Generic Closet* would be what it is without the folks named above. But there are likely people I have forgotten to mention, and for that, I apologize. But do know that it is only a reflection of my faulty brain, not a reflection of your importance to me and this book.

THE GENERIC CLOSET

INTRODUCTION

Television in Black and Gay

ON NOVEMBER 5, 2008, NEWSPAPERS, websites, and blogs reported the historic election of Barack Obama as the first Black president of the United States. On November 4, Californians also went to the ballot box to decide on Proposition 8, a ballot measure that would define marriage as a relationship between one man and one woman. The proposition was approved, nullifying the right to marriage that California's lesbian and gay couples had been granted in a California Supreme Court decision in May 2008. The *Washington Post* reported that 70 percent of Black California voters supported the ban on same-sex marriage, and 94 percent of these same voters supported Obama's candidacy.[1] The discourse engendered by these polling data was summed up by Jesse M. Unruh of the Institute of Politics at the University of Southern California: "You can make the argument that Barack Obama passed Proposition 8. . . . Had turnout among African-American voters been along more traditional lines, Proposition 8 probably would have failed."[2] In other words, the mantra went something like, "Black folks showed up to support Obama but did not support gay rights—homophobes!" When think tanks and investigative reporters really crunched the numbers, they found that some of these conclusions were overblown. As Ta-Nehisi Coates detailed, for example, 58 percent of California's Black voters—not 70 percent—supported Proposition 8, a figure comparable to the 59 percent of Latinx California voters who also supported passage of the proposition.[3] This is not to suggest that support for the proposition's passage was not high among California's Black voters or that Latinx voters should have shared the "blame" for its passage. Rather, it suggests that mythologies about Blackness get taken up and reported, and those fallacies are taken as factual.

At the same time, the efficacy of the quick conclusions around Proposition 8 were useful because they fell into a familiar trope: "Black folks," as a monolithic group, were unquestionably and quantitatively antigay.

It may seem odd that a book on Black-cast sitcoms and Black gayness begins by discussing the 2008 US presidential election, but that event is useful to illuminate and unpack the central concerns of this book. First, and perhaps most important, this lens shows that Black people are not necessarily more antigay than white people but rather that they are imagined as such. And the linkages between Blackness and antigayness are activated across a number of political, social, cultural, and entertainment discourses. Todd Gitlin's theorizations about audiences are apt here. He suggests that network executives are really just educated guessers

> trying to read popular sentiment and tailoring their schedules toward what they think the cardboard people they've conjured up want to see and hear.... These sentiments themselves are already heavily shaped . . . by the immense weight of mass culture's formulas as they have accumulated over the years.... The trick is not only to read the restless public mood, but somehow to anticipate it and figure out how to encapsulate it in a show. No one comes to such arcane work innocent of ideas about what the market will bear, ideas that circulate constantly through the standardized channels of executive culture. The executive "instinct," much praised in the industry, is a schooled instinct, formed in experience and concentrated by that common culture.[4]

Gitlin brings into focus how an event as seemingly dissociated from the world of entertainment television as the passage of Proposition 8 in California feeds and bleeds into imaginations about who Black viewers are and what kind of content they will consume. In other words, if the epistemology of Blackness equals antigayness, then network executives feel content greenlighting programming that would conform to such "knowledge."

The audience for Black-cast sitcoms is often constructed and imagined as "traditional" Black families—father, mother, and children. Most Black-cast sitcoms discussed in this book aired during the "family viewing hour." Established by the Federal Communications Commission (FCC) in the 1970s as a way to police (vaguely defined) decency and decorum in television content, the family viewing hour suggested that children and families might be watching television between 8:00 p.m. and 9:00 p.m. Eastern time (ET) and that content should reflect "family values." *Moesha* (UPN, 1996–2001) debuted on Tuesdays at 8:00 p.m. ET, at the start of the family viewing hour. Although the series briefly moved to 8:30 p.m. and then to Monday nights, it remained within the family hour for the entirety of its run, thus *Moesha* was imagined as a "family" series. *All of Us* (UPN, 2003–2006; CW, 2006–2007), like *Moesha*, aired at 8:00 p.m. ET and then moved to 8:30 p.m. for the season after its premiere before moving from Sundays to Mondays, but it remained at 8:30 p.m. ET. Although *Good News* (UPN, 1997–1998) aired at 9:00 p.m. ET, it was sandwiched between broad-based series like *Malcolm & Eddie* (UPN, 1996–2000) and its parent series *Sparks* (UPN, 1996–1998); thus, I argue, *Good News* continued to be imagined as a family series, particularly because of its depiction of Black family and religiosity. Because of the nature of syndication, *Are We There Yet?* (TBS, 2010–2013) did not air at a specific time, but given its urtextual history as a family-friendly film and its need to be as inoffensive as possible for syndicators, it also clearly fits this imagined family audience. Televisual flow, thus, imagines the Black viewer as a "family viewer" alongside an imagined Black antigay viewer.

The outlier is *Let's Stay Together* (BET, 2011–2014). The series aired outside of the family viewing hour (it premiered at 11:00 p.m. ET), which suggests the inclusion of racier content. On the one hand, *Let's Stay Together* created a story arc for Black gay character Darkanian that spanned far more episodes than any similar story lines in the other series discussed within *The Generic Closet*; perhaps this suggests the imagination of a different audience segment than the traditional family. On the other hand, as a late-night series, it remains bound by the narrative constraints of the Black-cast sitcom, unlike a Black-cast primetime soaps such as *The Haves and the Have Nots* (OWN, 2013–present), *Being Mary Jane* (BET, 2013–2019), and *Empire* (Fox, 2015–2020), which are mostly targeted at Black women.

Conversely, white viewers are segmented and can, and often do, have content created for their specific niche tastes. Networks typically court the segment of white viewers Ron Becker terms "socially liberal, upwardly mobile professional" viewers—the SLUMPY demographic.[5] This group is imagined to be far more tolerant of LGBT people and thus "worthy" of and receptive to LGBT programming, such as *Will & Grace* (NBC, 1998–2006; 2017–present), *Tales of the City* (PBS, 1994; Showtime, 1998, 2001; Netflix, 2019), *Modern Family* (ABC, 2009–2020), and *Sex Education* (Netflix, 2019–present). As the discursive understanding of Proposition 8 makes clear, Black folks are rarely imagined in such ways because Blackness is understood as monolithic.

The Black-cast sitcom is similarly bound to such discursive imaginings of Blackness and Black audiences. Black gayness's movement within the Black-cast sitcom is a specific industrial construct rooted in an "understanding" of Black folks' intolerance of homosexuality, often thought to derive from their (again, monolithically construed) religiosity. Thus, the Black-cast sitcom functions unlike any other contemporary genre with respect to Black gayness. As this book's title suggests, the Black-cast sitcom erects a "generic closet" around Black gayness. The generic closet, as I have argued elsewhere, "refers to the ways the Black-cast sitcom functions as an industrial representation of an imagined, monolithic Black audience, and, as such, contains Black gayness into specific coming-out episodes/story arcs before discarding these characters for other 'mainstream' stories."[6] I will return to a deeper theoretical discussion of the generic closet later. For now, I want to reiterate that the generic closet is an industrial construction of imagined Black audiences and their relationship to Black gayness.

The generic closet is found within channels', platforms', and networks' engagement with Blackness. It shapes practices in writers' rooms, spurs deployment of the laugh track, and can be observed within the reception practices of Black gay men. *The Generic Closet* is concerned with the discursive circulation of Black gay maleness within the Black-cast sitcom and the knowledge Black gay bodies are called on to produce within it. Foucault asserts that "power produces knowledge . . . that power and knowledge directly imply one another, that there is no power relation without the correlative constitution of a field of knowledge, nor any knowledge that does not presuppose and constitute at the same time power relations."[7] In *The Generic Closet*, I seek to understand the systems of power that produce ideologies about Black gayness and the relationship of knowledge production to Black gay audience reception, production, comedy, and Black masculinity.

With these cultural, social, and industrial issues in mind, *The Generic Closet* undertakes a *circuit of media study* approach to examine the various sites where Blackness, broadly—and Black gayness, specifically—are produced. Julie D'Acci notes, "Some analyses [tend to] overlook the conditions and specific shaping forces of production; the conditions and intricacies of reception; and . . . the specificities of the televisual form (from narrative structure to genre to the operations of televisual techniques)," which results in analyses that do not fully consider the multiple spaces where meaning can be made.[8] In *The Generic Closet*, I attempt to heed D'Acci's warning by examining aspects of sociocultural and industrial contexts, production, postproduction, and audience reception. In particular, I study the production of episodes of Black-cast sitcoms with Black gay characters to more fully understand the ways Black gayness is created and "lives" in Black-cast sitcom worlds. In so doing, I build on John T. Caldwell's approach by incorporating interviews with industry personnel to centralize Blackness (both the Blackness of industrial workers and the

Blackness of their subjects and imagined audiences).[9] In addition, *The Generic Closet* builds on Roderick A. Ferguson's suggestion that a *queer of color* analysis investigates "how intersecting racial, gender, and sexual practices antagonize or conspire with the normative investments of nation-states and capital."[10] The book is dually concerned with how the intersections of Blackness, maleness, and homosexuality function within the confines of hegemonic culture and how those intersections are deployed within a capitalist media culture. In particular, this book investigates the history of how Black-cast sitcoms make and circumscribe spaces for Black gayness within the genre's normative ranks.

I want to take a moment to step back to assert the importance of this area of study. When laypeople and scholars talk about gayness on television, they tend to mean white gayness. This flattening of gayness is constitutive, for as Melanie E. S. Kohnen argues, "queer visibility in the mainstream media depends on discourses of whiteness."[11] When gayness is conflated with whiteness, the discussion loses the specificity inherent in the different trajectories of Black gayness and white gayness within television discourse. That Black and white gayness in Black-cast and white- and multicultural-cast sitcoms have developed differently should come as no surprise. However, when media scholars turn their attention to gayness on television, they often exonminate whiteness.[12]

Suzanna Danuta Walters claims, for example, "In this era of liberal gay visibility, contemporary culture has other motifs to choose from, and the coming-out story no longer represents both the beginning and the end of how gay identity is imagined in popular media."[13] Walters's assertion appears to be valid for white-cast sitcoms when they feature Black gay characters. White- and multicultural-cast sitcoms tend to subscribe to post-racial and post-gay ideologies. These ideologies suggest that both race and gayness no longer matter as axes of difference and that we are all simply human. These presumptions manifest in the rare instance that Black gay characters appear in white- and multicultural-cast sitcoms, by engaging in little, if any, discussion of their Blackness and focusing primarily on their gayness. Examples include *Spin City* (ABC, 1996–2002), *Brooklyn Nine Nine* (Fox, 2013–2018; NBC, 2019–present), and *Sirens* (USA, 2014–2015), which fit within the *respectable gay* model. The respectable gay model follows Amber B. Raley and Jennifer L. Lucas's theorization that respectable LGBT characters would be seen in "diverse roles that go beyond the socially acceptable stereotypes" and are seen "interact[ing] with children and hav[ing] romantic relationships."[14] Conversely, the *sissy regular* model can be observed in series like *Don't Trust the B**** in Apartment 23* (ABC, 2012–2013). This model, according to Stephen Tropiano, is represented by a sitcom with a costarring or series regular male character that embodies stereotypically feminine behaviors.[15] As I demonstrate throughout this book, whereas gay men in white- and multicultural-cast sitcoms have become post-gay (implicitly gesturing toward a post-coming-out state of being), that presentation has not been extended to Black gay men in Black-cast sitcoms, who are not even granted regular or recurring status within the Black-cast sitcom.

When examining the representational landscape of Black gay characters in Black-cast sitcoms, a very different history appears. Only twenty-five episodes of Black-cast sitcoms have aired since 1977's *Sanford Arms* (NBC, 1977) that included such characters (see app. A). Although Black gay characters have appeared in a plethora of series and broadcast eras, they have remained narratively and industrially trapped in what I call the *pedagogical gay* model. These Black gay characters are called on to educate the (presumably Black) audience about homosexuality while reifying the boundaries of hegemonic Black masculinity. The short-lived *Sanford Arms*, a spinoff of *Sanford and Son* (NBC, 1972–1977), featured a pedagogical Black gay character, Travis. He drew on a broader move to decouple femininity as a stereotypical marker of gayness for one-off characters in television—a strategy seen in other "relevance" programming of the 1970s. Travis was a civil rights attorney fighting for the rights of gay communities and, by all outward appearances, looked "normal"—or in other words, his gayness could not be read onto his body via costume or a "swish act." Travis was pedagogical in that he challenged viewers to think differently about what a Black gay man could be within the context of a Black-cast sitcom.

Because Black audiences are imagined as less liberal or more antigay than SLUMPY audiences, the television industry appears to suggest that Black-cast sitcom audiences are not ready for a recurring Black gay character. This industry lore about the Black viewer shapes "what gets produced as well as how, where, and when productions get watched."[16] In an effort to parse the industry lore around Black-cast sitcoms, I not only examine what and how Black gayness is produced but also explore how Black gay men—the very bodies these Black-cast sitcoms claim to episodically represent—watch and make meaning from these representations.

THE PRIMACY OF THE BLACK-CAST SITCOM

Throughout this book (and in its subtitle), I employ the term *Black-cast sitcom*. Because of the difficulty in pinning down some defining criteria with respect to Black-cast sitcoms, I want to discuss what I mean when I use the term. This book is about Black-cast sitcoms, not Black-cast comedies. I distinguish the Black-cast sitcom from the Black-cast comedy by its use of a laugh track—whether that laugh track is "real" or created in postproduction. Thus, *Insecure* (HBO, 2016–present), which has a recurring Black gay male character, is not considered within this book because it does not employ a laugh track.

When asked, some of the Black gay men I interviewed for *The Generic Closet* understood the Black-cast sitcom in three broad ways: (1) the primary racial background of the cast, (2) the racial background of the majority of the actual (versus imagined) audience, and (3) the show's interest in engaging issues related to Black American experiences. Charles, who will be introduced in greater detail in chapter 4, where I center Black gay men's reception practices, articulated these three main criteria. He said that a Black-cast sitcom is one that has "members of the cast who identify, or the audience identifies, as being Black or African American . . . [and] speaks about issues specific to the Black community."[17] Charles begins with a discussion of the cast composition, revealing that the visual recognition of the cast as Black folks signals a Black-cast sitcom to him. He went on to discuss the idea that the audience is African American. In this sense, Charles signals the importance of reception practices. To Charles, a series like *The Cosby Show* (NBC, 1984–1992) is less of a Black-cast sitcom because although it had a primarily Black cast, it did not have a primarily Black audience. In fact, Janet Staiger argues that *The Cosby Show*'s comedic style "paralleled its white middle-class ambiance."[18] Such ambivalence ultimately meant that a series like *The Cosby Show*, unlike *Moesha*, *Good News*, *All of Us*, *Are We There Yet?*, and *Let's Stay Together*, did not mediate Black communities' specific issues.

In *The Generic Closet*, I use a definition similar to Robin R. Means Coleman's and Charlton D. McIlwain's: "Black situation comedy describes programming that employs a core cast of African American characters and focuses on those characters' sociocultural, political and economic experiences."[19] Instead of deploying "black situation comedy," as Coleman and McIlwain do, I use the term *Black-cast sitcom* to denote my focus on the racial makeup of the primary cast. In addition, I follow the tradition of scholars who call musicals with Black casts not *Black musicals* but *Black-cast musicals* to focus on the racial makeup of the cast and not necessarily the race of those involved in production.[20] At the same time, when examining the Black-cast sitcom, I want to heed Tricia Rose's call to "foreground . . . the historical context for the creation, dissemination, and reception of Black popular forms."[21] Thus, in *The Generic Closet*, I am not only principally concerned with the Black-cast sitcom as image production but also interested in exploring the histories of networks, startup networks (netlets), channels, and series; the negotiations within the writers' rooms; the production of the laugh track; and audience reception practices.

Kristal Brent Zook details the unprecedented ways Black writers and producers were utilized in the creation of Black-cast television series in the 1990s, such as *In Living Color* (Fox, 1990–1994) and *Living Single* (Fox, 1993–1998).[22] Zook explains that Black writers and producers often exercised a significant degree of agency with respect to the series and scripts they created. However, as actor, writer, and producer Tim Reid noted, there is "always somebody else you've got to answer to in network television.... There's this guy and this guy's boss. Then that division and that division's boss. Then the network."[23] As Reid underscores, the television production buck does not stop at the level of series production. And the higher one climbs from the series level, the less likely it becomes that an executive greenlighting a series will be Black. In this way, many Black-cast sitcoms that make it to air represent an idea of the Black image and a commodification of Blackness, a standpoint that undergirds this book. Put more eloquently by James Baldwin, "This country's image of the Negro, which hasn't very much to do with the Negro, has never failed to reflect with a frightening accuracy the state of mind of the country."[24] What I point to here is that the Black-cast sitcom is undergirded by the ideologies of the largely white television industry from which the Black-cast sitcom is granted existence on the airwaves. This white hegemonic (mis)understanding of Blackness often results in Black-cast sitcom humor that is "based on race and is a parody of Blackness."[25]

When Black gay bodies are used in the Black-cast sitcom form, they are filtered through existing (il)logics of white media industry executives. Given the imagined inextricable linkage of antigay sentiment among Black cultures and the monolithic industrial imagining of Blackness, these antigay ideologies come to represent Black people and thus come to function as a kind of Black public sphere. Catherine Squires posits that a Black public sphere consists of "mediated spaces where people can gather and share information . . . [in an attempt to convey] that dominant publics should reject pejorative definitions of a marginal group's identity, cultural practices, rights, and privileges."[26] To be sure, the Black-cast sitcom is often greenlit by and filtered through white network executives' minds. However, because of the bodies on screen and often because of the racial makeup of its writing and production staff, the form is imagined as a Black public sphere that can be taken to task for the ways it mediates Black bodies. The Black-cast sitcom not only rejects "pejorative definitions" of Blackness but also is imagined as a discursive housing for Black ideologies about race, gender, class, sexuality, and cultural politics.

The primacy of the Black-cast sitcom is rooted in the intersectional linkages of ethnicity, sexuality, and humor. In defining "representational intersectionality," Kimberlee Crenshaw details the interconnected ways "images are produced through a confluence of prevalent narratives of race and gender, as well as a recognition of how contemporary critiques of racist and sexist representation marginalize women of color."[27] In adopting a Black feminist stance, Crenshaw acknowledges that she is particularly interested in Black women. *The Generic Closet* adopts representational intersectionality to examine how the intersections of race, gender, and sexuality—namely, Blackness, maleness, and gayness—interlink to marginalize Black gay men in the Black-cast sitcom.

The sitcom broadly—and the Black-cast sitcom, specifically—seeks to find humor in situations that often include marking one character as "comic." Understanding the theories of humor, explored in chapter 3, helps to explain how, why, and when the comic is marked within a Black-cast sitcom. I propose that the Black-cast sitcom uses humor as a means to reify "the status quo either by denigrating a certain sector of society . . . or by laughing at the alleged stupidity of a social outsider"—in this case, the Black gay man.[28] Even as the Black-cast sitcom hails Black gayness in an episodic fashion, the genre can use humor not only to position Black gayness as an outsider but also to reify its deviation from Black normativity. The centrality of this kind of humor is particularly important and illuminating when discussing the inclusion of new characters, especially Black gay characters, into the Black-cast sitcom structure.

STEREOTYPING, CONTROLLING IMAGES, AND THE BLACK GAY IMAGE

As much as I loathe scholarly discussions of stereotype, particularly the positive/negative binary, I would be remiss if I did not engage with them briefly. In particular, I argue that the mediation of Black gayness is tied to the specific boundaries of Black masculinity and its own mediation. Stuart Hall theorizes the primacy of the stereotype as fixing, essentializing, reducing, and naturalizing differences.[29] In the process, the stereotype engenders a binary system for drawing boundaries around what is inside and what is outside.

Ronald L. Jackson and Celnisha L. Dangerfield assert that Black men's bodies are stereotyped in one of three ways: as "(1) violent, (2) sexual, and (3) incompetent."[30] Such stereotyping of heterosexual Black men was activated to demonstrate their difference from their white heterosexual male counterparts. Historically, these scripts have become a permanent fixture in the representational landscape and have helped determine Black masculinity's coherence and legibility. The virile and violent Black man initially appeared as a necessity for white Americans in the late eighteenth and early nineteenth centuries to justify slavery. The presumption was that if Black men were made free, they would rape white women (and, perhaps more horrifically in these minds, produce mixed-race children). Kobena Mercer asserts that a history of oppression rooted in colonialism and slavery has led Black men to adopt "certain patriarchal values such as physical strength, sexual prowess and being in control as a means of survival against the repressive and violent system of subordination to which they have been subjected."[31] In 1970s Blaxploitation films and in contemporary rap music, Black heterosexual men attempted to reclaim imagery of Black men as virile and violent by refashioning those terms as a source of pride among Black heterosexual people generally and Black heterosexual men specifically.

In the process of this reclamation, this "new" Black masculinity was also rearticulated through its binary opposite. Steve Estes argues that because manhood was systematically denied to Black men by white men, Black men had to find an abject object to stereotype in order to refute their own stereotyping.[32] Achieving political power and social status for Black men involved adhering to particular scripts for Black masculinity—and these scripts did not include masculinities that deviated from heterosexuality. Predictably, the oppositional boogeyman was the Black gay man. Marlon Riggs asserts,

> What lies at the heart . . . of black America's pervasive cultural homophobia is the desperate need for a convenient Other *within* the community, yet not truly *of* the community, an Other onto which blame for the chronic identity crises afflicting the black male psyche can be readily displaced, an indispensable Other that functions as the lowest common denominator of the abject, the base line of transgression beyond which a black man is no longer a man, no longer black, an essential Other against which black men and boys maturing, struggling with self-doubt, anxiety, feelings of political, economic, social, and sexual inadequacy—even impotence—can always measure themselves and by comparison seem strong, adept, empowered, superior.[33]

Heterosexual Black masculinity is preserved because to not conform is to be constructed as "gay." The ultramasculine performances of Black masculinity "claim visibility for their hardness only at the expense of the vulnerability of black women and the feminization of gay black men."[34] By staking claim to heterosexual sexual prowess and making femininity abject in both women and gay men, the very notion of a Black masculinity is reified. E. Patrick Johnson asserts that "much of the rhetoric of Black Nationalism disavows the black homosexual as antiblack in order to maintain the fiction of a coherent black male hetero-sexuality and to assuage the specter of the homosexual Other within."[35] The performance of a hegemonically approved Black masculinity works within a psychoanalytic framework wherein desire and fear exist in tension with one another. Although these prescriptions of "failed" Black masculinity certainly can function discursively within white gayness, Black gayness is understood as both failed masculinity *and* failed Blackness, making the Black gay man neither "manly" enough nor "Black" enough.

Words like *fag(got)*, *punk*, *soft*, and *fruity* are associated with homosexual-ity, whereas *strength* and *sexual prowess* become generally conflated with het-erosexual masculinity, specifically heterosexual Black masculinity. The terms associated with homosexuality serve as the hegemonic force to shore up the imaginary and porous boundaries of Black masculinity.

To understand the Black gay image means that Black masculinity must also be understood as a monolithic conceptualization. The imagination of all Black heterosexual masculinities as antigay dances just at the edges of *The Generic Closet*. Black gayness within the Black-cast sitcom occupies a subject position as the abject other that works to discipline Black heterosexual masculinity. Thus, Black gayness works as a controlling image that, as Jasmine Cobb and Robin R. Means Coleman theorize, functions "as justifications for various op-pressions by distorting reality through reducing the stereotyped subject to a controlled object."[36] In *The Generic Closet*, I extend Coleman and Cobb's controlling images to suggest that Black masculinity, and the protection of its porous boundaries, is part of the function of controlling images of Black gay-ness and its mediation within the Black-cast sitcom.

STUDYING BLACK GAYNESS ON TV

The Generic Closet is a book about Black gayness. I deliberately use the phraseol-ogy *Black gay* versus *gay Black* throughout this book. This move is feminist in its marrying of the political and the personal. It is political in its attempt to center Blackness as a major axis of identity for Black gay men in Black-cast sitcoms. I understand the scholarly tension between Black gay and gay Black identities. Gregory Conerly elucidates that this hierarchy of identities is a "central conflict many African American lesbians, bisexuals and gays experience in dealing with two identities that are often at odds with each other."[37] The difference between these two identities, according to Darieck Scott, is that gay Black men have "political, social and cultural allegiances . . . to 'white' gay politics, to 'white' gay men and to 'white' cultural forms," whereas a Black gay man's identity is rooted in Blackness, including Black culture, Black politics, and presumably a romantic preference for other Black gay men.[38] This debate between Black gay and gay Black is reductive in "real life." However, for the purposes of *The Generic Closet*, I deploy the term *Black gay*.

Using *Black gay* is personal in my own belief that I could presumably conceal my gayness (how well I am able to do that is debatable). For example, in any situation into which I walk, my Blackness and maleness are the clues someone encountering me for the first time uses to read my body. My gayness might not be detectable until I speak or stand a certain way or perform a certain act. Therefore, within this book, I lead with the Blackness of the characters and real-life men I study. In so doing, I stake Black gay men's (and my own) position as an integral component of intersectional Blackness.

The Generic Closet contributes to the little existing research that specifically addresses Black gay televisual representation. Other studies have focused on a single representation of Black gay men within a single media text, whereas this project puts these representations in conversation with one another. The inquiries into images of Black gay men in television are often sections within book chapters: Walters briefly discusses *Spin City* in *All the Rage*, as does Steven Capsuto in *Alternative Channels*.[39] In addition, Herman Gray devotes a section of a chapter in *Watching Race* to *In Living Color*, and E. Patrick Johnson does the same in *Appropriating Blackness*.[40] And Samuel Chambers analyzes *Six Feet Under* (HBO, 2001–2005).[41] All of these authors use textual analysis as their primary methodology. While each author gestures toward sociocultural contexts, each is primarily interested in the image rather than production and audience reception.

Even when scholars turn to lengthier examinations of Black gayness, they typically retain a focus on examining the image alone. Guy Mark Foster explicitly discusses matters of race and how they can become conflated with desire in his examination of *Six Feet Under*.[42] Johnson (re)turns to *In Living Color* and Eddie Murphy to examine "negro faggotry."[43] Gust A. Yep and John P. Elia examine notions of "authentic blackness" on *Noah's Arc* (Logo, 2005–2006).[44] These authors are largely bringing specific theoretical approaches to bear on texts without examining other forces that shape the ways Black gay images are created, distributed, understood, and consumed—an undertaking attempted in *The Generic Closet*.

CLOSETS, GENERIC AND OTHERWISE

This project hinges on a theorization of the "generic closet." To do that work, it is necessary to work backward, beginning with the concept of "the closet."

The closet is principally related to queer knowledge production in a hetero-normative culture. Foucault contends that in the eighteenth and nineteenth centuries, "the sexuality of those who did not like the opposite sex" came under scrutiny and marked a time when "these figures, scarcely noticed in the past" were called on to "step forward and speak [and] make the difficult confession of who they were."[45] Foucault's mention of "stepping forward" became the root of the theoretical understanding of the closet as an organizing principle for gay men and lesbians. But Eve Sedgwick locates the predominance of "the closet" within a public/private binarism that emerged and was made possible by "the post-Stonewall gay politics oriented around coming *out* of the closet."[46] Such a configuration presupposes that being "in" the closet is cloaked within darkness, seclusion and, often, deceit. Conversely, coming out of the closet represents—and within a post-Stonewall gay politic, represented—liberation from the confines of secrecy and darkness, and such liberation is typically achieved via a speech act. Being "out of" or "in" the closet is determined by speech acts—either the utterance of "I'm gay" (or some such declaration) or what Sedgwick calls "the speech act of silence," which separate the out from the in.[47] More importantly, the closet is understood as an important organizing logic for the lives of gay folk. Jeffrey McCune summarizes that "the closet has become a universal apparatus that describes an oppressive space where indi-viduals dwell" and where "the given solution for finding freedom" is "within the process of 'coming out.'"[48]

The "freedom" associated with coming out is not just applicable within the lives of "real" people. It shapes and is shaped by television's engagement with gayness. The speech act of saying "I'm gay" is generative in a way that Sedg-wick's speech act of silence is not. "I'm gay" engenders drama and knowledge production that can be deployed within a series. Lynne Joyrich stresses that the closet has become "an implicit TV form—a logic governing not only the ways in which gays and lesbians are represented but also the generation of narratives and positions on and for TV."[49] Furthermore, as Walters argues, "Because 'coming out' does present a before and after, it presents a problem for those coming out, for their friends, for their family, for the plot itself."[50] Thus, as Joyrich and Walters forward, coming out not only is useful as a televisual means of knowledge production but also generates drama—whether in series categorized generically as dramas or sitcoms. The overarching import of the closet (and, more importantly, coming out of it) remains a useful industrial framework through which gay representation can be examined.

However, the closet, as many scholars of color have observed, is a decidedly white concept. Marlon B. Ross forcefully asserts that such a white configuration of the closet "rests on the banishment of the problem of racial-class difference, which would unravel [the] fantasy of a homosexual identity consolidated into a total community solely through its subject's *identical* experiences of coming out."[51] In attempting to universalize the closet and its import, as Ross points out, the particularities of deviations from the ways whiteness is believed to navigate the closet become illegible. However, Dorie Gilbert Martinez and Stonie C. Sullivan suggest that "race, African American culture, a continuum of gay cultures, gender, and individual characteristics distinguish the gay identity experience of African American gays from that proposed by existing gay identity models, particularly related to the integration of one's gay identity and the coming out process."[52] Mirroring Martinez and Sullivan, William G. Hawkeswood found in his 156 interviews with Black gay men in Harlem that "coming out was not a major concern, because their homosexuality, and later their gay identity, had always been assumed by family and friends. There was no need to 'come out.' Folks in their social networks had gradually taken for granted their sexual orientation."[53] Sedgewick states that "for many gay people [the closet] is still the fundamental feature of social life; and there can be few gay people, however courageous and forthright by habit, however fortunate in the support of their immediate communities, in whose lives the closet is not still a shaping presence"; however, Martinez, Sullivan, and Hawkeswood suggest that the significance of the closet for white gay men is not always as important for Black gay men.[54] The differences in the universal import of the closet (or more aptly, coming out of the closet) across race are important when set alongside television's engagement with gayness. In *The Generic Closet*, I argue that these differences become particularly pronounced when discussing the Black-cast sitcom.

The *generic* in the term *generic closet* is rooted in the word *genre*. Genre is an organizational system based on similarities, not unlike the *Sesame Street* song "One of These Things Is Not Like the Other." Foucault suggests that schematic categorizations are culturally constructed and arbitrary while, importantly, allowing for a communal reading of resemblances.[55] These shared readings of similarities help to shape expectations.

When discussing genre and television, Jason Mittell advises that genre is not located solely within the text but "within the complex interrelations between texts, industries, audiences and historical contexts. Genres transect the boundaries between text and context, with production, distribution, promotion, exhibition, criticism, and reception practices all working to categorize media texts into genres."[56] For Mittell, and for my purposes within this book, the generic is a discursive formation that threads through texts generally but the Black-cast

sitcom specifically. It is visible in its functions as an industrial repository for ideologies related to an imagined monolithic Black audience.
This ideological repository is conjured by network executives and discursively reverberates throughout the various stages of and workers
within production, including showrunners and writers, who are principally concerned with keeping their series on air and the ratings stable.
It is also located within industrial practices that structure the style in
which series are filmed. For example, Black-cast sitcoms are shot with a
three-camera setup on a soundstage with an in-studio audience or a laugh
track. This industrial practice, as I will discuss in chapter 1, is rooted
in cost savings.

The generic is evident in Black-cast sitcoms' placement on particular
networks, streaming platforms, netlets, and stations over others. For example, within the late 1990s, it is no coincidence that the lion's share of
Black-cast sitcoms were broadcast on UPN or that historically new networks and channels turn to Blackness when they are entering the television landscape. It is observed in Black-cast sitcoms' pairing with particular programs on particular evenings at particular times (what Raymond
Williams theorized as "flow," or "planned flow").[57] As I discuss in greater
detail in chapter 1, CBS did not pick up *Moesha* because it could not find
a show to pair it with. And the generic dictates the ways Black audiences
are imagined and how advertising promoting Black-cast sitcoms is developed. I argue throughout this book that understanding these industrial
machinations—technically "outside" a particular Black-cast sitcom or a
corpus of Black-cast sitcoms—is central to understanding genre and, thus,
the *generic* of the *generic closet*.

The generic closet is thus concerned first and foremost with the industrial
imagination of Black audiences; I argue that this perspective structures Black
gay narrative development within the Black-cast sitcom. It functions within
what I am calling, building on an extending Lynne Joyrich's work, the "three
Ds": (1) detection, (2) discovery/declaration, and (3) discarding. Joyrich theorizes her classificatory system as an epistemology of television's engagement
with white gayness. I extend her useful scheme to both nuance it and make
it specific to Black gayness but also to reflect the industrial focus of how the
generic closet functions within the Black-cast sitcom. Joyrich suggests that
detection offers up "hints of sexuality" that function as "clues to be traced."[58]
These clues compose the first act of the three-act structure of the Black-cast
sitcom's "gay episode." Detection becomes what Linda Seger calls the act 1
"set-up," in which the main goal "is to tell us all the vital information we need

to get the story started."[59] Within the detection act, the central question of a character's (homo)sexuality is raised. Act 1 raises those questions not directly but by presenting something as slightly "off" with a character within the gay episode. This "offness" can range from a character being too polite or perfect (*Moesha, Good News, All of Us* and *Let's Stay Together*) or wearing colors out of step with approved scripts of Black masculine sartorial choices (*Are We There Yet?*). These characters are somehow out of sync with Black-cast sitcoms' mediation of Black masculinity, which lays the foundation for the detective work the Black-cast sitcom must do to ferret out Black gayness.

The detective work is important because it leads to the second act of the three Ds: discovery/declaration. Seger suggests that within the second act of a "good script," six things happen, three of which are useful to my theorization of the discovery/detection phase. First, the narrative action turns to a new direction. Second, central questions are raised anew. Third, a character has a moment of decision or makes a commitment to something.[60] If the central question in act 1 is "Is he gay?" then act 2 rephrases and reframes the question as, "Are you gay?" The shift in the subject and verb in the central question moves it from speculative to inquisitive. As such, within the discovery/declaration phase, the questions the cast has raised about a Black gay character's sexuality are affirmatively answered, typically in a speech act (also known as the declaration), because it has been asked directly of the character.

Discovery also reveals that, as C. Riley Snorton notes, "in the context of blackness, the closet is not a space of concealment, but a site for observation and display."[61] Put another way, the relationship of Black gayness to the closet is about external knowledge production. The discovery of gayness is made possible because Black gayness was never centralized within publicity around what are ostensibly the "gay episodes," a topic I will discuss in chapter 1. Nor is Black gayness a chief narrative concern within the writers' room, as I discuss in chapter 2. The discovery/declaration of gayness within the Black-cast sitcom is only a narrative catalyst: it brings heterosexual friendships or relationships back together and demonstrates the coolness of the core (heterosexual) cast. Thus, for the generic closet, the relationship of discovery/declaration to the closet is paramount for the visibility of Black gayness. Importantly, discovery/declaration requires the speech act that accompanies coming out, particularly in its televisual form, because it is difficult (but not impossible) without it for act 1 to move to act 2, which in turn makes the third act possible.

Act 3, discarding, resolves the narrative problems and answers central questions; most importantly, "the tension lets up, and we know that everything is all right."[62] As this book demonstrates (particularly in chap. 2), detection in act 1 situates Black gayness as a narrative problem that must be solved. The immediacy of the narrative problem and the question "Is he gay?" sets the narrative rules for Black gay inclusion in the series. Once the Black gay character, through the central question, has been discovered to be gay, his narrative utility is exhausted. In other words, the simplicity of the central question reduces Black gayness to a binary answer, "yes" or "no," rather than a more open-ended one. Seger's gesture toward knowing "everything is all right" is also important to discarding and the generic closet. Because the sitcom generally, and the Black-cast sitcom specifically, must return to stasis at the end of each episode, the "all rightness" of act 3 is in its discarding of the Black gay *other* so that the series can continue on its merry heterosexual or heterosexist way.

The three Ds, as a representational strategy, doggedly adhere to a three-act structure that industrially shapes narrative development of Black gay characters within the Black-cast sitcom. They are also an epistemological strategy that contains, constrains, and controls the parameters within which Black gayness is granted tenure within the Black-cast sitcom. That does not mean industry workers (chap. 2) and Black gay men (chap. 4) do not use tactics to try to escape the three Ds and the generic closet's hegemonic pull. But it does mean that the generic closet exposes the politics of the Black-cast sitcom, a distinct genre that is bound within ideologies and mythologies about Black heterosexual audiences. The Black-cast sitcom creates specific narrative conditions under which Black gayness is permissible. The deployment of Black gayness, once those narrative conditions have been met, must be discarded from and forgotten within the heteronormative Black-cast sitcom universe they disrupted for an episode or so.

THE EPISODES

Methodologically, the texts chosen for *The Generic Closet* were selected in three ways. First, building on research by Ron Becker, Steven Capsuto, and Stephen Tropiano, I used their books and indexes to select episodes of shows that featured Black gay characters on Black-cast sitcoms. Second, I searched episode guides to see which texts these authors may have missed because they were not focused specifically on Black gay men or the Black-cast sitcom or because their research was conducted before certain series or episodes aired. Third, I pared the list of fifteen series based on those episodes of each series that featured Black gay characters in a role that served a narrative function. For instance, an episode of the series *Martin* (Fox, 1992–1997), "DMV Blues," was excluded because the Black gay character is primarily in the background and delivers one line that is ultimately of little consequence to the central plotlines. In addition, the *Cosby* (CBS, 1996–2000) episode "Older and Out" was excluded because the Black gay character does not provide any of the narrative thrust for the episode (rather a white gay character does so). In addition, I excluded series that featured episodes concerning characters thinking a character is gay or those episodes that feature a character pretending to be gay. When applying that criterion, two episodes of *Tyler Perry's For Better or For Worse* (hereafter *For Better or Worse*; TBS, 2011–2013; OWN, 2013–2017) were excluded because one episode, "The Will and the Grace," dealt with a character who alleged he was gay to get romantically closer to the series' female protagonist. The episode "Tommy" was also excluded because it did not feature a gay character but rather the suspicion that a character might be gay because his mother caught him wearing her makeup. The *Guys Like Us* (UPN, 1998–1999) episode "In and Out" and the *For Your Love* (NBC, 1998; The WB, 1998–2002) episode "House of Cards" were removed because characters were pretending to be gay. Based on this set of criteria, my sample included ten possible series: *Sanford Arms* (NBC, 1977), *Roc* (Fox, 1991–1994), *Moesha* (UPN, 1996–2001), *Good News* (UPN, 1997–1998), *The Parkers* (UPN, 1999–2004), *Girlfriends* (UPN, 2000–2006; The CW 2006–2008), *All of Us* (UPN, 2003–2007), *The Game* (The CW, 2006–2009; BET, 2011–2015), *Are We There Yet?* (TBS, 2010–2012), and *Let's Stay Together* (BET, 2011–2014).

Because I wanted to study the production of these series, the sample was further limited by the death of either episode writers and showrunners and, more importantly, the willingness of writers and showrunners to speak with me for this project. With these criteria in place, *The Generic Closet* studies five series: *Moesha*, *Good News*, *All of Us*, *Are We There Yet?*, and *Let's Stay Together*. Below are synopses of each episode within *The Generic Closet*.

- *Moesha* (UPN): The "Labels" episode, which aired on October 1, 1996, concerns Moesha meeting and briefly dating Hakeem's cousin Omar. After meeting Omar's flamboyant friend, Moesha begins to spread the rumor that Omar is gay.
- *Good News* (UPN): On the pilot episode of the series, which broadly concerns the trials and tribulations of a church attempting to rebuild its membership after the departure of a beloved pastor, the new pastor is confronted with a parishioner who seeks help in coming out to his mother. The episode originally aired August 25, 1997.
- *All of Us* (UPN): In this two-part episode of *All of Us*, series star Robert discovers that his biological father is gay. The episodes,

"Like Father, Like Son, Like Hell" and "My Two Dads," aired November 13 and 20, 2006.

- *Are We There Yet?* (TBS): "The Boy Has Style" aired January 19, 2011. The episode concerned Lindsey Kingston's high school crush and her parents' suspicion (and ultimate confirmation) that he is gay. The Black gay character Cedric is a player on the high school football team.
- *Let's Stay Together* (BET): The first episode in which Darkanian appears is "Leave Me Alone." The episode aired April 24, 2012, and featured Darkanian, a closeted Black gay man and professional football player. In the episode, Darkanian begins to woo Crystal. The Darkanian story line continues in the May 22, 2012, episode, "No Wedding and a Funeral," which finds Crystal moving into one of Darkanian's "extra" apartments in downtown Atlanta. In the season 2 finale, "Wait . . . What?" Crystal discovers that Darkanian is gay when his long-term boyfriend visits the apartment in which Crystal lives. The episode aired June 5, 2012. In the March 26, 2013, season 3 premiere, "See, What Had Happened Was . . ." Darkanian asks Crystal to be his "beard"—an offer she accepts. In the episode "Buyer Beware," Darkanian and Crystal continue their public relationship, although Crystal begins to have sexual needs that Darkanian cannot fulfill. The episode aired May 14, 2013. In the season 3 finale, "Babies, Blindness and Bling," Crystal is caught kissing a man who is not Darkanian, leading to a media brouhaha. She is required to hold a press conference where she apologizes for her adulterous relationship. At the press conference, Darkanian proposes marriage. The last episode in which Darkanian appears is "Game Over," in which Darkanian comes out as gay. The episode aired April 1, 2014.

OVERVIEW OF CHAPTERS

In *The Generic Closet*, I use various methodologies to explore the sites that illuminate the ways meaning about Black gayness is made within the Black-cast sitcom. Chapter 1 engages with broadcast and cultural history to illuminate the ways UPN, TBS, and BET emerged and how network leadership decided to mediate Blackness on the respective networks. Ultimately, this chapter demonstrates the ways the mainstreaming of hip-hop and Black culture and industrial jockeying for audiences converged to give rise to the series under examination within this book.

In chapter 2, I use production studies to examine the ways Black gay characters are written for Black-cast sitcoms. The interviews with writers and showrunners that form the basis of this chapter show the ways cultural and industrial forces operate within episodes of Black-cast sitcoms featuring Black gay characters. In this chapter, I pay particular attention to the ways controlling images of Black gay men in television shapes the way writers craft their episodes and the level of agency they are afforded as they write. This chapter is concerned with the reification of particular ideologies via the cultural norms of commercial television narratives and encoded when writers are writing Black gay characters.

Chapter 3 draws from and builds on sitcom genre theory, television sound studies, and humor theory to examine how the Black-cast sitcom marks Black gay bodies as comic. Chapter 3 contends that the laugh track, as an electronic substitute for the audience, instructs at-home audiences about how they should view homosexuality, regardless of the message conveyed by the script itself. The laugh track works to create a heterosexual "us" versus a homosexual "them," particularly with respect to the "proper" performance of Black masculinity. Within this analysis, I consider the laugh track as part of the postproduction process because although some series were filmed in front of a live studio audience, laughter and the laugh track can be moved around in postproduction, and some series create their soundtracks entirely in postproduction. An examination of these series provides a clear ideological link between what the producers of each series believe to be humorous.

Chapter 4 employs a reception study of Black gay men's understanding of Black gay characters. Specifically, the Black gay men's meaning-making of Black gay images is the star of this final chapter. This chapter illuminates their difficult and negotiated relationship to historical stereotypes of Black gay men and acknowledges these viewers as postmodern subjects who are not only interested in the text but also are aware of the ways series can gesture toward preferred meanings via the use of the laugh track. There is merit in gauging the reception of other viewers, perhaps heterosexual Black men or gay white men, and comparing and contrasting the ways these groups make meaning vis-à-vis Black gay male representation. However, this chapter is predicated on letting the voices of Black gay men be heard without having to draw differences or similarities in their meaning-making process with other viewers to validate the "realness" of their reception processes. I used in-depth interviews with twenty self-identified Black gay men for this chapter.

Finally, I conclude by drawing linkages among the various sites where meaning is made and speculate on how my findings illuminate the conditions under which Black gay representation in Black-cast sitcom exists in this cultural moment. Specifically, I ask, does the generic closet still exist within the Black-cast sitcom, and if so, why does it still exist?

Taken together, the chapters within *The Generic Closet* illuminate how Black gayness has been (and continues to be) mediated within the Black-cast sitcom by undertaking historical, industrial, discursive, and reception analyses. Through its pages, *The Generic Closet* engages not only how Black gayness has been mediated but also why it has been mediated in the ways it has.

NOTES

1. Chris Cillizza and Sean Sullivan, "How Proposition 8 Passed in California—And Why It Wouldn't Today," *Washington Post*, March 26, 2013, https://www.washingtonpost.com/news/the-fix/wp/2013/03/26/how-proposition-8-passed-in-california-and-why-it-wouldnt-today/?noredirect=on&utm_term=.45b3f70508e0.

2. Valerie Richardson, "Gay Rights Left on Sidelines after Election," *Washington Times*, November 18, 2008, https://www.washingtontimes.com/news/2008/nov/18/gay-rights-abandoned-on-sidelines-after-election/.

3. Ta-Nehisi Coates, "Proposition 8 and Blaming the Blacks," *Atlantic*, January 7, 2009, https://www.theatlantic.com/entertainment/archive/2009/01/prop-8-and-blaming-the-blacks/6548/.

4. Todd Gitlin, *Inside Prime Time* (Berkeley: University of California Press, 2000), 203–204.

5. Ron Becker, *Gay TV and Straight America* (New Brunswick, NJ: Rutgers University Press, 2006), 158.

6. Alfred L. Martin Jr., "Generic Closets: Sitcoms, Audiences, and Black Male Gayness," in *The Comedy Studies Reader*, ed. Nick Marx and Matt Sienkiewicz (Austin: University of Texas Press, 2018), 235.

7. Michel Foucault, *Discipline and Punish: The Birth of the Prison*, trans. Alan Sheridan (New York: Vintage Books 1995), 27.

8. Julie D'Acci, "Cultural Studies, Television Studies, and the Crisis in the Humanities," in *Television after TV: Essays on a Medium in Transition*, ed. Lynn Spiegel and Jan Olsson (Durham, NC: Duke University Press, 2004), 422.

9. John T. Caldwell, *Production Culture: Industrial Reflexivity and Critical Practice in Film and Television* (Durham, NC: Duke University Press, 2008).

10. Roderick A. Ferguson, *Aberrations in Black: Toward a Queer of Color Critique* (Minneapolis: University of Minnesota Press, 2004), 4.

11. Melanie E. S. Kohnen, *Queer Representation, Visibility, and Race in American Film and Television: Screening the Closet* (New York: Routledge, 2016), 3.

12. Critical race theory work borrows from and extends Roland Barthes' theorization of exnomination to explain how the bourgeoisie fail to name themselves as such in a bid to make the bourgeoisie seem "natural." Whiteness similarly rarely names itself but is instead imagined as the default that stands in for normativity. See Roland Barthes, *Mythologies*, trans. Annette Lavers (New York: Farrar, Straus, and Giroux, 1972), 139.

13. Suzanna Danuta Walters, *The Tolerance Trap: How God, Genes, and Good Intentions Are Sabotaging Gay Equality* (New York: New York University Press, 2014), 36.

14. Amber B. Raley and Jennifer L. Lucas, "Stereotype or Success? Prime-Time Television's Portrayals of Gay Male, Lesbian, and Bisexual Characters," *Journal of Homosexuality* 51, no. 2 (2006): 24–25.

15. Stephen Tropiano, *The Prime Time Closet: A History of Gays and Lesbians on TV* (New York: Applause Books, 2002), 238.

16. Timothy Havens, *Black Television Travels: African American Media across the Globe* (New York: New York University Press, 2013), 4.

17. Charles, interview with author (Austin), February 15, 2014.

18. Janet Staiger, *Blockbuster TV: Must-See Sitcoms in the Network Era* (New York: New York University Press, 2000), 149.

19. Robin R. Means Coleman and Charlton D. McIlwain, "The Hidden Truths in Black Sitcoms," in *The Sitcom Reader: America Viewed and Skewed*, ed. Mary M. Dalton and Laura R. Linder (Albany, NY: SUNY Press, 2005), 125.

20. Arthur Knight, *Disintegrating the Musical: Black Performance and American Musical Film* (Durham, NC: Duke University Press, 2002).

21. Tricia Rose, "Black Texts/Black Contexts," in *Black Popular Culture*, ed. Gina Dent (Seattle: Bay Press, 1992), 223.

22. Kristal Brent Zook, *Color by Fox: The Fox Network and the Revolution in Black Television* (New York: Oxford University Press, 1999).

23. Ibid., 6.

24. James Baldwin, *Nobody Knows My Name* (New York: Vintage Books, 1992), 143.

25. Robin R. Means Coleman, *African American Viewers and the Black Situation Comedy* (New York: Garland Press, 2000), 68.

26. Catherine Squires, "Rethinking the Black Public Sphere: An Alternative Vocabulary for Multiple Public Spheres," *Communication Theory* 12, no. 4 (2002): 448.

27. Kimberlee Crenshaw, "Mapping the Margins: Intersectionality, Identity Politics, and Violence against Women of Color," *Stanford Law Review* 43, no. 6 (1991): 1283.

28. Simon Critchley, *On Humor* (New York: Routledge, 2002), 12.

29. Stuart Hall, "The Spectacle of the Other," in *Representation: Cultural Representations and Signifying Practices*, ed. Stuart Hall (London: Sage, 1997), 258.

30. Ronald L. Jackson and Celnisha L. Dangerfield, "Defining Black Masculinity as a Cultural Property: An Identity Negotiation Paradigm," in *Intercultural Communication: A Reader*, ed. Larry A. Samovar and Richard E. Porter (Florence, KY: Wadsworth, 2002), 123.

31. Kobena Mercer, *Welcome to the Jungle: New Positions in Black Cultural Studies* (London: Routledge, 1994), 137.

32. Steve Estes, *I Am a Man! Race, Manhood and the Civil Rights Movement* (Chapel Hill: University of North Carolina Press, 2005).

33. Marlon Riggs, "Black Macho Revisited: Reflections of a Snap! Queen," in *Out in Culture: Gay, Lesbian, and Queer Essays on Popular Culture*, ed. Corey K. Creekmur and Alexander Doty (Durham, NC: Duke University Press, 1995), 471. Emphasis in original.

34. Stuart Hall, "What Is This 'Black' in Black Popular Culture," in *Popular Culture: A Reader*, ed. Raiford Guins and Omayra Zaragoza Cruz (London: Sage, 2008), 292.

35. E. Patrick Johnson, *Appropriating Blackness: Performance and the Politics of Authenticity* (Durham, NC: Duke University Press, 2003), 32.

36. Jasmine Cobb and Robin R. Means Coleman, "Two Snaps and a Twist: Controlling Images of Gay Black Men on Television," *African American Research Perspectives* 13, no. 1 (2010): 86.

37. Gregory Conerly, "Are You Black First or Are You Queer?," in *The Greatest Taboo: Homosexuality in Black Communities*, ed. Delroy Constantine-Simms (Los Angeles: Alyson Books, 2001), 7.

38. Darieck Scott, "Jungle Fever: Black Identity Politics, White Dick and the Utopian Bedroom," *GLQ* 1, no. 3 (2004): 300.

39. Suzanna Danuta Walters, *All the Rage: The Story of Gay Visibility in America* (Chicago: University of Chicago Press, 2001), 105; Steven Capsuto, *Alternative Channels: The Uncensored Story of Gay and Lesbian Images on Radio and Television* (New York: Ballantine Books, 2000), 375.

40. Herman Gray, *Watching Race: Television and the Struggle for Blackness* (Minneapolis: University of Minneapolis Press, 1995), 141; Johnson, *Appropriating Blackness*, 66.

41. Samuel A. Chambers, *The Queer Politics of Television* (New York: Tauris, 2009), 38.

42. Guy Mark Foster, "Desire and the 'Big Black Sex Cop': Race and the Politics of Intimacy on HBO's *Six Feet Under*," in *The New Queer Aesthetic on Television: Essays on Recent Programming*, ed. James Keller and Leslie Stratyner (Jefferson, NC: McFarland, 2006), 109.

43. E. Patrick Johnson, "The Specter of the Black Fag: Parody, Blackness, and Hetero/Homosexual B(r)others," *Queer Theory and Communication* 45, nos. 2–4 (2003): 232.

44. Gust A. Yep and John P. Elia, "Queering/Quaring Blackness in *Noah's Arc*," in *Queer Popular Culture: Literature, Media, Film, and Television,* ed. Thomas Peele (New York: Palgrave Macmillan, 2007), 1.

45. Michel Foucault, *The History of Sexuality: An Introduction,* vol. 1 (New York: Random House, 1990), 39.

46. Eve Kosofsky Sedgwick, *Epistemology of the Closet* (Berkeley: University of California Press, 2008), 14.

47. Ibid., 3.

48. Jeffrey Q. McCune Jr., *Sexual Discretion: Black Masculinity and the Politics of Passing* (Chicago: University of Chicago Press, 2014), 3–4.

49. Lynne Joyrich, "Epistemology of the Console," in *Queer TV: Theories, Historic, Politics,* ed. Glyn Davis and Gary Needham (New York: Routledge, 2009), 27.

50. Walters, *All the Rage,* 105.

51. Marlon B. Ross, "Beyond the Closet as a Raceless Paradigm," in *Black Queer Studies: A Critical Anthology,* ed. E. Patrick Johnson and Mae G. Henderson (Durham, NC: Duke University Press, 2005), 177.

52. Dorie Gilbert Martinez and Stonie C. Sullivan, "African American Gay Men and Lesbians: Examining the Complexity of Gay Identity Development," *Journal of Human Behavior in the Social Environment* 1, nos. 2–3 (1998): 244.

53. William G. Hawkeswood, *One of the Children* (Berkeley: University of California Press, 1997), 139.

54. Sedgwick, *Epistemology of the Closet,* 68.

55. Michel Foucault, *The Order of Things: The Archaeology of the Human Sciences* (New York: Routledge, 2001).

56. Jason Mittell, *Genre and Television: From Cop Shows to Cartoons in American Culture* (New York: Routledge, 2004), 10.

57. Raymond Williams, *Television: Technology and Cultural Form* (New York: Routledge, 2008).

58. Joyrich, "Epistemology of the Console," 28.

59. Linda Seger, *Making a Good Script Great,* 2nd ed. (Hollywood: Samuel French, 1994), 21.

60. Ibid., 28–29.

61. C. Riley Snorton, *Nobody Is Supposed to Know: Black Sexuality on the Down Low* (Minneapolis: University of Minnesota Press, 2014), 18.

62. Seger, *Making a Good Script Great,* 33.

ONE

—ʍ—

BUILDING AND REBUILDING GENERIC CLOSETS WITHIN THE BLACK-CAST SITCOM INDUSTRY

IN THE OCTOBER 2012 ISSUE of *Out* magazine—one of the national magazines that specifically and explicitly target lesbian, gay, bisexual, and transgender readers—the editors wrote "The Big Gay TV Timeline" as part of a package they called "Primetime: How the Evolution Was Televised." The piece began with gay images on television in 1965 with Paul Lynde and his first appearance on *Bewitched* (ABC, 1964–1972), not as Uncle Arthur but as a "jumpy driving instructor."[1] The package traces representations of gay men and lesbians on television through eras, genres, episodic representations, and recurring characters. It even covers female characters who were not gay but were the object of gay men's adoration like Dorothy, Rose, Blanche, and Sophia from *The Golden Girls* (NBC, 1985–1992). As it does this work, it also makes one thing clear: the history traced by *Out* is rooted in whiteness and white television. *Out* mentions Black gay characters including Carter Heywood from *Spin City*, Keith Charles from *Six Feet Under* (HBO, 2001–2005), and Snoop and Omar from *The Wire* (HBO, 2002–2008), but no characters from Black-cast television are mentioned within that history. The magazine inexplicably does not even mention *Noah's Arc* (Logo, 2005–2006), which has historical import if only for its distinction as the first television series to feature a main cast entirely comprising Black gay characters.

I want to use *Out*'s version of gay television history to situate the concerns engaged in this chapter. First, Black television's relationship to Black gayness is vastly different than white television's relationship to gayness. In other words, the "Gay '90s" (as dubbed by the September 8, 1995, *Entertainment Weekly* cover) were the *white* gay '90s, rooted in the differences in how white and Black audiences are industrially imagined: white audiences are segmented and partly imagined as liberal with a tendency to consume content with LGBT characters, whereas Black audiences are understood as conservative and antigay. Second, some of these different audience imaginations have their nexus in how Black television, in a bid for a kind of televised Black authenticity, draws on the rise of hip-hop commodification, which is always already understood as antigay (however problematic that generalization might be). Third, Black television is precarious within the media industries. Jennifer Fuller argues that Black television representation is "shaped in part by the contemporary workings and limits of television production."[2] To be sure, the media industries are no longer necessarily segregated by race, but they remain "mediated by racial hierarchies and commercial imperatives."[3] In other words, when Fox loaded up on Black-cast series, only to dump those series once it had secured broadcasting rights to Sunday Night Football in 1994, it served as a "lesson" for Black-cast sitcoms. Black-centered television production, like the film industry's temporary engagement with cinematic Blackness in the 1970s and 1990s, would be allowed only as long as white executives thought reaching Black viewers was a valuable endeavor and one that would continue to serve as a market differentiator.

The tethering of whiteness and gayness, the mediation of Black homophobia, and the precariousness of Black television converge with an additional industrial practice that comes to bear on the Black-cast sitcom: flow. Initially conceptualized by Raymond Williams, *flow* describes the television industrial process of scheduling not only programming but also the commercials between the programming. As Nick Browne succinctly sums it up, flow imagines a television network or channel as a "relay in a process of textualizing the interaction of audience and advertiser."[4] Scheduling helps to make sense of television's flow and is industrially shaped by programming shows with similar tone within close proximity.[5] Brett Mills further illuminates the industrial logic behind this pairing system when he asserts that comedy is an "industrial tool for cohering specific audience groups, with the implication that such groups find similar things funny, and have similar responses to particular character types."[6] But Amanda Lotz rightly argues that this scheduling strategy of pairing "like with like becomes problematic when networks assume that similar ethnic identities among casts equates to similar content."[7] Lotz's discussion of flow is important to some of the concerns that undergird this chapter, particularly the industrial practice of "Black blocking."

Black blocking extends Lotz's notion of channels, networks, and streaming platforms using ethnicity as a marker of similarity by positing that it increases precarity for the Black-cast sitcom. Put another way, if a channel or network only programs Black-cast content on, say, Monday night, and assuming the schedule

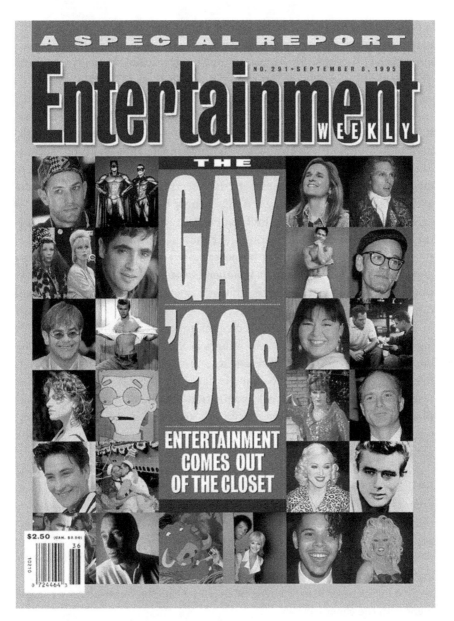

Fig. 1.1. *Entertainment Weekly* cover proclaiming the 1990s the "Gay '90s" because of the explosion of LGBT representation within television.

is filled with sitcoms, that means only six Black-cast programs can be on the network or channel at any given time versus a white- or multicultural-cast series, which is understood as "universal" and programmable virtually anywhere. The net result is reinforcement of the precariousness of Black-cast content, which serves to structure and discipline the kinds of "risks" these series take.

Through an examination of the industrial histories of UPN, TBS, and BET, this chapter proposes that the Black-cast sitcom creates and recreates the generic closet—not necessarily because of some innate antigayness but because of the precarity of Black television production. Showrunners do not want to take a chance on "risky" content, with *risk* referring to a sustained engagement with Black homosexuality. Veteran showrunner Ed. Weinberger encapsulates this precarity: "I don't think [BET has] encouraged gay Black characters because they are fearful of alienating their audience. I think they're afraid that there is still a prejudice [about homosexuality]."[8] Importantly, Weinberger gestures toward an industrial *imagination* of Black audiences rather than any semblance of audience research. Thus, the generic closet's enduringness is rooted in fiction, not necessarily fact.

As I will argue throughout this chapter, precarity becomes an organizing logic for Black-cast sitcoms. It encourages productions to color inside the industrial lines drawn around Black-cast television, and this approach reconnects to how audiences are understood and imagined, without the benefit of market research. And thus the (lack of) imagination of urbane (versus "just" urban) Black audiences, an overreliance on hip-hop's (partial) homophobia, and Black television's precarity are interlocking discourses that result in building and rebuilding the generic closet.

This chapter is a deep dive into the industrial weeds of UPN, TBS, and BET. It is important to understand how these networks come to Blackness in order to understand how they come their (brief) engagement with Black gayness. This historical sketch shifts the question from "How did Black gayness appear within Black-cast sitcoms?" to "Why did Black gayness appear within Black-cast sitcoms?" More to the point, this chapter underscores the industrial logics that underpin the creation of Black-cast sitcoms and their subsequent limited inclusion of Black gayness by detailing the Black-cast sitcom's engagement with the generic closet.

To explore the creation of *Moesha, Good News, All of Us, Are We There Yet?,* and *Let's Stay Together* and their reification of the generic closet, it is first necessary to understand the post-network television environment, which began in 1986. At that time, Fox launched with a few hours of programming in a bid to become the fourth broadcast network (after DuMont's failed attempt at being a fourth network in the 1940s and 1950s) and break up the "Big Three" networks' (ABC, CBS, and NBC) monopoly over TV content. Roberta Pearson theorizes this era as TVII, which dates "roughly from the 1980s until the late 1990s . . . [and] is the era of channel/network expansion, quality television, and network branding strategies."[9] The multichannel environment encouraged startup networks (netlets) and channels to take "risks" within their programming—a risk that was often rooted in representations of Blackness as a means to attract critical attention and underserved demographic segments (always with an eye toward selling those demographics to advertisers). Jennifer Fuller details how "the proliferation of broadcast and cable channels in the 1980s and 1990s increased the competition for audience shares and threatened to muddle distinctions between the growing number of cable channels and broadcasting networks. In response, channels made greater efforts to remain distinct and cultivate viewer loyalty. . . . Broadcasters began to select and promote their line-ups not just in terms of what shows might be successful in certain time slots, but as a way to create a network brand."[10] I quote Fuller in detail here because her understanding of the interconnectivity between Black representation and network branding is important to the work I undertake in this chapter and in *The Generic Closet* more broadly. Because Blackness is a brand strategy to promote product differentiation, it retains its precariousness: when the brand needs to differentiate in a new way, that strategy will be abandoned.

Fox recognized a hole—and a potential branding strategy—in Black television representation as the major three networks became whiter (in terms of their series) in the 1980s. The major networks had Black-cast hits like *Benson* (ABC, 1979–1986), *Gimme a Break* (NBC, 1981–1987), and *The Cosby Show* (NBC, 1984–1992), among others, but for many Black viewers, these programs did not ring true to their lived experiences. Jannette Dates finds that the series *Benson* "fit the pattern that scripted African American male characters as innocuous true-believers in the system, who supported, defended, and nurtured mainstream, middle class values, concerns, and even faults" before contending that on *Gimme a Break*, Nell Carter played a "proud but servile, cocky but nurturing, loyal" mammy.[11] In their reception study of *The Cosby Show*, Sut Jhally and Justin Lewis acknowledged that some critics believed "the Huxtables' charmed life [was] so alien to the experience of most black people that they [were] no longer 'black' at all."[12] Ultimately, the success of *The Cosby Show* resulted in a whitewashed television environment in which Blackness was enacted and deployed within television's established white cultural norms. Put simply, many of these Black-cast series were largely understood as series with Black faces but white sensibilities.

Donald Bogle notes that Fox "struggled to be a contender in the network arena ... [and] realized it needed a solid viewer block that would ensure strong ratings."[13] As such, Fox began its foray as a broadcasting powerhouse by featuring sitcoms with Black bodies and sometimes Black writing staff and producers, including *In Living Color* (Fox, 1990–1994), *The Sinbad Show* (Fox, 1993–1994), *Roc* (Fox, 1991–1994), and *Martin* (Fox, 1992–1997). By 1993, when Fox began broadcasting seven days a week, it "was airing the single largest crop of black-produced shows in television history."[14] These shows included greater engagement with African American culture than those previously mentioned, albeit partially to attract young, urban audiences.[15] It is important to note that although Fox attempted to use Blackness to attract Black viewers, it was dualcasting for young, white male audiences. Katherine Sender defines *dualcasting* as a strategy to "target two specific audiences."[16] While Sender's discussion centers Bravo's courtship of white gay men and white heterosexual women with *Queer Eye for the Straight Guy* (Bravo, 2003–2007), her assertion that dualcasting can simultaneously increase a channel's profile and diversify its programming is applicable here. This practice begins to lay the groundwork for networks' engagement and disengagement with Blackness at will because courting Blackness is understood as a means to a commercial end.[17]

Of the early series Fox produced, *In Living Color* through its "Men On ..." sketches and *Roc* were the only two series to engage with Black gayness. The "Men On ..." sketches featured Blaine Edwards and Antoine Merriweather (portrayed by Damon Wayans and David Alan Grier, respectively) reviewing film, television, and culture in the style of Gene Siskel and Roger Ebert. They loved everything that featured men and greeted anything with women by saying, in unison, "Hated it!" The sketches spawned a pop culture phenomenon with their pithy resignification of Siskel and Ebert's "two thumbs up" as "two snaps up." Despite their problematic representation of Black gay men, which included dialogue delivered with an affected lisping speech pattern and liberal use of vernacular associated with Black gay communities, the characterizations were almost universally understood as funny, and Antoine and Blaine became popular, recurring characters on the series.

More germane to the subject matter of *The Generic Closet*, *Roc* was a Black-cast sitcom that centered on a working-class Black family in Baltimore headed by Charles S. Dutton as the titular character and patriarch. The series featured four episodes with a Black gay character, Roc's uncle Russell. The character was played by Richard Roundtree, best known as the titular character in the *Shaft* trilogy (1971, 1972, dir. Gordan Parks; 1973; dir. John Guillermin) and the television series (CBS, 1973–1974). The first episode on which Russell appears

Fig. 1.2. Blaine Edwards (Damon Wayans) and Antoine Merriweather
(David Alan Grier) from *In Living Color*'s "Men On . . ." sketches, in which
they play black gay cultural critics in the vein of Siskel and Ebert.

revolves around his coming out and marrying his white partner, in what is believed to be television's first wedding between two men (*The Golden Girls* had a 1991 commitment ceremony episode, but the word *marriage* was never used). The episode won the GLAAD Media Award for Outstanding Comedy Episode in 1992. Two of the other episodes are fairly inconsequential with respect to Russell's involvement, although in each episode he is introduced to new characters to whom he has to come out as gay (and heterosexist comedy ensues from the incongruity of a "masculine-presenting" Black man being gay). In the final episode, Russell and Chris decide to move to Paris where they expect to encounter less discrimination than had become (and remains) de rigueur within American culture.

In the mid- to late 1990s, while Fox was targeting Black viewers to ratings success and sporadically engaging with Black gayness, the major networks began recognizing the increased marketability and ratings potential of

Fig. 1.3. A promotional photo from the *Roc* episode "Can't Help Loving That Man," in which Roc's uncle Russell weds his partner Chris in what is understood as television's first wedding ceremony between gay people. Photo by Fox Broadcasting.

programming with white gay characters on series targeted at SLUMPY viewers. This explosion did not include Black gay characters in Black-cast sitcoms; the major networks' white-cast sitcoms featured mostly white gay characters like *Ellen* (NBC, 1994–1998) and *Will & Grace*, despite *Roc* writer Jeffrey Duteil's assertion that *Roc*'s audience was "overwhelmingly supportive" of the episode on which Russell and Chris wed.[18] And although Duteil recalled Fox executives saying that "they couldn't be more pleased with the way [the episode] turned out," Russell remained a temporary presence on the series.[19]

This chapter grapples with the tensions between increases in Black-cast television production and gay representation across white- and multicultural-cast sitcoms by engaging the industrial histories of five Black-cast sitcoms that featured Black gay characters. In this chapter, I am interested in exploring why the 1990s had increases in both Black television production and representations of white gayness but never an increase in the production of Black gayness—in a word, *intersectionality*. In the sections that follow, I trace the creation of UPN's, BET's, and TBS's entries into original programming through Blackness to underscore how the episodes of *Moesha, Good News, All of Us, Are We There Yet?*, and *Let's Stay Together* engage with Black gayness, precarious Black-cast television production, and the branding of Black culture.

BUILDING UPN'S BLACK BRAND (AND THE GENERIC CLOSET) WITH *MOESHA, GOOD NEWS,* AND *ALL OF US*

The company that ultimately became UPN took a circuitous route to arrive at the slate of Black-cast programming for which the network would become known. In the early 1990s, Paramount Network Television, a division of Paramount Pictures, was a major player in television production and also struck lucrative deals to sell syndicated programming to networks. While Paramount Network Television was financially riding high, the division was increasingly concerned that the FCC would scale back the Fin/Syn rules, which were designed to limit the amount of programming that ABC, CBS, and NBC owned and aired during prime time. Fin/Syn initially gave rise to a number of independent producers including Norman Lear's Tandem/TAT Productions, Mary Tyler Moore and Grant Tinker's MTM Enterprises, and Paramount Television. However, with the FCC revisiting those rules—and ultimately abolishing them in 1993—Paramount Television began searching for options to replace revenue streams from programs it produced, including *Cheers* (NBC, 1982–1993) and *Star Trek: The Next Generation* (First Run Syndication, 1987–1994). One option was to launch a fifth network where Paramount could vertically integrate its television production and distribution by owning, making, and airing its own content. Paramount Television and Chris-Craft Industries announced this endeavor in October 1993.

While scrambling to secure enough affiliates and coverage (a fight with competing Warner Brother's netlet, The WB), Paramount Television and Chris-Craft Industries—now called United Paramount Network (UPN)—began production on a slate of original programming in preparation for its launch. Much like Fox before it, UPN ultimately assembled a schedule of original programming designed to air on a few nights per week—in this case, Monday and Tuesday nights—presumably to avoid competing with the other networks' top programming, particularly NBC's juggernaut Thursday night comedies.

UPN debuted on Monday, January 16, 1995. Ron Becker argues that by 1995, the networks (meaning ABC, CBS, Fox, and NBC) had entered a phase of full-fledged acceptance and representation of gay and lesbian characters on television.[20] Network executives no longer considered theses representations toxic; in fact, they were valued for their ability to attract lucrative niche audiences that wanted to demonstrate their "coolness" by consuming television content with gay and lesbian characters.[21] While other networks and advertisers were courting SLUMPY viewers, UPN counterprogrammed with *Star Trek: Voyager* (UPN, 1995–2001), a series ostensibly targeted at young, white males. The gamble proved fruitful as the series debuted with 21.3 million viewers, a feat that was "impressive by any network's standards."[22] Thanks to those stellar ratings, UPN "bested its rivals decisively on its premiere night . . . averaging a 14.5 rating/20 share in 29 metered markets."[23] However, its second night of programming took the wind out of the new netlet's sails. The original series *Marker* (UPN, 1995) and *The Watcher* (UPN, 1995) barely registered with viewers, sending the upstart network into a frenzy to figure out how to deliver more hits like *Star Trek: Voyager*.

Taking a page from Fox's playbook, UPN began exploring Black-cast sitcoms in a bid to capture the African American viewers that Fox had abandoned. To begin the 1994 television season, Fox—once home to a number of Black-cast sitcoms—canceled four of its six Black productions: *The Sinbad Show, Roc, South Central* (Fox, 1994), and *In Living Color*. This left *Martin* and *Living Single* as the only two Black-cast sitcoms on the network (these series would be canceled in 1997 and 1998, respectively). In place of these Black-cast sitcoms were prime time dramas like *Melrose Place* (Fox, 1992–1999; The CW, 2009–2010) and *Party of Five* (Fox, 1994–2000), which focused on younger, white characters (and audiences).

Bogle suggests that programmers at UPN "were aware that shows designed for African American audiences appealed not only to Black and urban viewers . . . but often to a young white audience too."[24] In this way, UPN and its rival The WB could dualcast their programming to kill two demographic birds with one production stone using Black-cast programs as crossover shows, just as Fox had done before it. As Kelly Cole details, UPN had a problematic relationship with its branding as a "Black network" because its executives thought it too limiting, particularly because advertisers typically pay less to capture Black viewers.[25] Ultimately, however, UPN acquiesced and, at least initially, provided programming that appealed to Black and urban audience segments, demographics that were underserved by the four major networks.

For UPN's winter 1996 midseason, the network debuted two Black-cast sitcoms: *Minor Adjustments* (NBC, 1995; UPN, 1996) and *Moesha*. *Minor Adjustments* originally began life on NBC. Once it was canceled, UPN picked up the series' first thirteen episodes, including the seven that had initially aired on NBC before its cancellation, and ordered six additional episodes.[26] *Minor*

Adjustments also failed to find an audience on UPN and was canceled at the end of its first season, but *Moesha* became a bona fide hit.

Moesha *and the Brand(y)ing of (Crossover) Black Culture at UPN*

Moesha was originally developed for CBS. According to its showrunner Ralph Farquhar, *Moesha* was "originally about some kids in a garage. It was much younger, it was like a fourteen-year-old girl and stuff like that. So, when I came in and began re-shaping what ultimately became *Moesha*, we introduced a step mom to create some sort of conflict, and we developed a bunch of characters that were older and it became an edgier piece."[27] Farquhar maintains that because the show was initially being developed for CBS, he had to be cognizant of making the show appeal to a "general" (i.e., white) audience versus alienating those viewers. This was evident in his interview with me:

> [Vida Spears, Sara Finney and I] weren't trying to create the show for Black people, but certainly a show for the general audience, that cast a different light on the Black family dynamic. It was obviously post-*Cosby* [*Show*], which was the gold standard in terms of family shows, and depictions of Negroes on TV for sure. But there were a lot of us who felt there were slightly more genuine portrayals that could also appeal to a broad audience, and so the notion of having a family, which was fairly typical, where you know the father was on his second marriage, and you had a stepmom. So, it introduced those dynamics that a lot of TV shows avoided at the time. And that it happened to be a Black family, that presented maybe a more grounded version of the Black middle class where we didn't attempt to dodge their Blackness.[28]

Farquhar speaks to the double bind of televisual Blackness in which series with Black casts have to attempt to be specific enough to attract Black viewers but "universal" enough to attract white and mainstream audiences, who, as I mentioned previously, advertisers typically pay more to reach.

Farquhar also gestures toward the ways Black representations have a call-and-response relationship to the Black media that came before it—with *Moesha* responding to and repairing the "wrongs" of *The Cosby Show*. The success of *The Cosby Show* demonstrated that Black-cast sitcoms could attract "blockbuster" ratings, but the series also had to reckon with how Black viewers' reception of the series and its "authenticity" would be shaped.[29] For example, in their audience reception study of *The Cosby Show*, Jhally and Lewis noted, "So powerful is the desire among blacks to escape the negative world of stereotyping that the representation of social reality, the reality of which most of them are a part, becomes a necessary sacrifice. The question of whether the Huxtables are typical or atypical, black or white, real or unreal, is resolved in terms of the broader concerns of the black audience, the desire to overcome TV racial stereotyping. Blacks are willing to accept the unreality because of the broader role played by *The Cosby Show*."[30] Jhally and Lewis's interviewees reported that they knew *The Cosby Show* represented a Blackness that was untethered from their own everyday Blackness, but given the historical mediation of Blackness, *The Cosby Show* provided a necessary fiction.

Conversely, *Newsweek* writers Allison Samuels and Rick Marin indicated that *Moesha*'s South Central Los Angeles setting breaks from the three typical categories of Blackness within Black-cast sitcoms: "poor black folks (*Good Times* [and] *Sanford and Son*), poor folks getting rich (*The Jeffersons* [and] *The Fresh Prince of Bel-Air*), [and] rich black folks who wear really expensive sweaters ([*The*] *Cosby* [*Show*])."[31] In this way, Farquhar underscores that *Moesha*'s production team wanted to correct the fiction *The Cosby Show* forwarded. "We didn't dodge *Moesha*'s Blackness. And that was probably more represented in the fact that Brandy had braids [in her hair], which was a standard of beauty that was avoided on TV at the time. That was initially an issue, but that was very important to us that she look that way and had that authentic feel about her."[32] Within the context of Farquhar's implication that *Moesha* was designed to appeal to the universal, *Newsweek* found *Moesha* specific and "unapologetically ethnic" because it used "black slang and cultural references without footnotes. If you don't know that 'booty' means bad, and 'knockin' boots' is a euphemism for sex, or you've never heard of Zora Neale Hurston, then you're 'whack'—and you don't want to know what that means."[33] Concurrently, part of *Moesha*'s specificity was that it was at times "unapologetically ethnic" but that it only excluded those who were not well versed in the particularities of mid-1990s Black urban culture. Like Farquhar's earlier comment, *Moesha* was a general audience series that could appeal not only to Black audiences but also to a youthful white audience that was consuming Black culture through hip-hop videos broadcast on *Yo! MTV Raps* (MTV, 1988–2004).

Even as CBS was interested in *Moesha*'s concept, it was greenlit as a casting-contingent series, meaning that in order for Farquhar, Spears, and Finney to shoot a pilot, they had to cast the series' axial character, Moesha Mitchell. Demetrius Bady, a freelance *Moesha* writer, told me that because of the network's logic about Black viewers and crossover white audiences, only singers were considered for the series' titular character. "I read that script before they even got Brandy. I remember UPN would only pick it up if they got a singer. . . . To this day, we all know that if you're going to get a [Black-cast] show off the ground you have to have a singer."[34] Here, Bady posits that the

Fig. 1.4. The similarities between Will Smith's music video for "Parents Just Don't Understand" (*left*) and the opening credits for *The Fresh Prince of Bel Air* (*right*).

requirement for a popular Black music personality is an attempt for networks to engage in Black representation but not alienate white viewers by gesturing toward the crossover appeal of such entertainers.

In the 1990s, several cultural trends emerged that proved important to *Moesha*'s central character's casting. First, Black and hip-hop culture emerged as a force within American popular culture in the late 1980s and early 1990s. *The Cosby Show* spinoff *A Different World* (NBC, 1987–1993) followed up its folksy season 1 theme song sung by Phoebe Snow with versions by "Queen of Soul" Aretha Franklin in seasons 2–5 and then R&B group Boyz II Men in season 6. The shift in the series theme song, particularly from seasons 2 through 6, highlights the shift from the kind of crossover appeal of Aretha Franklin to the more urban (but still crossover) appeal of Boyz II Men and the New Jack Swing sound. *Yo! MTV Raps* also signaled the mainstreaming of rap and hip-hop music, particularly for young, white, suburban boys and men. This emergence was particularly prescient in television series like *The Fresh Prince of Bel-Air* (*Fresh Prince*; NBC, 1990–1996), starring Will Smith (a.k.a. the Fresh Prince). His song "Parents Just Don't Understand" took the sensibility of hip-hop rhythms and created a universal hit that centered the disjuncture between youth and their parents versus social ills like poverty, crime, and urban life, as hip-hop from artists like the Sugar Hill Gang and Public Enemy had done. In fact, the music video for "Parents Just Don't Understand" served as the creative referent for *Fresh Prince*'s credit sequence and theme song.

In addition, some of the early Fox network series, like *In Living Color* and *Roc* gestured toward how television networks were moving away from Huxtable-centered representations of Blackness and toward youth-centered, hip-hop representations. Specifically, *In Living Color*'s theme song was rapped by hip-hop artist Heavy-D, and, *Roc* costar Rocky Carroll introduced the new mid–second season theme song, "Live Your Life Today"—sung by the R&B group En Vogue (also known colloquially as "The Funky Divas")—by saying, "now you can't confuse us with *Murder, She Wrote*."[35] The theme songs for many Black-cast sitcoms of the 1990s not only were infused with hip-hop and R&B sounds but also used those sounds as a sonic landscape to convey the series' hipness and urbanity.

From its initial development, music generally—and the hip-hop sound, specifically—were part of *Moesha's* DNA. Farquhar explained, "Our production scheme was a little bit more challenging than most multicamera shows because we did a lot of single-camera scenes, including concert scenes. Music played a very important part in the show, so we shot some things at locations and on stage."[36] Because of her abilities as a singer, Norwood also performed the theme song for the series, written in the New Jack Swing style with which Brandy had become associated.

Most importantly for *Moesha*, the prior success of Black rap and R&B artists like Smith (*Fresh Prince*) and Queen Latifah (*Living Single*) demonstrated how success in the music industry could translate these elements of Black culture into mainstream sitcom success. Certainly, Brandy had worked in television previously on the short-lived sitcom *Thea* (ABC, 1993–1994); however, the minor role she played was of little consequence. Norwood's 1994 eponymous debut record, featuring the singles "I Wanna Be Down" and "Baby," helped to position her as "the country's hottest teen recording star."[37] The insistence on having a singer in the lead role was, in some ways, rooted in the network's desire for the series to appeal to a youthful demographic and for synergistic profits.

Nevertheless, Norwood's successes were largely confined to Black audiences, a demographic UPN executives were reticent to target because "it is a cold fact of the television advertising business that programs that attract a largely minority audience command lower advertising rates, from a smaller pool of advertisers, than shows with broader appeal."[38] This conundrum returns to the casting-contingent terms of *Moesha's* pickup at CBS. Brandy was largely unknown to the white executives at CBS because she was understood as a Black singer, not a "universal" Black singer in the vein of Whitney Houston or Janet Jackson. Farquhar recalls,

> I told CBS, "We have Brandy," and the network is like, "Well, who's that?"
> So, I said, 'Let's take a meeting,' and fortunately the *Seventeen* magazine with Brandy on the cover was just out. She was only the second Black girl to be on

quiz: are you a boyfriend addict?

seventeen

April 1995

how to
dump
him

best
friend
envy

hair
1 cool cut,
2 hot looks

teen
moms
3 girls'
stories

are you
depressed?

brand new

Brandy diva

alternahunks
from Green Day to Beck

U.S. $2.50 Can. $2.75

Fig. 1.5. Brandy on the cover of *Seventeen* magazine, a cover appearance that *Moesha* showrunner Ralph Farquhar says helped get the series the greenlight from CBS. Photo by Jesse Frohman. Permission granted by Jesse Frohman and Hearst Magazines.

the cover of *Seventeen*, the first being Whitney Houston, so I just bought a bunch of copies of the magazine, put them in all their seats when we met with each other and that was something they understood. A Black girl on the cover of a very white magazine meant something. They got it immediately. About thirty seconds into the meeting, they greenlit the show.[39]

Seventeen signaled Brandy's crossover into mainstream youth culture and it also paved the way for her foray into crossover television. Although CBS ultimately ordered the pilot, they were unable to find a space for it on the network's schedule. *Moesha* was a series clearly targeted at a teenage demographic, even if it was a family domesticom, and CBS's fare generally skewed toward older (white) audiences with hit series like *Touched by an Angel* (CBS, 1994–2003) and *Walker, Texas Ranger* (CBS, 1993–2001). CBS's failure to find a space on its schedule for *Moesha* was more deeply rooted in issues of flow in a pre-DVR world. Once CBS's option expired on *Moesha*, Farquhar began taking meetings with anyone who would listen to his pitch.

Ultimately, Farquhar found himself in an enviable position: two networks, ABC and UPN, were interested in placing *Moesha* on their schedules. Farquhar recalls that "ABC offered us six episodes on the air, and they had notes and some creative concerns. UPN gave us thirteen episodes on air and had no concerns. It seemed like we could have a chance to grow and develop at one place versus the other, so we went with UPN."[40] Because UPN had no reservations about the series, Farquhar and his writers' room proceeded with *Moesha* as a series that tackled issues, similar to his series short-lived Fox series *South Central*, particularly those facing a contemporary urban audience. Farquhar says, "We tackled all sorts of issues on *Moesha*: we did the thing where Moesha dated this white boy and some people didn't like the fact that a Black and white couple went out on a date. So, we dealt with a lot of topics. I think we dealt with them in a pretty entertaining way though. Like, never trying to give a lesson, but you know, ultimately one was delivered."[41] Farquhar imagined *Moesha* as a series that certainly had a point of view and wanted to deliver its ideology to audiences but did not want to do so in a way that audiences would construe as "preachy."

With its debut on January 23, 1996, *Moesha* delivered UPN's second hit series, after *Star Trek: Voyager*'s success almost a year earlier, and a new branding direction for the budding netlet. Farquhar says *Moesha*

was a huge hit for [UPN]. They had had no success in the half-hour-sitcom genre. In fact, they had jettisoned their entire line up that they had premiered with, and that that initial demo was to go after men, with the comedies and none of the comedies succeeded. So, they were really at a loss. They had *Star Trek [:Voyager]* in the beginning and they had some hour-long shows that were working, but they had no traction in the half hour, so *Moesha* comes out the box with a Black young woman, and they were like OK, great, anything Black we are going to put on the air.[42]

As an anonymous television industry insider said in an interview with *Arizona Republic*, "UPN needed to do something a little different . . . so they went to the Fox model, going young and ethnic when you're starting out. Those are the easiest groups to get initially."[43] To replicate *Moesha*'s success, UPN began reevaluating its programming strategy, ultimately deciding to load "two nights of its three-night schedule with six sitcoms featuring predominantly African American casts," with *Moesha, In the House* (NBC, 1995–1996, 1999; UPN, 1996–1998), *Goode Behavior* (UPN, 1996–1997), *Sparks* (UPN, 1996–1998), *Malcolm & Eddie* (UPN, 1996–2000), and *Homeboys in Outer Space* (UPN, 1996–1997) in the 1996–1997 TV season, much to the chagrin of some television critics.[44] This pushback was evident during the Television Critics Association's July 1996 press junket, in which several critics admonished UPN's new series as "modern day Stepin Fetchit material," reserving particular ire for *Goode Behavior* and *Homeboys in Outer Space* for their stereotypic depictions of Blackness.[45] However, the network thought they were providing programming for an audience not being served by the other four broadcast networks and continued to target African Americans with their programming. In the subsequent television season, however, its Black-cast programming would be limited to one of its three evenings of programming. *Moesha* clearly demonstrates the ways the emergence of commodified Blackness worked to shape how series would develop on UPN. As I will demonstrate in chapters 2 and 3, the industry's imagination of a monolithic hip-hop Black audience ultimately shaped how the series would engage with Black gayness: as one and done. Put more succinctly, Black gayness would remain trapped in the generic closet on *Moesha*.

Moesha dealt with Black gayness in the second season episode, "Labels," written by Demetrius Bady. The *TV Guide* episode synopsis of the episode reads, "With Q [Moesha's ex-boyfriend] seeing other women, Moesha accepts a date with a guy who has the potential of being a true soul mate—Hakeem's cousin Omar."[46] As I will explore in chapter 3, the episode description fails to mention that Omar might be gay. This omission is narratively useful because it makes the discovery of gayness more dramatic within the context of *Moesha*. The show was the first US television series to feature a Black gay teenager and, as I will discuss in chapter 2, to have an episode written by a Black gay writer.

Its engagement with Black gayness (and its failure to mention Black gayness in the so-called Gay '90s) indicates the show's reticence to promote the episode's gayness for fear of softening the ratings of one of UPN's few hit shows.

This exclusion is particularly fascinating because the same issue of *TV Guide* for the week in which "Labels" aired also featured a story about *Ellen* and how its producers, "led by Ellen DeGeneres herself, are lobbying . . . [producer] Touchstone Television . . . for the character to come out of the closet."[47] Later in that television season, Ellen Morgan (the character) and Ellen DeGeneres went on to come out as lesbian, becoming the first lesbian axial character in television history. This juxtaposition highlights the differences in the deployment of queerness in the Gay '90s across white- and Black-cast sitcoms and the efficacy of the generic closet for Black-cast sitcoms.

After two seasons on the air, *Moesha* had transcended its status as "only" a Black-cast sitcom; thus, UPN used the show to build its white-cast teen programming, including series like *Clueless* (ABC, 1996–1997; UPN, 1997–1998) and *Veronica Mars* (UPN, 2004–2006; The CW, 2006–2007; Hulu, 2019). Signaling the differences in the imaginations of Black versus white teen audiences, *Veronica Mars* would frequently engage with gay story lines throughout its three-season run on UPN. As I explore more deeply in chapter 2, *Moesha* would never return to gayness, Black or otherwise, despite Bady's attempts to pitch gay characters and story lines.

Good News *for Straight Black Viewers and the Birth of UPN's Black Block*

Out of the gate, *Good News*'s "Pilot" episode engaged Black gayness within a Black church and notions of Christianity. A "risky" endeavor, the episode's B-story revolved around Eldridge, the son of one of the series' main characters, wanting to come out to his mother and bring his boyfriend to Sunday church service. Despite Eldridge's relationship to one of the series' major characters, the episode marked the beginning and the end of Black gayness on the show. A year after (mostly) white SLUMPYs saw Black gay Carter Heywood each week on *Spin City* and in the year in which Ellen DeGeneres would come out as lesbian on *Ellen* and in real life, the generic closet was still alive and well within the Black-cast sitcom generally and on *Good News* specifically. This section investigates *Good News*'s industrial history to center its discursive attachments to Blackness and antigay Black audience imaginations.

Good News was greenlit as UPN completed its first year of Black blocking its programming on Monday nights. In need of companion series for modest hits *In the House*, *Sparks*, and *Malcolm & Eddie*, UPN leaned on *Sparks* executive producer Ed. Weinberger for a new series. Weinberger pitched *Good News*, a spin-off from his *Sparks* and similar to his NBC hit *Amen* (NBC, 1986–1991). Like *Amen*, *Good News* was set within a Black church. Instead of *Amen's* Philadelphia setting, *Good News* took place in South Central Los Angeles, similar to *Moesha*. The series centers on a congregation dealing with the loss of its founding pastor and the installation of a new pastor. Weinberger recalls, "My relations with the network at the time were such that if we were able to do a decent pilot, I was assured that the series would be picked up. . . . They trusted my tastes and they trusted my judgment, for whatever reasons that may be."[48] Just as Weinberger's *Sparks* relied on established sitcoms stars James Avery, who had just completed a successful run as Uncle Phil on *Fresh Prince*, and Robin Givens, known for her role on *Head of the Class* (ABC, 1986–1991), UPN ordered the pilot for *Good News* based on known talent. The project was greenlit because gospel singer Kirk Franklin was attached, recalling *Moesha's* reliance on known talent to mitigate the risks associated with developing a new Black-cast series. At the time, Franklin was riding high from his success with a seventeen-voice choir called "Kirk Franklin and the Family." The group, formed in 1992, released its debut record in 1993. It spent almost two years on the Gospel charts and crossed over to the R&B charts. Two additional hit records followed, with the record "Whatcha Lookin' 4" earning Franklin a Grammy Award for Best Contemporary Soul Gospel Album. In other words, Franklin was a well-established entertainer, and UPN could use his success in gospel and R&B musical forms to mitigate the risks associated with producing new television programming—particularly for a start-up network hungry for more hit series.

Weinberger imagined *Good News* as an issues-based show, in the vein of many series on which he had worked previously and its network mate *Moesha*. He explained,

> I wanted the show to deal with issues. I thought it would be a fresh approach given that my hero was a minister. I wanted him to have a point of view that was forward and progressive, but most importantly, Christian. . . . But I also had to remember that it was also a comedy show done in front of an audience. There was a limit to how deep I could go or how probing or how pious or meaningful. It was a need to entertain, so all of this had to be done to the medium of comedy. There always has to be a comic attitude, whatever these issues were.[49]

Weinberger insinuates the limitations of comedy in dealing with issues, which can be serious for only a moment before returning to a series' jokes-per-page quota. In this way, comedy (and, as I explore in chap. 3, the laugh track) always undercuts the seriousness of whatever issues a sitcom aims to tackle. And because sitcoms, particularly Black-cast sitcoms like *Good News*, must return to stasis at the conclusion of each episode, the issues raised must be concluded at the end of the thirty-minute episode. At the same time, Weinberger thought homosexuality and the hegemonic understanding of the Black church were important enough to center them within the series' pilot episode. The inclusion of homosexuality ultimately cost him series star Kirk Franklin, a topic I explore in chapter 2.[50]

Weinberger wanted the series to be bold and signaled that boldness by putting a Black gay "character into the church."[51] Weinberger's characterization of homosexuality as "bold" has a dual function. First, he gestures toward the discourse that Black churches (in particular) are antigay. Therefore, putting a Black gay character within a story centered within a Black church is considered a bold move, given how Blackness and religiosity have become linked with antigayness in popular discourse.[52] At the same time, Weinberger's "boldness" also speaks to the relative absence of Black homosexuality within Black-cast sitcoms, although homosexuality on white- and multicultural-cast sitcoms had become de rigueur by the time *Good News* entered production. Although Franklin ultimately left (or was fired from) the series for his objection to the "Pilot" episode's inclusion of Black gay content, it also speaks to the power held by series showrunners (a topic to which I return in chap. 2), particularly ones with as much industrial capital as Weinberger, and the willingness or desperation of UPN to find a hit to add to its stable of programming. Weinberger undoubtedly worked within the generic confines of the Black-cast sitcom, but he could essentially fire his series star (or let the series star decide to leave) rather than change the content of an episode. In the UPN world in which Black music stars and established Black-cast sitcom actors were understood to be the order of the day, Weinberger's clout allowed him to continue with *Good News* by recasting the lead role with a relatively unknown actor, David Ramsey.

Good News premiered on August 25, 1997, as part of UPN's Monday night Black-cast sitcom programming block, which at this time also included the third season premiere of *In the House* starring rapper LL Cool J, the second season premieres of *Malcolm & Eddie* with former "*Cosby* kid" Malcolm Jamal Warner, and *Sparks*. The opening credits clearly situated the show within Black church traditions by its invocation of Black gospel music. As Beretta Smith Shomade details, there are "connections between R&B, gospel, and hip hop within black popular culture [because] gospel is the foundation for both of the other two genres."[53] But unlike *Moesha*, which featured a kind of commodified Blackness in its use of New Jack Swing music, the *Good News* theme song signals a connection to Blackness somewhat separate from other commodified Black music forms. After all, while gospel music may be popular, it does not typically reach the level of crossover popularity that R&B and hip-hop were consistently reaching.

TV Guide, glossing over the notion that there was a gay story line in the *Good News* pilot, synopsizes the episode as dealing with "a beleaguered young minister, who, in the opener, takes over the pastorship of an urban church."[54] It is important to note that the TV description is not generated by *TV Guide* but the network—or in this case, UPN. As an industrial paratext, the episode's description gestures toward the series' engagement with the generic closet—Black gayness is so temporary within the series that to discuss it is to raise the potential for an imagined homophobic Black audience to dismiss the series, jeopardizing its potential longevity.

The reviews for the pilot episode were mixed. Caryn James at the *New York Times* concluded that "*Good News* is one of the three new UPN sitcoms . . . and the only one with a hope of matching the appeal of the network's *Moesha*."[55] *Los Angeles Times* critic Howard Rosenberg panned the series, saying "caricatures really hit the fan on this series . . . [and] exaggerates everything else in such extreme that satire is not even a possibility."[56] The mixed reviews did not deter 5.5 million viewers from tuning into the premiere episode. Soon thereafter, UPN ordered nine additional episodes, bringing the series to a total of twenty-two episodes for its first season. However, low ratings throughout the season resulted in its cancellation after its inaugural season.

Ultimately, the industrial history of *Good News* demonstrates how Blackness could be commodified in very specific ways. The argument could be made that *Good News* was "just" a bad show. Because the show ultimately did not have known talent top-lining the series and used gospel music in the series' theme song, it deviated from the models of Blackness that were finding success within these new netlets. In addition, in a series designed to deal with issues, Weinberger imagined gayness as an issue that should be dealt with once—coming out *and* introducing a boyfriend or partner—rather than over two different episodes.

In the season immediately following the cancellation of *Good News*, UPN and The WB both began programming five nights of original programming. However, UPN quickly discovered that more is not always better. The season was abysmal (ratings-wise) for UPN and included flops like *The Secret Diary of Desmond Pfeiffer* (*Desmond*; UPN, 1998) and *Love Boat: The Next Wave* (UPN, 1998–1999). Not only was *Desmond* a ratings failure, but the series was also the subject of boycotts because, as organizations like the NAACP and the Brother-hood Crusade alleged, the show displayed "a callous disregard for the suffering of blacks during the slavery era by using the Lincoln White House and the Civil War as a backdrop for a sitcom."[57] With its turn to five nights of programming, the network abandoned most of its Black-cast sitcoms, keeping well-performing but aging series *Moesha* and *Malcolm & Eddie*. The two Black-cast sitcoms paired with those series were *Moesha* spin-off *The Parkers* (UPN, 1999–2004), featuring eventual Oscar-winner Mo'Nique and *Moesha* breakout star Count-ess Vaughn, and *Grown Ups* (UPN, 1999–2000), a short-lived multicultural-cast sitcom starring Jaleel White (best known as Steve Urkel on *Family Matters*; ABC, 1989–1998). For the 1999–2000 television season, the network turned most of its energy to courting young (white), adult males with *WWF Smack-down* (UPN, 1999–2006; The CW, 2006–2008; MyNetworkTV, 2008–2010; SyFy, 2010–2015; USA, 2016–present) and *Dilbert* (UPN, 1999–2000). Even as the network had five nights of programming, for the second consecutive year, it still segregated Black-cast sitcoms to its Monday night "Black block." This Black blocking ensured that UPN would generally have no more than four Black-cast sitcoms on its schedule at any given time but also prompted the network to always find new Black-cast sitcoms to fill out this block when others failed (the last hour of programming, from 10:00 p.m.–11:00 p.m. ET was reserved for local programming).

UPN's segregation strategy was still in effect during the 2000–2001 tele-vision season. With *Moesha* having been canceled, the network picked up D. L. Hughley's canceled ABC sitcom *The Hughleys* (ABC, 1998–2000; UPN, 2000–2002) and greenlit a new Black-cast sitcom *Girlfriends* (UPN, 2000–2006; The CW, 2006–2008) and aired them all on Monday nights. Although the so-called Gay '90s were largely over, UPN (and its rival The WB) failed to engage in any significant way with the veritable explosion of gay representation, although *Girlfriends* would include two Black gay characters. Series showrunner Mara Brock-Akil told me, "Because I've always had gay men in my life—my children have gay uncles—it never occurred to me to not include gay characters in the stories I'm telling."[58] But even with Brock-Akil's gesture toward the inclusivity of homosexuality, *Girlfriends* would gesture toward Black gayness but always within the context of the Black-cast sitcom's generic closet. The two Black gay characters, Peaches and Ronnie, were never central to the story lines the show chose to tell, and they were deployed solely for their sassy retorts before sim-ply being written off the series, never to return. *All of Us*, which debuted two seasons after *Girlfriends*, would continue to reassert the efficacy of the generic closet.

*Breaking Out of UPN's Black Block (but not the Generic
Closet) with "A-List" Talent for* All of Us

All of Us, a series about a blended family that was executive produced by Will Smith and Jada Pinkett Smith, allowed Black gayness temporary visibility for two episodes in 2006. In the episodes "Like Father, Like Son, Like Hell" and "My Two Dads," series star Duane Martin, who played Robert, discovers that his biological father is gay. Even in the construction of the episode synopsis—a topic explored more deeply in chapter 2—the generic closet is at work. The discovery of Luther's (Robert's biological father) gayness sets in motion the three-act structure necessary for the generic closet's operation. This section engages Daniels and Littleton's discursive positioning of *All of Us* as "a cut above the garden-variety UPN sitcom," alongside its continued reliance on the generic closet as a representational and industrial strategy for engaging Black gayness.[59]

Produced through the Smith's production company Overbrook Entertainment, which had produced the films *Wild Wild West* (1999, dir. Barry Sonnenfeld) and *Ali* (2001, dir. Michael Mann), *All of Us* was based loosely on the Smiths' lives as a blended family. More than that, it traded on hip-hop's (re)signification of comedy (not only resonant in series like *Fresh Prince* and Queen Latifah's stint on *Living Single* but also in films like the *House Party* franchise) to sell the series. PopMatters writer Cynthia Fuchs details the ways "hip hop and TV seem[ed] rather like they were made for each other, what with their many interconnections in . . . any number of TV shows . . . that use hip hop to signify everything from sophistication to club culture, comedy to coolness."[60] Will Smith was most famous as the "Fresh Prince" through both his rap music career and his six-year stint on *Fresh Prince*. Jada Pinkett Smith was known for her work on three seasons of *A Different World* (NBC, 1987–1993) and the film *Set It Off* (1996, dir. F. Gary Gray). The involvement of Betsy Borns lent *All of Us* television production credibility through her work on *Roseanne* (ABC, 1988–1997) and *Friends* (NBC, 1994–2004). UPN's pick up of *All of Us* also fulfilled then-senior vice president of comedy development Kim Fleary's vision of working with Borns. Fleary also described the Smiths as being "so passionate about the idea because it was inspired by their lives. That's always attractive to me as a developer."[61]

All of Us, much like Smith's sitcom debut *Fresh Prince*, traded on the twin pillars of Black authenticity and autobiography. Just as the series was ramping up to premiere, a *Jet* magazine cover story tethered the Smith family's autobiography and a sense of Black authenticity as central to the series' premise.

Smith explained, "The show is really just loosely based on our experience. . . . It's more about blended families. We worked with a couple of psychologists, and we took the basis of our experiences, and we talked to our friends and parents and had focus groups and went out and really got an essence of the struggles of blended families."[62] Smith's comments work to center autobiography and authenticity in two key ways. First, he centers the autobiographical component of the series, implying that the show's rootedness in his family members' "real" lives transfers onto the series to make it seem real by extension. Second, Smith's recounting the ways psychologists, focus groups, and "real people" offered input gestures toward the accuracy and authenticity the series attempted to achieve. Much in the way Bill Cosby consulted psychologist Alvin Poussaint to ensure that *The Cosby Show* promoted particular images of televisual Blackness, Smith attempts to tether *All of Us* to a similar set of traditions. Part of *All of Us*'s claim to quality was also rooted in the notion that the Smiths "maintained a semi-regular presence on the set, reviewed scripts, and contributed to the writing process—particularly during the first season," as a way to ensure that their vision for the series was executed.[63]

The series' pick-up also made good on UPN's then-Entertainment President Dawn Ostroff's articulation of the network's goal to "be in business with A-list talent."[64] The notion of the Smiths' "A-list" status is important because their star texts (both as separate actors and as a Hollywood "power couple") make the series plausible in an increasingly crowded landscape with the advent of cable channels like HBO and Lifetime producing original content. In addition, the series relied on known talent with series lead Duane Martin, who had found success on the Patti LaBelle–led Black-cast sitcom *Out All Night* (NBC, 1992–1993) and episodic appearances on Black-cast sitcoms like *Fresh Prince*, *Living Single*, *Girlfriends*, and *One on One* (UPN, 2001–2006).

Premiering September 16, 2003, the series broke from UPN's segregation of Black-cast sitcoms on Monday nights. Monday night still featured a night programmed with two hours of Black-cast sitcoms including *The Parkers*, rapper Eve's eponymous new series (UPN, 2003–2006), *Girlfriends*, and the sophomore season of *Half & Half* (UPN, 2002–2006). The Tuesday night block sandwiched *All of Us* between *One on One* (which was moved to be a Black-cast block mater with *All of Us*) and the short-lived eight-episode run of *Rock Me Baby* (UPN, 2003). The night concluded with *Mullets* (UPN, 2003), a short-lived white-cast sitcom starring John O'Hurley and Loni Anderson. While *All of Us* may have been described as "a cut above," Alessandra Stanley at the *New York Times* called it an "agenda sitcom" that felt like an attempt to present "a sympathetic self-portrait [of Will Smith] that exempts the father—and his comely fiancée—from guilt," gesturing toward the real-life relationship of Will Smith, Jada Pinkett, and Smith's ex-wife Sheree Zampino.[65] Fuchs found that the series included "romantic tensions, petty competitions, banal jealousies, and enough general good-heartedness to resolve all issues by the end of the weekly 30 minutes."[66] However, tepid reviews did not matter for the series' ratings. Shortly after its debut, *All of Us* was picked up for a full season after becoming the network's highest rated series, with 4.5 million total viewers, and "improv[ing] the Tuesday 8:30–9 p.m. time period compared with last season in viewers and all key demos."[67] UPN's programming strategy seemed to work by mitigating the risks associated with new programming by tethering the Smiths' extra- and intertextual persona to *All of Us* in order to shore up its chances for success.

Like the other Black-cast sitcoms UPN picked up in its early history, *All of Us* would engage with Black gayness but only within the context of a specific coming-out story arc. Much as Fox before it, UPN strategically targeted Black and "hip" viewers with Black-cast sitcoms. Although episodes of *Moesha, Good News, The Parkers, All of Us,* and *Girlfriends* would feature Black gay characters in an episodic fashion, they failed to sustain such representations, gesturing toward the limits of Black gayness as "hipness" for an imagined Black viewer. UPN's Black-cast sitcoms lagged behind white- and multicultural-cast sitcoms' engagement with gayness, seemingly stuck in the early 1990s, whereas *Ellen, Will & Grace,* and *Spin City* weekly visited white SLUMPY viewers' homes; no such profile existed for the Black viewers that UPN was courting.[68] As I have argued elsewhere, "The television industry has made no space for the imagining of a BLAMPY viewer—ones who are black, liberal, affluent, metropolitan professionals and who understand that gayness can be a part of the fabric of black television families. These black gay characters are imagined as temporary intruders designed to reify broad cultural understandings of blackness broadly and the black family unit specifically."[69] Even with the emergence of cable as a provider of original content, Black-cast sitcoms would remain disengaged from sustained representations of Black gayness as part of the Black-cast sitcom experience, although Black gayness would resurface as TBS began courting Black viewers, like Fox and UPN had done before it. And in the process of courting these Black viewers, the network would, once again, rely on the generic closet to represent gayness.

BUILDING A BRAND ON BLACKNESS AT TBS: *ARE WE THERE YET?* AND THE GENERIC CLOSET

"Are you gay?" Terry Crew's character Nick asks this question of Cedric, a potential suitor for his daughter Lindsay, about halfway through the 2010 *Are*

We There Yet? episode "The Boy Has Style." This question leads to the discovery and declaration of Cedric's gayness and, thus reasserts the series' engagement with the generic closet. As a Black-cast series greenlit as TBS sought to establish itself through original programming, *Are We There Yet?* trafficked in discourses similar to those of UPN in its quest for market differentiation. TBS's move from syndicator to producer of original content demonstrates the vitality of Black audiences and the commercial efficacy of Black content. As this section details, TBS's engagement with Blackness was not necessarily through hip-hop sensibilities but rather through the mass marketing and the commodification of Blackness using known properties and known talent. Simultaneously, TBS, and *Are We There Yet?*, by extension, continued to imagine a Black audience as antigay for its Black-cast content.

Like The WB and UPN, TBS developed after the demise of the network era as a competitor with the big three networks. By the 1990s, TBS made a number of syndication agreements that would help position the network as a force within broadcasting. Similar to many other media companies caught up in the consolidation and conglomeration of the 1990s, TBS was acquired by Time Warner in 1996. With that merger, TBS began solidifying its position as a superstation making major deals to run syndicated content on the network, including the first broadcast rights for hit films (many outside the Time Warner family of companies) and deals to rerun popular sitcoms like *Home Improvement* (ABC, 1991–1999), *Friends, The Drew Carey Show* (ABC, 1995–2004), and *Seinfeld* (NBC, 1989–1998).

By 2004, TBS had established itself as a major player in cable programming and began branding itself under the tagline, "Very Funny," a move that saw many channels and networks under the Time Warner conglomerate creating clearly delineated brands in an increasingly crowded television marketplace. Thus, TBS remade "their daily program schedule to play up contemporary co-medic content, principally in the form of reruns of popular broadcast-network sitcoms . . . as well as comic films like the *Austin Powers* movies, *Legally Blonde* and *Men in Black*."[70] Continuing to build its viewers with popular comedic fare, TBS began seriously considering expansion of its original programming in this era.

In particular, TBS struck a deal with fellow Atlanta-headquartered company Tyler Perry Studios for first-run distribution rights for *Tyler Perry's House of Payne* (*House of Payne*; TBS, 2006–2012), produced by Debmar-Mercury Productions. Rather than pursuing the "traditional" mode of television development, where the studio makes a pilot, it gets picked up for an initial thirteen episodes and is either renewed or canceled, the TBS deal with Debmar-Mercury resulted in an initial order for ten episodes immediately and exclusively for TBS. The additional ninety episodes (to reach the "magic" hundred episodes needed for syndication) would be produced shortly thereafter. That pioneering deal led TBS and Debmar-Mercury to develop a number of similar deals for Tyler Perry–produced television shows and *Are We There Yet?* Reflecting on the deal among Tyler Perry, TBS, and Debmar-Mercury, *Are We There Yet?* showrunner Ali Leroi explains that "the idea is that when you deal with that volume of programming, you can sell it off into markets. It's a financially lucrative deal to know that you'll have a large number of episodes available to sell. Usually when you do network television, they don't know beyond the first season whether or not they'll ever get to [100 episodes]. So, to go into the deal knowing that you're going to produce at least 100 episodes, which makes something a viable syndication property, really just changed the way the production was done."[71] *Are We There Yet?* was greenlit in a "10–90" deal, a model that "calls for a test run of 10 episodes on a cabler, and if those episodes hit pre-determined ratings targets, the cabler is obligated to pick up 90 more to be produced over two years. That allows Debmar-Mercury to then sell the off-network rights to local stations, which means the show (in success) is churning out profits barely two years after its premiere."[72]

Producing a series for syndication typically means that the series should be episodic versus serial—or have stories that are self-contained within an episode versus ones that stretch across multiple episodes. The episodic nature of most syndicated series conforms to a fairly standard programming tool—*stripping*—meaning that episodes are run daily (or weekly in the case of *Are We There Yet?*) in the same time slot.[73] Stripping is also partially how the generic closet is constituted within *Are We There Yet?* Because the series "has no memory" (as is the case with most thirty-minute sitcoms), the assumption is that recurring characters are impossible (particularly Black gay ones).

Are We There Yet?'s 10–90 deal required a more truncated production schedule than "traditional" series designed to air roughly twenty-three weekly episodes. In this model, showrunner LeRoi contends that the first ten-episode run was completed with about six weeks of preproduction, which included episode writing. The production schedule was such that in a four-day production week, the series could shoot three episodes on its soundstage in Stamford, Connecticut. Part of the hastened production pace was rooted in the plan for the series to air two episodes weekly (rather than the single episode that most multicamera series air per week). In addition, it was a cost-cutting decision for the production. LeRoi adds, "it's all financial because when you're shooting shows at that pace, it's incredibly difficult to shepherd in an audience, have a warm-up comic, and so forth. And in television production, time is money."[74]

As was the case with *Moesha*'s Brandy Norwood, *Good News* and Kirk Franklin, and *All of Us* relying on Duane Martin and the Smiths, the main reason TBS picked up *Are We There Yet?* was based on its recognizability as a property. Although the film version of *Are We There Yet?* (dir. Brian Levant, 2005) was largely panned by critics, it grossed $98 million worldwide and spawned the sequel *Are We Done Yet?* (dir. Steve Carr, 2007), which grossed $58 million worldwide. The films largely traded on the success and popularity of Ice Cube, who had ironically transitioned from an antigay, misogynistic gangsta rapper who rapped that "true niggas ain't gay" to an actor in "family-friendly" fare with the *Friday* and *Barber Shop* film franchises, demonstrating the continued utility of rap, hip-hop, and Black culture for Black-cast television and film content into the new millennium. LeRoi underscores that "part of making a deal like [the *Are We There Yet?* deal] is having some sort of property that has a built-in marketing component."[75]

Once the deal was secured, as TBS began ramping up marketing efforts in advance of the series premiere, one of the print ads it used both touted Ice Cube's role as one of the series' executive producers and featured the rapper, actor, and producer alongside the cast. A second ad featured only the cast but included a call-out with Ice Cube's photo and his credit on the series as an executive producer. The advertising underscores how the series' success seemed to be predicated on Ice Cube as a visible author who functioned as a "built-in marketing component" that TBS and Debmar-Mercury counted on to sell the series to viewers and potential syndicators. While some viewers may have been familiar with Terry Crews (who was cast as patriarch Nick Persons) from his work on *Everybody Hates Chris* (UPN, 2005–2006; The CW, 2006–2009) or Essence Atkins (who was cast as matriarch Suzanne Kingston) from her role on the UPN series *Half & Half*, the initial ads traded on the connection to Ice Cube rather than the sitcom's story or its actors. In fact, one of the stories announcing the series featured a quote from Ice Cube about Terry Crews taking over the role he originated cinematically but nothing from the actor himself.[76]

The June 2, 2010, premiere of the series, which featured two back-to-back episodes, was met with mixed reviews. The *New York Daily News* said the show "traps a buoyant cast in a sitcom that's slow out of the gate," while *Variety* claimed "the occasionally stilted dialogue doesn't make it easy for the cast, which otherwise performs passably. Still, the series' overall sweetness makes up for a number of its failings."[77] Demonstrating the ways critical discourse and Black viewership are often out of sync, the series debuted with 3.2 million viewers,

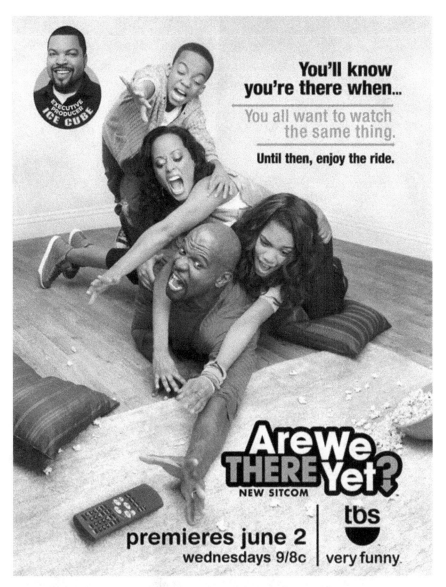

Fig. 1.6. Advertisement for *Are We There Yet?* that draws on Ice Cube's star text as a means to sell the series to viewers. Permission granted by Turner Broadcasting System, Inc.

Fig. 1.7. Advertisement for *Are We There Yet?* that features Ice Cube alongside the cast as a means to sell the series to viewers. Permission granted by Turner Broadcasting System, Inc.

1.6 million of whom were in the coveted eighteen-to-forty-nine-year-old demographic. The second episode increased to 3.3. million total viewers and 1.7 million viewers aged eighteen to forty-nine. Its third episode, which aired the following week, attracted 2.6 million viewers. Ultimately, the series performed well enough that TBS greenlit the "back ninety" episodes of *Are We There Yet?*, which averaged 2.8 million viewers in its first ten-episode airings.

Within the back ninety, *Are We There Yet?* included an episode featuring a Black gay character and story line. "The Boy Has Style" was the first time a Black-cast TBS series engaged with homosexuality. But importantly, it is *an* episode, hence rebuilding and reifying the generic closet for Black gayness on yet another network. There were certainly "gay episodes" and gay characters within its (largely white-cast) syndicated fare, including *Friends* and *Sex and the City*, but the fleeting inclusion of a Black gay character is important for two reasons.

First, while the "explosion" of gay television representation seen in the Gay '90s was important, the early 2000s continued a trend similar to those Gay '90s series but mostly with cable networks, leading *Vanity Fair* to declare that TV was having a "gay heat wave" on the cover of its December 2003 issue.[78] Despite this declaration, the major networks' engagement with gay representation began to wane in the late 1990s and early 2000s when *Ellen* was canceled in 1996 because of low ratings (also wrapped up in the discourse that the show had gotten "too gay" since DeGeneres and her on-screen alter ego had come out as lesbian), *Spin City* concluded its run in 2002, and *Will & Grace* signed off in 2006 (although it returned to airwaves in 2017). However, cable networks would pick up where the broadcast networks left off with series like *Queer Eye for the Straight Guy* (Bravo, 2003–2007; Netflix [as *Queer Eye*], 2018–present), *Queer as Folk* (Showtime, 2000–2005), *Noah's Arc* (Logo, 2005–2006), and *The L Word* (Showtime, 2004–2009, 2019–present). By the early 2010s, few series featuring gay characters had achieved mainstream recognition or multiseason runs on the major networks, save *Modern Family* (ABC, 2009–2020).

Second, with its move into original programming, TBS was specifically targeting Black and urban viewers. There was some crossover appeal to *Are We There Yet?*, with both its choice of property and the network's Tyler Perry series, but Black and urban viewers were a top priority with the network's new slate of programming. To gesture toward its Wednesday night Black and urban viewer programming block, *Are We There Yet?* was paired with *House of Payne* before it and the George Lopez chatfest *Lopez Tonight* (TBS, 2009–2011) immediately following it. The programming flow made sense within the assertion by Michael Wright, TBS's programming chief, that "the cornerstone of our development is what's already working. We take an audience that's already coming and program to them."[79] Wright's comments telegraphed the network's historical programming of Black-cast sitcom reruns including *Amen* (1997–2002), *Cosby* (2000–2005), *The Cosby Show* (1999–2008), *A Different World* (1999–2002), *Family Matters* (1995–2003), and *Fresh Prince* (1999–2004, 2007–2014), among others. In addition, the flow of Black-cast programming also carries with it the attendant unfounded industry lore about Black viewers and their intolerance of homosexuality. At the same time, the programming block ghettoized TBS's Black and urban programming in much the same way Fox, UPN, and The WB had done before it.[80]

Once TBS reached a critical mass of viewers that would demonstrate value to advertisers, they slowly but surely began canceling Black-cast sitcoms and replacing them with white- and multicultural-cast sitcoms, or what I have elsewhere "Fox Formula 3.0."[81] In 2011, TBS canceled the Tyler Perry series *Meet the Browns* (2009–2011), and in 2012, *House of Payne* ended its six-year run. After producing its hundred episodes, TBS ordered no new episodes of *Are We There Yet?* Those Black-cast series were replaced by series with mostly white casts like *Sullivan & Son* (2012–2014) and ABC's canceled Courteney Cox vehicle *Cougar Town* (ABC, 2009–2012; TBS, 2013–2015). TBS's brief engagement with Black-cast sitcoms underscores the precarity associated with Black-cast television production. The ease with which networks cancel Black-cast series also helps to explain the caution series producers exercise when engaging with "taboo" topics like Black homosexuality. In other words, the precarity of Black-cast series coupled with the imagined conservatism of Black audiences rebuilds the generic closet over and over again. This cautiousness was also the order of the day at BET, a network ostensibly more dedicated to and invested in representing Blackness than "mainstream" networks.

BET(TING) ON BLACKNESS AT BLACK ENTERTAINMENT TELEVISION

It is impossible to discuss Black television without a discussion of Black Entertainment Television (BET). BET launched in 1980 as an independent Black network owned by former Washington, DC, lobbyist Robert L. Johnson. At the time of its launch, BET "stood as a much-needed and desired platform for visioning African-American imagery in general and black artistic talent specifically."[82] This period was also marked by the founding of cable channels like Nickelodeon, HBO, CNN, Bravo, and MTV. Derek Kompare argues that these new networks mostly "thrived on the stuff of repetition, offering schedules filled with . . . reruns."[83] This model is most regularly employed by new cable networks because of the relatively low cost of procuring existing material vis-à-vis producing original content. BET was no exception: it initially featured older films centered on Black protagonists, sporting events, and public affairs series, initially eschewing music videos as viable programming for the network. According to Beretta E. Smith-Shomade, within a year of its launch, the network debuted *Video Soul* (BET, 1981–1996), and by 1983—the year BET began twenty-four-hour programming—it "televised six hours of music videos" focusing on Black music and artists still largely neglected on MTV.[84] Darnell M. Hunt submits that BET had historically relied "upon the rotation of music videos and other low-cost, recycled programming in order to offset relatively low subscriber and advertising rates in its bid for profits."[85] This programming strategy was a financially winning combination, and by 1999, BET "was lauded by *Forbes* magazine as one of the best small businesses in America," boasting subscribers in more than fifty-five million American homes.[86]

With the increase of cable channels in the 1990s, many of which began producing original content, audiences and viewer shares were increasingly fragmented. The lingering and continuing effects of the proliferation of home video and DVD added to the major network's woes with respect to capturing market share. Becker concluded that by the early 1990s, the networks "saw their ad revenues and sense of invulnerability decline, [while] cable actually saw ad rates and revenues increase at double-digit rates."[87] HBO intermittently produced original movies and series, but its importance as a source of original programming is often placed in 1999, when its series *The Sopranos* (1999–2007) won four prime time Emmy Awards. By the time *Sex and the City* (HBO, 1998–2004) won the Best Comedy Series Emmy in 2001, the other networks were on notice that something (allegedly) new, different, and exciting (as far as "quality" discourses were concerned) was happening at HBO, and viewers were fleeing network fare in favor of the "edgier," more specifically targeted content offered by cable networks. By 2005, cable channels were "capturing over 50 percent of the daily viewing audience" as they continued to multiply and dissect the viewer demographic pie into smaller pieces.[88]

Although BET seemed to be riding high in the late 1990s and early 2000s, Black sentiment about the network was often less than sunny. As Smith-Shomade found in a Spelman College focus group, some of her respondents' "comments suggested not only negatively transformed visual imagery [via music videos and other network programming] but also BET's impact and viability on the lives of citizens, both in public and private spaces."[89] Satirist Aaron McGruder turned his ire toward BET as well. In a *Boondocks* comic strip, his protagonist, Huey, a child Black Nationalist, questioned his allegiance to the Black

Nationalist principle that companies like BET would continue to "act in the best interest of Black America."[90] The *Washington Post*'s Paul Farhi synthesized the problems at BET: "At a time when the NAACP has been challenging the major networks for inadequate black representation, some African Americans [were] expressing disenchantment with BET. They gripe[d] that BET's schedule [was] rife with lowbrow and shopworn programs, that . . . often traffic in the very stereotypes blacks have complained about on other networks," ultimately exposing the import of "respectable" Black images to some of BET's viewers.[91] Although there was growing discontent with BET and its programming, the network continued to grow and prosper, although the 2000s would see a number of Black-focused cable networks, including ASPiRE, Centric, and TV One attempting to fill the "positive" image gap many saw as deficient at BET.

After the passage of the Telecommunications Act of 1996, which was meant to open up marketplace competition in the telecommunications industry, mergers, acquisitions, and media conglomeration became the orders of the day. Larger companies merged with or acquired independent networks, film studios, and production companies in a bid to augment weaknesses in their demographic portfolios and to stave off competition. In 2000, BET was no exception as Viacom purchased the network for a reported $2.34 billion, bringing BET under a conglomerate that also owned music video channels MTV, VH1, and CMT.[92] Almost immediately, questions were raised about the sale of the network and what impact a white-owned conglomerate would have on a previously Black-owned network. In an ABCNews.com article, James Winston, then-executive director of the National Association of Black Owned Broadcasters, expressed concern that under its new ownership, "there will not be African-American ownership at the very top, and I think that makes a difference."[93] Some of those fears were quickly realized. In March 2001, the network abruptly dismissed Tavis Smiley, host of its news and public affairs program *BET Tonight* (1998–2002), which was canceled in 2002. The same year, the network canceled its long-running public affairs program *Teen Summit* (1982–2002). Soon the network began airing more music video and inexpensively produced reality television programming, mirroring programming on its sister networks MTV and VH1, and raising the ire of some of its Black viewers who wanted the network to traffic in "respectable" Black images.

Part and parcel of the kinds of images BET produced and distributed were those that were decidedly and aggressively heterosexual. As Smith-Shomade argues, "On BET, heterosexual masculinity maintain[ed] a ratcheted up personification. While allusions to homosexuality surfaced periodically [in music videos] . . . the notion and discussion of homosexuality garnered very limited airtime on BET."[94] BET was heavily invested in a hip-hop masculinity that resisted certain tropes of Black masculinity while it concomitantly embraced patriarchy and heteronormativity (and its corollary antigayness).[95] Hip-hop's relationship to Black masculinity cannot necessarily be understood as mono-lithic; BET's approach to Blackness and its intersection with gayness was simi-lar to rapper Beanie Sigel's warning that gay men should "keep that shit all the way in the closet around me."[96] Furthermore, as writer Demetrius Bady recalls, "I went to pitch over at BET. A gay person at the network told me that I should not write any gay characters. That's their directive because they think their audience would never accept a recurring gay character, which I just think is ludicrous."[97] BET's directive to not include ongoing homosexuality within the confines of any series on the network underscores that BET imagines that its audience, of both Black viewers and white viewers interested in commercial-ized Black culture, are not tolerant of gay content.

By 2011, BET found that it needed to shift its programming strategy away from music videos and inexpensive reality programming. TV One launched as a rival network in January 2004, but BET initially dismissed the network, pontificating, "We've been challenged . . . but BET reigns supreme."[98] TV One was hitting singles and doubles with its programming, particularly *Unsung*, an "answer" to VH1's *Behind the Music*, with entertainers who may not have achieved mainstream success but were important to Black popular culture. In 2010, TV One premiered its first original sitcom *Love that Girl!* (2010–2014), which in its first season reportedly cost about $1.2 million per episode, about "half what one episode of a successful-ish broadcast sitcom costs these days."[99] In addition, as detailed in the previous section, TBS had been striking gold with *House of Payne, Meet the Browns, Are We There Yet?*, and *For Better or Worse*.

Realizing that BET was behind the curve on Black-cast original program-ming and that TV One and other Black-focused start-up channels were eating into its market share, BET executives began developing a number of original Black-cast sitcoms. BET Networks' CEO Debra Lee told *Broadcasting and Cable* that BET's new programming was meant to "respect, reflect and at the same time, elevate" its program offerings in an effort to differentiate itself from other Black-focused networks.[100] Part of Lee's comments relied on "uplift" discourses in Black media image production, but at the same time, Lee asserted that BET's brand strategy was different than what was offered at other Black-focused net-works.[101] The result was a slate of original programming that *Broadcasting and Cable* summarized as series "that support[ed] families and embrace[d] and encourage[d] their dreams, focusing on the issues that are important to them while providing the 'freshest' talent in entertainment."[102] Not only does Lee center "family" in her comments, she also centers the importance of known talent within the quest for new programming.

BET's "focus on family" also gestures toward the generic closet. The convergence of this family focus and BET's resignification of hip-hop homophobia signaled that the network would not engage with homosexuality in any sustained fashion. BET demonstrated its new brand strategy with unscripted series *The Family Crews* (2010–2011) and *Tiny and Toya* (2009–2011). *The Family Crews* centered on the family and home life of actor Terry Crews, whereas *Tiny and Toya* followed the series' titular stars (one a former member of the R&B group Xscape) as they navigated life and parenthood. By 2011, Loretha Jones, then-president of BET original programming, said reality programming was limited in its storytelling ability and that scripted series "allow us to tell very detailed stories in a very broad way, and it allows us to expand on the experience of what you get to see of African-American life."[103] To be sure, this approach is partly rooted in a general Black viewer objection to the ways Blackness appears in reality television. Racquel Gates suggests,

> One criticism made of reality television is that it promotes "negative" images of African Americans more effectively than television programs such as the sitcom or drama because, unlike these fictional offerings, reality TV masks itself as documentary, which straightforwardly presents, rather than represents, people and situations. The problem, critics argue, is the claim that what appears on the screen is an accurate depiction of real people with no intrusion by scripts, producers, or any of the other elements of fictionalized representation. Without the acknowledgment that these representations are constructed fictions, such images run the risk of being interpreted as truthful and accurate reflections of essentialized racial identities.[104]

The relay between Black audiences and Black representation undoubtedly weighed on BET, which had been under fire for its (over)reliance on "gangsta" rap music videos versus programming that would "uplift." I argue that it was the rating success of some unscripted programming that allowed BET the ad revenue to move from unscripted to scripted series.

BET's turn to scripted series began with the network announcing that it would resurrect the canceled CW series *The Game* (The CW, 2004–2009; BET, 2011–2015), which coincidentally included two episodes in its original run that featured a Black gay character: "Stay Fierce, Malik" and "Do the Wright Thing." The network had purchased syndication rights to the program after The CW canceled it and realized that the show retained an active fan base. In fact, some

BET reruns of *The Game* garnered "higher numbers than they did when they originally aired on The CW.... BET's senior vice president of original programming, Charlie Jordan Brookins, said, 'This is the beginning of building what scripted programming means to BET.'"[105] BET demonstrated its ongoing commitment to moving away from unscripted programming by also greenlighting *Let's Stay Together* (2011–2014) as a flow companion series to *The Game*. Even as BET turned to scripted series, it retained the imagination of its audiences as antigay. Thus, on the rare occasion that BET's original series engaged with Black gayness, they remained tightly linked to the generic closet.

SCRIPTING THE GENERIC CLOSET ON *LET'S STAY TOGETHER*

Let's Stay Together was a multicamera sitcom shot in Atlanta. Executive produced by Jacque Edmonds Cofer, *Let's Stay Together* was originally developed as an autobiographical series titled *Oldywood*, based on Edmonds Cofer's relationship with her husband. She says, "Because we were not young when we got married, I wanted to do a show that deals with those sorts of challenges. Then, when we got it to BET they wanted to tailor it to a younger audience. So, we changed it to *Let's Stay Together* ... The only other change was that the original concept was based on the challenges of being a newlywed, but BET wanted the primary couple not to be married at the beginning of the series so that we could show progression from being engaged to being married."[106] The series was described in BET's press release as "an updated, urban-romantic comedy that takes an unconventional look into the lives of five young, ambitious African Americans. The series centers on a married couple, an engaged couple and a single sister who all take courageous steps as they navigate life, love and matrimony."[107] By featuring African Americans at varying life stages (single, engaged, and married), BET hoped it could create a series broad enough to retain (and perhaps build on) *The Game*'s audience.

With *The Game* and *Let's Stay Together* and the Malcolm Jamal Warner–led *Reed between the Lines* (BET, 2011), BET (re)entered the original scripted programming space for the first time since its failed *Somebodies* (2008). But like the "pedigree" required to jumpstart a Black-cast show, *Let's Stay Together* also relied on a number of known variables to attempt to secure its success. First, the project came from Queen Latifah's production company Flavor Unit, which had produced successful Black-cast films *The Cookout* (dir. Lance Rivera, 2004), *Beauty Shop* (dir. Bille Woodruff, 2005), and *Just Wright* (dir. Sanaa Hamri, 2010) and was venturing into television, having already signed a deal for *Single Ladies* (VH1, 2011–2014; Centric, 2015) to debut on BET sister network VH1.

In addition, Edmonds Cofer had worked as an executive producer on series including *Moesha* and *Living Single* and as a supervising producer on *Martin*. Furthermore, half of the series' axial couple, Malinda Williams, had costarred on the successful television adaptation of *Soul Food* (Showtime, 2000–2004).

Even as BET wanted to substantively enter the original programming game, it needed to figure out how to do so cost-effectively. One such measure was to take advantage of Georgia's tax incentives for film and television production. BET had been shooting its program *Sunday's Best* (2007–2015), an *American Idol*-style singing competition for gospel singers, in Atlanta, and with the continuation of tax incentives and the 2010 opening of EUE/Screen Gems Studios, BET seized the opportunity to produce its programming for a fraction of the cost associated with "typical" Hollywood production. Toni Judkins, TV One's senior vice president of original programming, summed up the explosion of Atlanta-based television production: "Shows aren't just shot in L.A., they're in Atlanta . . . and they're creating opportunity where opportunity was not available. . . . One of the things we say is how do you make a dollar out of 50 cents. It's what [TV One is] attempting to do, and I believe it's what BET is doing as well."[108] Thus, *Let's Stay Together*'s production was centered in Atlanta.

When *The Game* and *Let's Stay Together* debuted on BET on January 11, 2011, the industry was stunned. On The CW, *The Game* typically averaged 2.1 million viewers.[109] Its BET debut attracted a staggering 7.7 million viewers, with *The Game* distinguished as the highest rated basic cable series ever, while *Let's Stay Together* drew 4.4 million sets of eyeballs.[110] BET quickly renewed both series for another season.

In 2014, Edmonds Cofer decided to create a story line—one that would stretch across six episodes and two seasons—featuring a Black gay character. The story line was different than the one-off episodes exemplified in *Moesha*, *Good News*, *All of Us*, and *Are We There Yet?* Indeed, *Let's Stay Together*'s engagement with homosexuality would ultimately renovate the inner workings of the Black-cast sitcom's generic closet. As I detail in chapter 2, within production, Darkanian was never imagined as central to *Let's Stay Together*. In fact, the last episode on which he appears is aptly titled, "Game Over," signaling the end of the series' engagement with Black gayness and returning Darkanian, and Black gayness by extension, to the generic closet.

INDUSTRIAL GENERIC CLOSETS

This chapter provided an overview of some of the significant industrial developments of Black-cast sitcoms during television's post-network era. The

Blaxploitation films of the 1970s rescued the film industry from the brink of bankruptcy with relatively cheaply produced Black-cast films that returned stellar box office receipts. Similarly, the television industry in the 1990s through the 2010s continued to commodify Black audiences as a reliable source of differentiation and revenue when they were financially on the ropes. Fox, UPN, TBS, and even BET turned to Black audiences when they wanted to solidify their positions within the marketplace. And with the exception of BET, Black audiences are *only* temporarily commodified before networks, channels, and streaming platforms move on to wider and whiter audience segments.

The temporary commodification of Black audiences is well known to Black audiences themselves, who, as I have argued elsewhere, tend to approach Black media production with a sense of civic duty that is "tethered to a politics of representation as well as an industrial knowledge of" Black media production's "importance to the future of blackness in Hollywood."[111] In other words, many Black viewers often feel if they consume enough Black-cast media, then Hollywood will produce more and, conversely, if they do not, it can mean the end of Black-cast production.

The industrial development of and reliance on the generic closet is undergirded by unfounded imaginings of antigay Black audiences. The post-network era has been exemplified by the illusion of seemingly endless choices for original TV content. However, as choices have proliferated and avenues for telling "different" stories emerged, Black gay stories have infrequently been told in the ways afforded white gayness. As television turned from broadcasting to "narrowcasting" and white- and multicultural-cast sitcoms disassembled the closet for its white lesbian and gay characters, the Black-cast sitcom constructed, reconstructed, and reified its generic closet.

Media industry workers are also disciplined by the commodification of Black audiences. The laborers who work in the film and television industries specialize in very particular tasks and roles (writer, producer, director, lighting designer, camera person, etc.) and are "socialized to the norms and values of the industry."[112] These workers generally know what is permissible within the twenty-two-minute Black-cast sitcom episode. And if he or she wants to get a writing credit for an episode, he or she will need to color inside the lines of the series' predetermined norms and values—an issue that is integral to chapter 2. As Michel Foucault argues, "discipline 'makes' individuals; it is the specific technique of a power that regards individuals both as objects and as instruments of its exercise."[113] This socialization suggests that these creative roles, while specialized, are ultimately part of a system that operates by a set of rules that require adherence if one wishes to continue to work and contribute to the culture industries. It is this threat of "never working in this town again" that, in many cases, drives workers to learn and adhere to the industry's systems and norms and alleviates deviance.

NOTES

1. "The Big Gay TV Timeline," *Out*, October 2012, 61.
2. Jennifer Fuller, "Branding Blackness on US Cable Television," *Media, Culture, and Society* 32, no. 2 (2010): 286.
3. Herman Gray, "The Endless Slide of Difference," *Critical Studies in Mass Communication* 10, no. 2 (1993): 191.
4. Nick Browne, "The Political Economy of the Television (Super) Text," *Quarterly Review of Film and Video* 9, no. 3 (1984): 178.
5. Williams, *Television*.
6. Brett Mills, *Television Sitcom* (London: British Film Institute, 2005), 5.
7. Amanda Dyanne Lotz, "Segregated Sitcoms: Institutional Causes of Disparity among Black and White Comedy Images and Audiences," in *The Sitcom Reader: America Viewed and Skewed*, ed. Mary M. Dalton and Laura R. Linder (Albany, NY: SUNY Press, 2005), 146.
8. Ed. Weinberger, interview with author (Austin, TX), March 19, 2013.
9. Roberta Pearson, "Cult Television as Digital Television's Cutting Edge," in *Console-ing Passions: Television as Digital Media*, ed. James Bennett and Niki Strange (Durham, NC: Duke University Press, 2011), 107.
10. Fuller, "Branding Blackness," 286.
11. Jannette L. Dates, "Commercial Television," in *Split Image: African Americans in the Mass Media*, ed. Jannette L. Dates and William Barlow (Washington, DC: Howard University Press, 1993), 295, 297.
12. Sut Jhally and Justin Lewis, *Enlightened Racism: The Cosby Show, Audiences, and the Myth of the American Dream* (New York: Routledge, 1992), 2–3.
13. Donald Bogle, *Prime Time Blues* (New York: Farrar, Straus, and Giroux, 2001), 441.
14. Zook, *Color by Fox*, 4.
15. Ibid.
16. Katherine Sender, "Dualcasting: Bravo's Gay Programming and the Quest for Women Audiences," in *Cable Visions: Television beyond Broadcasting*, ed. Sarah Banet-Weiser, Cynthia Chris, and Anthony Freitas (New York: New York University Press, 2007), 314.
17. Ibid.
18. Curtis M. Wong, "This TV Sitcom Broke New Ground by Portraying a Same-Sex Wedding in 1991," *Huffington Post*, March 27, 2019, https://www.huffpost.com/entry/matt-baume-roc-gay-wedding-1991_n_5c9955afe4b0d42ce35fde67.

19. Ibid.

20. Ron Becker, *Gay TV and Straight America* (New Brunswick, NJ: Rutgers University Press, 2006), 158.

21. Ibid.

22. Susanne Daniels and Cynthia Littleton, *Season Finale: The Unexpected Rise and Fall of The WB and UPN* (New York: Harper Books, 2007), 9.

23. Steve Coe, "UPN Beats . . . Everybody. Debuts at Number One for Its First Night with New *Star Trek* Show," *Broadcasting and Cable*, January 23, 1995.

24. Bogle, *Prime Time Blues*, 430.

25. Kelly Cole, "From Homeboys to Girl Power: Media Mergers, Emerging Networks and 1990s Television" (PhD diss., University of Wisconsin–Madison, 2005), 133.

26. Joe Flint, "UPN Adds 2 Affiliates, 2 Sitcoms to its Lineup," *Daily Variety*, December 11, 1995, 14.

27. Ralph Farquhar, interview with author (Denver), June 1, 2016.

28. Ibid.

29. Janet Staiger defines blockbuster TV "as a series program that achieved audience ratings markedly higher than those of any of its contenders, week after week"; *Blockbuster TV*, ix.

30. Jhally and Lewis, *Enlightened Racism*, 122–123.

31. Allison Samuels and Rick Marin, "Brandy: Keeping It Real," *Newsweek*, March 24, 1996, http://www.newsweek.com/brandy-keeping-it-real-175802.

32. Farquhar interview.

33. Samuels and Marin, "Brandy: Keeping It Real."

34. Demetrius Bady, interview with author (Austin), February 27, 2013.

35. The theme song debuted on *Roc*'s fortieth episode, "Second Time Around," which aired on January 17, 1993, the first new episode following its holiday break.

36. Farquhar interview.

37. "Singer Brandy Turns Actress in New TV Series *Moesha*," *Jet*, February 26, 1996, 59.

38. Daniels and Littleton, *Season Finale*, 107.

39. Farquhar, interview.

40. Ibid.

41. Ibid.

42. Ibid.

43. Stephen Battaglio, "UPN Catches FOX," *Arizona Republic* (Phoenix, AZ), February 19, 1998, C8.

44. Daniels and Littleton, *Season Finale*, 107.

45. Ibid., 114.

46. "Moesha," *TV Guide*, September 28, 1996, 120.

47. Daniel Howard Cerone, "Ellen May Be Telling Even Though Not Asked," *TV Guide*, September 28, 1996, 59.

48. Weinberger, interview.

49. Ibid.

50. Franklin has recently denounced his antigay stance; Jeannie Law, "Kirk Franklin Tackles Abortion, Homosexuality on 'Breakfast Club': 'Bible Is Not Homophobic,'" *Christian Post*, June 6, 2019, https://www.christianpost.com /news/kirk-franklin-tackles-abortion-homosexuality-on-breakfast-club-bible-is -not-homophobic.html.

51. Weinberger, interview.

52. Horace Griffin, "Their Own Received Them Not: African American Lesbians and Gays in Black Churches," *Theology and Sexuality* 12 (2000): 89.

53. Beretta Smith Shomade, "'Don't Play with God!': Black Church, Play, and Possibilities," *Souls* 18, nos. 2–4 (2016): 329.

54. "Close-Up," *TV Guide*, August 23, 1997, 10.

55. Caryn James, "New Minister in Town, No Angels in Tow: 'Good News' UPN, Tonight at 9," *New York Times*, August 25, 1997, C14.

56. Howard Rosenberg, "A Wobbly Start, That's for Sure," *Los Angeles Times*, August 25, 1997, http://articles.latimes.com/1997/aug/25/entertainment /ca-25696.

57. Cynthia Littleton, "UPN Pulls First 'Desmond Pfeiffer' Seg," *Variety*, September 30, 1998, https://variety.com/1998/tv/news /upn-pulls-first-desmond-pfeiffer-seg-1117480928/.

58. Mara Brock-Akil, "A Conversation with Mara Brock-Akil and Salim Akil" (interview at the ATX TV Festival, season 6, Austin, TX, June 11, 2017).

59. Daniels and Littleton, *Season Finale*, 305.

60. Cynthia Fuchs, *"All of Us/Eve,"* *Pop Matters*, October 13, 2003, http://www .popmatters.com/review/eve-2003/.

61. Leslie Ryan, "Making Room for *All of Us*," *Television Week*, May 5, 2003.

62. *"All of Us*: TV Show Explores the Lighter Side of Blended Families," *Jet*, November 3, 2003, 59.

63. Daniels and Littleton, *Season Finale*. 305.

64. Ryan, "Making Room for *All of Us*."

65. Alessandra Stanley, "A Rap Diva. A Painful Divorce. Cue the Laugh Track," *New York Times*, September 15, 2003, E6.

66. Fuchs, *"All of Us/Eve."*

67. Nellie Andreeva, "UPN All about *Eve, Us*," *Hollywood Reporter*, October 14, 2003, international edition.

68. See Becker, *Gay TV and Straight America*, for his definition of the white SLUMPY demographic networks were targeting in the 1990s.

69. Martin, "Generic Closets," 233.

70. Stuart Elliot, "TBS Puts Serious Money into Promoting Itself as a Place for Laughs," *New York Times*, April 22, 2004, C3.

71. Ali LeRoi, interview with the author, March 1, 2017.

72. Cynthia Littleton, "Fast-Tracked Sitcom May Be Way of Future," *Variety*, June 26, 2012, http://variety.com/2012/tv/columns /fast-tracked-sitcom-may-be-way-of-future-1118055951/.

73. Derek Kompare, *Rerun Nation: How Repeats Invented American Television* (New York: Routledge, 2004), 72.

74. LeRoi, interview.

75. Ibid.

76. Nellie Andreeva, "'Are We There Yet?' Heads to TV," *Hollywood Reporter*, July 15, 2009, http://uk.reuters.com/article/television-us-yet -idUKTRE56E1HU20090715.

77. David Hinckley, "Ice Cube's *Are We There Yet?* Feels Like a Trip Viewers Have Already Taken with Stale Humor," *New York Daily News*, June 1, 2010, http://www.nydailynews.com/entertainment /tv-movies/ice-cube-feels-trip-viewers-stale-humor-article-1.180480; Andrew Barker, "*Are We There Yet?*," *Daily Variety*, June 1, 2010, 12.

78. Mark Seliger, *TV's Gay Heat Wave*, December 2003, photograph, *Vanity Fair*, cover, December 2003.

79. Megan Angelo, "At TBS, Diversity Pays Its Own Way," *New York Times*, May 28, 2010, https://mobile.nytimes.com/2010/05/30/arts/television/30tbs .html.

80. Alfred L. Martin, Jr., "FOX Formula 3.0? TBS, *Cougar Town*, and the Disappearing Televisual Black Body," *Antenna*, June 18, 2012, http://blog .commarts.wisc.edu/2012/06/18/fox-formula-3-0-tbs-cougar-town-and-the -disappearing-televisual-black-body/.

81. Ibid.

82. Beretta E. Smith Shomade, *Pimpin' Ain't Easy: Selling Black Entertainment Television* (New York: Routledge, 2008), 75.

83. Kompare, *Rerun Nation*, 171.

84. Ibid., 76.

85. Darnell M. Hunt, "Making Sense of Blackness on Television," in *Channeling Blackness: Studies on Television and Race in America*, ed. Darnell M. Hunt (New York: Oxford University Press, 2005), 21.

86. Mark Anthony Neal, *Soul Babies: Black Popular Culture and the Post-Soul Aesthetic* (New York: Routledge, 2002), 164.

87. Becker, *Gay TV and Straight America*, 89–90.

88. Michele Hilmes, *Only Connect: A Cultural History of Broadcasting in the United States*, 4th ed. (Boston: Wadsworth, 2014), 388.

89. Shomade, *Pimpin' Ain't Easy*, 131.

90. Aaron McGruder, *The Boondocks: Because I Know You Don't Read the Newspaper* (New York: Andrew Keel, 2000), 93.

91. Paul Farhi, "For BET, Some Static in the Picture; Bob Johnson Wanted People to Turn on His Cable Network. He Got His Wish," *Washington Post*, November 22, 1999, C01.

92. Geraldine Fabrikant, "BET Holdings to Be Bought by Viacom for $2.34 Billion," *New York Times*, November 4, 2000, http://www.nytimes.com/2000/11 /04/business/bet-holdings-to-be-bought-by-viacom-for-2.34-billion.html.

93. Skip Wollenberg, "Viacom Acquires BET," ABC News, October 4, 2000, http://abcnews.go.com/Business/story?id=89100.

94. Shomade, *Pimpin' Ain't Easy*, 168.

95. Timothy J. Brown, "Welcome to the Terrordome: Exploring the Contradictions of a Hip Hop Masculinity," in *Progressive Black Masculinities*, ed. Athena D. Mutua (New York: Routledge, 2006), 199.

96. Andre Tartar, "XXL Magazine on Hip Hop Homophobia," *New York Magazine*, July 7, 2011, http://nymag.com/daily/entertainment/2011/07/xxl _magazine_on_hip hop_homoph.html.

97. Bady interview.

98. Allison Romano, "Holding Its Own; BET dismisses TV One as Serious Competition," *Broadcasting and Cable*, April 14, 2004, 12.

99. Lisa de Moraes, "For Black Sitcom 'Love That Girl!,' TV One May Be the Network of Its Dreams," *Washington Post*, January 6, 2010, http://www .washingtonpost.com/wp-dyn/content/article/2010/01/05/AR2010010503534 .html.

100. BCST Staff, "Remaking BET with Originals," *Broadcasting and Cable*, June 27, 2011, http://www.broadcastingcable.com/news /news-articles/remaking-bet-originals/112163.

101. Christine Acham, *Revolution Televised: Prime Time and the Struggle for Black Power* (Minneapolis: University of Minnesota Press, 2004).

102. BCST Staff, "Remaking BET with Originals."

103. Rob Owen, "Tuned In: TVOne, BET Debuts Sitcoms Slightly Used and New," *Pittsburgh Post-Gazette*, January 7, 2011, http://www.post-gazette.com/ae /tv-radio/2011/01/07/Tuned-In-TV-One-BET-debut-sitcoms-slightly-used -and-new/stories/201101070169.

104. Racquel Gates, "Keepin' It Reality Television," in *Watching While Black: Centering the Television of Black Audiences*, ed. Beretta E. Smith Shomade (New Brunswick, NJ: Rutgers University Press, 2013), 143.

105. Trevor Kimball, "*The Game*: Season Four Starts on BET in January 2011," *TV Series Finale*, October 12, 2010, https://tvseriesfinale.com /tv-show/the-game-season-four-bet-18759/.

106. Jacque Edmonds Cofer, interview with author (New York), March 7, 2016.

107. "BET Presents *Let's Stay Together*, a New Original Series That Gives an Updated, Urban Perspective on Love and Marriage Premiering Tuesday, January 11 at 11:00 p.m." (press release), BET, January 6, 2011, http://www .thefutoncritic.com/news/2011/01/06/bet-presents-lets-stay-together-a-new -original-series-that-gives-an-updated-urban-perspective-on-love-and-marriage -premiering-tuesday-january-11-at-1100-pm-323113/20110106bet01/.

108. Owen, "Tuned In."

109. Philiana Ng, "BET's 'The Game' Season Finale Draws 4.4. Million," *Hollywood Reporter*, March 30, 2011, http://www.hollywoodreporter.com /live-feed/bets-game-season-finale-draws-172832.

110. Philiana Ng, "'The Game' Series Premiere Huge for BET," *Hollywood Reporter*, January 12, 2011, http://www.hollywoodreporter.com/blogs /live-feed/game-season-premiere-huge-bet-70941.

111. Alfred L. Martin Jr., "Blackbusting Hollywood: Racialized Media Reception, Failure, and *The Wiz* as Black Blockbuster," *Journal of Cinema and Media Studies*, forthcoming.

112. Janet Staiger, "Authorship Approaches," in *Authorship and Film*, ed. David A. Gerstner and Janet Staiger (New York: Routledge, 2003), 41.

113. Michel Foucault, "The Means of Correct Training," in *Blackwell Reader on Contemporary Social Theory*, ed. Anthony Elliot (Oxford: Blackwell, 1999), 97.

SCRIPTING THE GENERIC CLOSET IN THE WRITERS' ROOM

AS I DISCUSSED IN CHAPTER 1, the media industries' investment in the generic closet is laid bare in its imagination of Black audiences for Black-cast sitcoms. This chapter investigates the enduring nature of the generic closet from the perspective of production within the writers' room. The three Ds—detection, discovery/declaration, and discarding—serve as a ready-made, industrially approved, three-act structure for the writers and showrunners interviewed for this book.[1] Some of the writers and showrunners push against the doors of the generic closet, but ultimately, no matter how much agency they have, they cannot break through to free Black gayness from it. Yet I do not want to suggest that they are dupes. Rather, they must often temper their politics with a desire to maintain gainful employment. In this sense, this chapter draws from and builds on Raymond Williams's culturally materialist concept of determination, in which structures of economic and social power set limits and exert pressure on cultural production, thereby controlling the potential, possibility, and parameters for change.[2]

Reconstituting the generic closet within the Black-cast sitcom separates the logic of "the closet" from its roots in liberation—the freeing discourse of confessing one's secret through a speech act to loved ones. I will discuss this perspective in greater detail later in this chapter. For now, it is important to begin a discussion of how coming out of the closet—typically understood as the beginning of one's life as a queer person—does not work here. Coming out of the closet for Black gay characters functions as an end. Unlike the warm familial embrace that awaits white gay characters across white- and multicultural-cast television, Black gay characters who come out within Black-cast sitcoms are shown the nearest exit, regardless of their alleged relationship to the rest of the series.

This chapter also analyzes how the Black-cast sitcom and its relationship to the generic closet functions as a "defensive truth,"[3] a term I initially theorized to discuss casting practices. I use it here to broadly reflect production practices. Defensive truths provide "a ready-made explanation" for production decisions, even as they adhere to recognizable industrial patterns, like the generic closet.[4] Through interviews with series executive producers and episode writers, this chapter details the commercial constraints of the business of Black-cast sitcom production on the creative hopes, dreams, and aspirations of the writers' room, particularly with respect to Black gayness. I want to be clear that I am not looking to the writers and executive producers for an absolute truth. My aims are (1) to highlight writers' and showrunners' experiences of bringing Black gay characters to Black-cast sitcoms; (2) to examine how the conventions and structures of the Black-cast sitcom play an important industrial role in the appearance of Black gayness within the narrative world; and (3) to explore how such constraints reconfigure, but never demolish, the generic closet.

Structurally, the writers' room is the well from which authorship springs. It is the place where episodic sitcom stories live and die and where gender, race, sexuality, and class are negotiated, ultimately shaping and reshaping the narratives and images granted tenure on television screens.[5] The study of television's writers' rooms has often centered on the managerial role of the executive producer, reified in Horace Newcomb and Robert S. Alley's seminal tome *The Producer's Medium: Conversations with Creators of American TV.*[6] I engage with the complex interplay between the showrunner and the individual writer(s) assigned the task of writing weekly episodes of Black-cast sitcoms, particularly as they engage with Black gayness. In this chapter, I explore the spaces and places where culture industry workers and the commercial imperatives of the media industries collide within the Black-cast sitcom.

For this chapter, I conducted interviews with five writers and four showrunners. These semi-structured, tape-recorded interviews were conducted by telephone from Austin, New York, and Denver (the institutional review board–approved interview script is included in app. D). Building on Alexander Doty's pioneering work, this chapter acknowledges that "attributing authorship . . . remains contested ground, as production records, interviews, (auto) biographies, official and unofficial credits, publicity, and various cultural reception practices will frequently be at odds in establishing the authorship of a text."[7] To circumvent some vagaries, I interviewed both writers and showrunners to attempt to reconcile sometimes differing accounts of the production context of Black-cast sitcom episodes with Black gay characters.

These media industry workers represent a number of axes of self-reported identity. Demetrius Bady, a Black gay man, worked on *Moesha* and entered the television industry in 1994 as an assistant on the short-lived sitcom *My Brother and Me* (Nickelodeon, 1994). In addition to *Moesha*, Bady worked as a staff writer on *Sister, Sister* (ABC, 1994–1995; The WB 1995–1998) and *All of Us* and was a staff writer for the first season of *Single Ladies* (VH1, 2011–2014; Centric, 2015). The writing positions Bady held across series as a freelance and staff writer are entry-level positions within the industry and allow executive producers to hire at minimum risk and cost.

Antonia March and Jacqueline McKinley, both heterosexual Black women, began working as a writing team in 1998 on *Smart Guy* (The WB, 1997–1999) and soon found their next jobs as staff writers and story editors and then as executive story editors on *The Bernie Mac Show* (Fox, 2001–2006). McKinley and March next held positions as coproducers and staff writers on *Are We There Yet?* and *All of Us*. Then the team worked as consulting producers and writers on the first-run syndicated Black-cast sitcom *First Family* (2012–2013) before working as executive producers and creators of the series *Here We Go Again* (TV One, 2016). They have most recently written episodes for *The Quad* (BET, 2017–2018), *Raven's Home* (Disney, 2017–present), and *Ambitions* (OWN, 2019).

Carla Banks-Waddles, a heterosexual Black woman, moved to Los Angeles in 1998 and attended the University of Southern California's writing program. She became a writer on the last season of Yvette Lee Bowser's *For Your Love* (NBC, 1998; The WB, 1998–2002). After the show ended, Banks-Waddles entered the Warner Brothers Writing Workshop and was hired as a writer on *That's So Raven* (Disney, 2003–2007), *The Bill Engvall Show* (TBS, 2007–2009), and *Fresh Beat Band* (Nickelodeon, 2009–2013). Because of a business relationship with Jacque Edmonds Cofer, she was hired as a staff writer on *Let's Stay Together* in 2013. She served as executive producer on the short-lived series *One Love* (Bounce, 2015) and worked as supervising producer on *Truth Be Told* (NBC, 2015). She is currently consulting producer for *Good Girls* (NBC, 2018–present).

With respect to the showrunners in this chapter, Ali LeRoi, a heterosexual Black man, entered the industry intending to become an actor but found his way into television and film production as a writer before being promoted to supervising producer on *The Chris Rock Show* (HBO, 1997–2000). Next, he served as producer on the film *Pootie Tang* (dir. Louis C. K., 2001) before moving to the late-night talk show *The Orlando Jones Show* (FX, 2003). Later, he reteamed with Rock as writer and producer for the film *Head of State* (dir. Chris Rock, 2003) and the autobiographical Black-cast sitcom *Everybody Hates Chris*

(UPN, 2005–2006; The CW, 2006–2009). Next, he developed and executive produced *Are We There Yet?* (2010–2012). He most recently served as writer of a 2016 episode of *Survivor's Remorse* (Starz, 2014–2017).

Edward "Ed." Weinberger, a heterosexual white man, began working in Hollywood as a writer in the mid-1960s on a number of television specials before creating and writing *The Bill Cosby Show* (NBC, 1969–1971). His high-profile jobs in Hollywood as a writer and producer include *The Tonight Show Starring Johnny Carson* (NBC, 1962–1992), *The Mary Tyler Moore Show* (CBS, 1970–1977), and *Taxi* (ABC, 1978–1982; NBC, 1982–1983). Weinberger began working almost exclusively in Black-cast sitcoms in the mid-1980s and through the 1990s with work on *Amen, The Cosby Show, Sparks,* and *Good News,* all series he both created and executive produced. His most recent series was *Belle's* for TV One, which was canceled in 2013 after one season.

Beginning work in Hollywood in the 1980s, Ralph Farquhar, a heterosexual Black man, found his first jobs as an episode writer on series including *Happy Days* (ABC, 1974–1984), *The New Odd Couple* (ABC, 1982–1983), and *Fame* (NBC, 1982–1983; syndication, 1983–1987). When the Fox network debuted in 1986, it provided opportunities for Black writers, including Farquhar, who became a supervising producer for *Married . . . with Children* (Fox, 1987–1997). Next, Farquhar was executive producer for a number of Black-cast sitcoms including *The Sinbad Show, South Central* (Fox, 1994), *Moesha,* and *The Parkers* and the "reality TV" spoof comedy *Real Husbands of Hollywood* (BET, 2013–2016).

Entering Hollywood through the Walt Disney fellowship program, Jacque Edmonds Cofer, a heterosexual Black woman, secured her first staff writer job on *Martin,* where she was quickly promoted to supervising producing for the last two seasons of the series. Her next job was as co–executive producer on *Living Single* before going to work as a consultant and executive producer on *Moesha.* After her stint on *Moesha,* Edmonds Cofer worked as a co–executive producer on a number of series, including *All about the Andersons* (The WB, 2003–2004) *Abby* (UPN, 2003), *Cuts* (UPN, 2005–2006) and *Reed between the Lines,* before entering a development deal with BET to create and develop *Let's Stay Together,* which ended in 2014. She is currently consulting producer for *Mr. Iglesias* (Netflix, 2019–present) and co–executive producer for *The Unicorn* (CBS, 2019–present).

In this chapter, I use in-depth interviews with these industry workers to unpack the tensions and representational politics involved with the Black-cast sitcom's episodic engagement with Black gayness. These industrial politics are often contested and negotiated but can be pushed only so far before they collide with the hegemonic forces of the television industry and the industrial imagination of Black audiences. Each writer and showrunner had a reason for creating the episodes in their series, mostly to try to make Black gayness mean something different—less stereotypic, more "positive"—than had been previously mediated for Black-cast sitcom audiences. This transcoding work has its limits. As Isaac Julien forcefully argues, attempting to create so-called "positive" Black gay images might be well intentioned but ultimately fails because "it will never be able to address questions of ambivalence or transgression."[8] In addition, many of the writers and showrunners felt they had a story to tell about Black gayness because they are gay themselves, they know and love someone who is gay, or they had dating experiences with gay men. These personal autobiographical details find their way into writers' rooms and onto the pages that are written and produced.

DECENTERING GAY NARRATIVES IN THE WRITERS' ROOM

There are two constants in Black-cast sitcom production. First, each series uses a writers' room where the writers, at all levels, come together to work on story pitches and ideas and, generally, to shape the way a script (or scripts) develop. Second, each series discussed here works within a logic that reduces Black gayness to its narrative utility. Each series has a Black gay character (or two), but the story lines are never ostensibly about those characters. Instead, the stories are concerned with the series regulars and their reactions to the presence of homosexuality (similar to Becker's discussion of white- and multicultural-cast sitcoms when they include one-off gay characters versus recurring or co-starring gay characters).[9] Because Black gayness is already predetermined as never necessarily central to the stories being told, it is ripe for ultimate discarding from the Black-cast sitcoms discussed in this book. Decentering gayness is an industrial strategy to include Black gayness but to do so in ways that are tertiary to the main thrust of the series, therefore, it can only ever be a temporary interloper. In more Althusserian terms, the Black-cast sitcom hails the Black gay subject into its universe as an ideological apparatus to shore up meanings about the structures of the Black family and the boundaries of Black masculinity.[10] I return to the decentering of Black gayness from a reception perspective in chapter 4. For now, this chapter reveals the configuration of writers' rooms and their uses of the generic closet as a conduit to marginalize Black gay story lines.

Moesha's writers' room typically had up to ten writers who contributed in various ways to the stories chosen for script development. *Moesha* showrunner Farquhar contends his writers' room management style meant that a writer would pitch an episode idea that he either approved or rejected. If approved, Farquhar says, "then we would break that idea in the room with the writers . . . and then after we break it, we send the writer out to come back with an outline. And then we give notes on that, and then the writer refines the outline, and then, after we get network notes, we go to script."[11] Farquhar states that with the "Labels" script, both he and the network were cognizant of not offending audience members and members of gay communities with the episode because he knew that the topic "would attract a lot of attention" given the proliferation of lesbian and gay representations in the Gay '90s.[12] Part of this caution is rooted in two important moments in LGBT activism and history. The first was the beginning of the Los Angeles chapter of the Gay and Lesbian Alliance Against Defamation's (now known simply as GLAAD) "Media Watch" column in the early 1990s, which was designed to catalogue and respond to problematic media representations of LGBT people.[13] The second was the nationalization of GLAAD, which began in 1993 and worked to centralize unified responses to LGBT political and media issues. In a 2012 acceptance speech at the GLAAD Awards, television producer and writer Shonda Rhimes centered the importance of GLAAD as a media watchdog group: "When someone says something they shouldn't say, GLAAD shows up and they're there before you even know that they needed to be there."[14] In this sense, Farquhar's caution about getting *Moesha's* foray into Black gay representation "right" is well placed because to raise GLAAD's ire is to have to deal with a public relations campaign instead of running the series. I suggest that Farquhar's caution is also partially rooted in industrial and discursive imaginings of Black audiences. As discussed in chapter 1, the precarity of Black-cast productions—even for one of UPN's hit series—is a constant consideration for Black-cast sitcoms.

This dual set of considerations, offending LGBT organizations and Black audiences, can be observed in the different ways episode writer Demetrius Bady and Farquhar describe the episode. Bady describes the episode as being concerned with "Moesha get[ting] caught up in the gossip about Hakeem's cousin's sexuality," whereas Farquhar understands the episode as about "people circulating stories about someone, and how that can affect someone. . . . And then, [it] just so happens that the story being circulated was about someone who was gay. . . . Rumors start. People whisper. People get hurt. And so, we wanted to make a story about, whether or not it was true, and then if it is true, what about it?"[15]

For Farquhar, the emergence of Black gayness within *Moesha* is secondary, whereas it is a primary concern for Bady—a Black gay man himself. Both Bady and Farquhar center "gossip," but Bady understands (homo)sexuality as central

Fig. 2.1. Members of *Moesha*'s writers' room on the set of the series. Demetrius Bady, writer of the "Labels" episode, is seated center. Photo provided to author by Demetrius Bady.

to how the episode's narrative unfolds, and Farquhar narratively thinks that the gossip could have been about almost anything—it just happened to be about gayness. Farquhar's approach to gayness is tinged with post-gayness, a position that understands the gossip within the episode's narrative as separate from an identity that can be "defined by sexuality alone . . . [but that] champions the idea that gay culture and mainstream culture cross-pollinate."[16] Within such a post-gay stance, the specificity of gossip about Black gayness serves a utilitarian purpose because it can be deployed as something understood as rumor-worthy within the context of the series. For Farquhar, centering gossip is implicitly a way to ensure that the series can properly discard Black gayness from *Moesha*'s narrative universe because the story was never about Black gayness—Black gayness simply became a conduit for a story centering gossip. Simultaneously, centering gossip versus gayness works to subsume Black gayness against the risk of offending or alienating Black audiences. Thus, the foundation of the generic closet for *Moesha* begins to be exposed—even with a Black gay writer at the helm.

Good News is an outlier in the sense that its showrunner, Weinberger, was also the writer of the "Pilot" episode, which included a Black gay character.

Weinberger indicates that gayness was central to the episode's narrative and that he attempted to decouple homophobia and Blackness, representing a "progressive" approach to Black gayness. Simultaneously, Weinberger told me Black gayness "was an interesting issue to deal with, but it was not going to be the issue of the series in the way that *Will & Grace* would want.... I went on to other stories.... To make gay or lesbian themes part of the series, that was never the intention; it was really once and out."[17] Weinberger points to the ways, under his purview, the Black-cast sitcom he created made no ongoing space for homosexuality. For him, Black gayness can exist only as an "issue"—Weinberger very much understood that there was no "post" in gayness. Gayness was a central identity with which the series must deal. His suggestion that Black gayness is "once and out" reveals an industrial investment in the generic closet. In other words, "once" a Black character reveals his gayness, he is not only "out" of the closet but also out of the series. Weinberger seems to suggest that Black gayness within a Black-cast sitcom is understood as so all-encompassing that it can be called on only to proclaim its deviation from heteronormativity.

Weinberger's episodic engagement with Black gayness seems rooted in a tolerance for homosexuality, an inclusion that Walters proposes "we would rather avoid. Tolerance is not an embrace but a resigned shrug."[18] The Black-cast sitcom's engagement with Black gayness is through an abject tokenism that acknowledges the existence of Black gayness and reifies its lack of place within the Black-cast sitcom and within the fabric of Blackness more broadly. Black gayness can be tolerated for an episode or two, but it can never be understood as an ongoing "normalized" presence within the Black-cast sitcom. When Black gayness does appear, it must always be a secondary concern for the series to reinforce the industrial power of the generic closet.

In a similar fashion, *All of Us*, a writers' room composed of roughly six writers, decenters Black gayness. The episodes focus on the clarity of a sexual declaration. Episode cowriter and series coproducer March states that "there was always a time where we wanted Robert to find out [that his biological father was gay] so that there was no mistake.... I just knew that we wanted it to be something that would not be mistaken, where Robert could say, 'Maybe I saw [my biological father kiss his partner] or maybe I didn't.' It was very clear."[19] The brief kiss shared between the two actors playing Black gay men in a romantic relationship does the work of outing them because presumably two men would not kiss unless they were in a romantic relationship. This sexual clarity is something on which the six writers in the writers' room and the series showrunner, Jeff Strauss, agreed. March's description of the narrative function of the Black gay character underscores how Luther's tenure within the series is predicated on his biological son discovering his gayness, not on anything that might signal his agency as a character who has a rightful claim to exist within the narrative space of the series, untethered from his utility to the core cast.

To further accentuate this point, March recalls that she and McKinley imagined the episode arc to be something that tackled homosexuality and Black men's responses to its presence. "We knew this was something really important, especially with dealing with gayness and Black men. I know everyone is always saying Black men are so scared about [gayness]. That's usually the belief. Everyone was so interested in it and got so into the show and the writing of it. It was really a good experience."[20] March's description of her experience writing a series of episodes with a Black gay character, and the all-Black cast's response to it, is worth celebrating. It breaks up the hegemonic belief that all Black folks, and specifically Black men, hold antigay beliefs. Concurrently, March discusses how the importance of including Black gay characters was not to demonstrate something about Black gay men but to discursively attempt to change the narrative about Black heterosexual men's relationship to Black gayness. In other words, extending Foucault's discussion of the panopticon, the generic closet securely confines Black gay characters so that they become "the object of information, never a subject in communication."[21] Black gay characters in Black-cast sitcoms are the "object of information" about sexualities and their deviance from what is understood as "normal." There is never an attempt to relate narratives from the perspective of the Black gay "other"; he is always providing information about the hegemonic confines of "authentic" Blackness and Black masculinity.

For *Are We There Yet?*, showrunner Ali LeRoi explained that the writers' room comprised six staff writers and another four to six writers working as freelancers. Because of the nature of the show's 10–90 deal (detailed in chap. 1) and the speed with which episodes had to be produced, LeRoi used a different managerial style than he had with any of the other shows on which he worked:

> The process that I used was [to] break stories over the course of a couple of weeks for the four or six writers I was working with. What we would do then is, as a group, we would bring in say another four writers, freelancers. Then we would break stories for them. So, at any given time, I could have six to eight writers working on stories. It was a way of overlapping the workflow. Some of it was internal and some of it was outsourced. Then it allowed us to keep a flow going. So that at any given time, I didn't have a situation where I had all of my staff working on stories and no one available to start generating new material or no one available to come down on [the set] when we're shooting to help with things like punch-up and rewrites.[22]

The speed at which production on the series had to happen gestures toward how the 10–90 model requires a different approach to getting the writing on a series done. Importantly, this speed generally helped writers to write their best version of the episode(s) they were assigned because they were allowed to go off and write rather than "group writing" within the room. LeRoi believes that this managerial style worked best because "I just think when you have a writer, you get the strongest version of their voice if you let them do the work instead of micromanaging their writing."[23]

He indicates that the nexus for the episode "The Boy Has Style" was pulled from his personal experience:

> When I was the showrunner on *Everybody Hates Chris* there was someone that worked in our office—handsome guy, really charming, lot of fun and I never thought twice about his sexual orientation. . . . This particular guy was interesting because he did not read in any way, shape or form, stereotypically gay. It came up one day offhandedly and it was funny to me because he was a guy that a lot of girls would look at and think that he's cute or whatever that kind of thing. Just the idea of a guy that there's no stereotypical tell so to speak.[24]

LeRoi posits that the "The Boy Has Style" episode is autobiographical; within Black-cast television production, Kristal Brent Zook describes that as concerning "collective and individual authorship of black experience[s]."[25] The story is also yoked to knowledge production about Black gayness, demonstrating its subordination to the concerns of the series' narrative universe. Cedric, the Black gay character within the episode, can only be imagined as having to, as Samuel Chambers describes, "deal with the asymmetrical power and knowledge relations that constitute closet space."[26] Episode cowriter McKinley revealed that the episode was autobiographical for her as well. This association demonstrates the ways the Black-cast sitcom's production engages with "group memories as well as individual ones," with both LeRoi's and McKinley's memories shaping the episode's narrative.[27] McKinley recalled,

> I pitched this story, which was based on my own dating experiences, but we did it in a teenage fashion. . . . [The guy I was dating] wasn't comfortable coming out. Now that we have teenage characters it would be handled a little differently. We really wanted [Cedric] to not be in the closet but he wasn't telling everybody on the street that he's gay. For him, it was "I just thought you knew. I'm sorry that you got hurt or . . . I know you have a crush on me . . ." That's how we handled that story.[28]

Within *Are We There Yet?* knowledge production about Black gayness is of paramount importance. In a sleight of hand, the episode writers and the executive producer suggested that the episode was not necessarily centered on Black gayness as an identity category but rather focused on the technologies for detection, which, ironically, help to (re)produce and confirm identity categories. In a nod to the generic closet's detection phase, the epistemological framework within which "The Boy Has Style" works positions homosexuality as something that needs to be ferreted out so it can be identified and expunged from the narrative universe of the series.[29] Cedric's homosexuality is clearly delineated with respect to the ways his gayness can be deployed and produce knowledge. It reifies the notion that gayness can be detected by a number of characteristics, including sartorial choices, and that gayness *should* be detectable and declared, not for Cedric, but for the benefit of the knowledge it produces for the core cast—they can be secure in the knowledge that they reduced gayness to a technology that can be successfully and reliably read onto Black gay bodies. George Simmel discusses fashion's use as a means to prop up cultural needs rather than practical ones.[30] In other words, clothing shifts from fulfilling a need for cloth to shield the body from environmental elements to a system built on and reified by hegemonic norms. Clothing color and texture are used as a technology to read sexuality onto the body.

"The Boy Has Style" becomes less about Black gayness and more about the notion that a failure to disclose gayness is understood as deceitful and that Black gayness within the Black-cast sitcom is legitimate only if it is disclosed. The queer politics of the writers' room insinuates that knowing one's own gayness is never enough—it can be made manifest only if it is proclaimed in a speech act. A. C. Liang theorizes that coming out is a speech act that brings a gay selfhood into being, that "alters social reality by creating a community of listeners and thereby establishing the beginnings of a new gay-aware culture."[31] What is important about Liang's theorization is that coming out is understood as an external act, not an internal one. The speech act, much like the Black-cast sitcom's insistence on such a speech act for the discovery/declaration phase of the generic closet, is principally concerned with knowledge production and the hearer of such knowledge's reaction to the speech act. The Black-cast sitcom engages with Black gayness in a manner similar to Marlon Riggs's theorization that hegemonic Blackness is constructed as an ideological framework "that enforces a rigorous exclusion of certain kinds of difference . . . [and] confines them within an easily recognizable . . . psychosocial arena."[32] The Black-cast sitcom's engagement with Black gayness is trotted out but never fully welcomed into the fabric of the series.

The writers' room for *Let's Stay Together* consisted of five staff writers and several freelance writers. Unlike the other Black-cast sitcoms in this book, *Let's Stay Together* functioned more as a serial than an episodic series, resulting in story arcs (including Darkanian's) stretching across several episodes and seasons.[33] According to staff writer Banks-Waddles, *Let's Stay Together*'s showrunner, Edmonds Cofer, would come in to discuss where the show would narratively travel over the course of a season. Once that broad arc was settled, Banks-Waddles said the writers' room would "pick a path of different ways to get there [and] how many episodes to get there."[34] As Banks-Waddles articulates, the serialized nature of *Let's Stay Together* allowed for more nuanced stories that could take longer to tell than the "average" episodic Black-cast sitcom, which must create and resolve narrative problems quickly.

Given how *Let's Stay Together* centers broad story arcs versus individual episodes, it is telling that Edmonds Cofer underscores the lack of importance of homosexuality in describing how Darkanian's story arc would play out:

> Crystal, the character that Kyla Pratt plays, we had her as a college student at Atlanta University, but she wasn't really focused. . . . Her father said he's not gonna pay her bills anymore if she couldn't just stay in school and pick a major. She's having goal issues as well as financial issues. So, we thought of the idea of what if she gets some kind of sugar daddy? And what are the ethics of that? Obviously, we didn't want her to be a call girl. But you know, if you have a rich boyfriend, that's kind of where it started.[35]

In Edmonds Cofer's retelling, Darkanian begins life in the *Let's Stay Together* writers' room as "simply" a sugar daddy-type who steps in to financially help one of the series regulars. That the character may not be heterosexual only occurred to the writers as a way to be socially relevant because retired National Basketball Association (NBA) player John Amaechi had come out as gay in 2007 and NBA player Jason Collins did the same in 2013. While homosexuality was initially understood as secondary, these events signaled an opportunity for the series to be topical and socially relevant, similar to the Norman Lear–produced series of the 1970s, like *Good Times, Maude,* and *All in the Family*. Edmonds Cofer recalled,

> We thought let's marry these two ideas where you have an athlete who has this image, and when he first comes on he's hitting on Kita, he's the super aggressive athlete stereotype. Crystal sees this and says "Rich boyfriend? Maybe he'll buy me a purse before I can get out of this." And she decided to start dating him. She sort of takes him up on his offer. . . . So, from that point you can see what Darkanian's motive was. He needed a girlfriend to flaunt

around town, she needed money, so it seemed like it was a good exchange. [That's] what we wanted to deal with whether he had been straight or not. If you're not emotionally invested in a relationship, what are the morals around that? It could have just been an old guy who was really into her, right?[36]

Edmonds Cofer gestures toward how the idea for Darkanian to be gay was an afterthought. In particular, Edmonds Cofer's suggestion that Darkanian could have just as easily been an "old guy who was really into [Crystal]" reveals homosexuality's lack of import within the context of the series. The series and its writers and showrunner are aware that Black gayness exists, but they are unwilling to center it within the series' narrative. Edmonds Cofer continued, "So, we wanted to keep the topic relevant to our audience, and I wanted to get the other characters' reactions to his coming out. We have Crystal, who's gonna be funny.... But then how do the other characters deal with someone who was one of their sports idols coming out to them and having to keep that secret? But, in general they were pretty cool because all of our characters were fairly progressive young people."[37] Edmonds Cofer centers the alleged progressiveness of the characters within *Let's Stay Together*'s narrative universe, suggesting an imagination of a "BLAMP" audience—Black, liberal, affluent, metropolitan, and professional—that would tolerate Black gayness.[38] However, Edmonds Cofer's characters are presumably progressive only enough to temporarily allow Black gayness within the series' borders. Black gayness is and can only be a narrative arc within the series, never something that exists within the series on a weekly basis.

Before any of the episodes discussed were written, gayness was already ideologically decentered from the Black-cast sitcom's universe. Through gossip, issues, and knowledge production, these episodes deploy gayness as a means to a heteronormative end. The struggles within the writers' room are fascinating tales of working within the constraints of the generic closet while pushing to write multivalent stories. Through those struggles, one thing is constant: Black gay characters and their stories are never an ongoing central concern for the series, even as they purport liberalism as a guiding principle—similar to Thomas Cripps's conceptualization of the function of "conscience-liberalism" within Hollywood. Such conscience-liberalism ultimately posits that Hollywood's liberalism is limited because it is ultimately beholden to the politics of production.[39] Conscience-liberalism helps explain the routinized ways the Black-cast sitcom welcomes Black gay characters into its universe to demonstrate that the characters who regularly inhabit the series' world are good people. The double-edged sword of conscience-liberalism is that it is achieved at the expense of the abject Black gay character. This section detailed how tangential Black gay characters are conceived initially to perform a specific narrative role for a limited episodic arc. In the next section, I examine the process of negotiating the writing of Black gay characters who are already decentered at their conception.

NEGOTIATING THE GENERIC CLOSET IN THE WRITERS' ROOM

If the Black-cast sitcom's ultimate goal is to expunge Black gayness, then the struggles around how the writers author such characters within industrial boundaries is worth examining. Caldwell rightly maintains that "negotiated and collective authorship is an almost unavoidable and determining reality in contemporary film/television."[40] And Jonathan Gray's theorization of "clusters of authorship" only deepens Caldwell's perspective by suggesting that television's authors both work in concert with one another and are often in contention with each other while writing television series.[41] In this section, I focus on the negotiations and labors of the culture industry workers I interviewed. I argue that they are attempting to work within the constraints of the Black-cast sitcom's generic closet to give new meanings to Black gayness. Therefore, I want to, as Matthew Tinkcom advises, "keep in mind the forces of production under capital, particularly in terms of how capital seeks to treat all labor as undifferentiable."[42] In other words, I assert in this section that the labor of the writers and showrunners who want to bring Black gay representation to television screens is fundamentally different from the labor of those studio executives who believe that their shows are simply what happens between Tide commercials. The writers and showrunners I interviewed are not without agency; however, their agency is circumscribed by industrial constraints.

Bady's "Labels" script went through workshopping that is indicative of the way television is made; however, he contends that the narrative structure remained relatively untouched with one exception: in Bady's draft of the script, Moesha attempts to kiss Omar. When he refuses her kiss, Moesha starts the rumor that Omar is gay, making the series' hero more culpable in beginning the rumor. Such a construction of Moesha as a rumor-starter because Omar rebuffs her advances would not necessarily set him up for a "deserved" expulsion from the series' narrative universe because the rumor would have been rooted in Moesha's hurt feelings. Instead, Farquhar and story editor Ron Neal added Tracy, a flamboyantly Black gay character, to the script, in a significant change to Bady's original script. Bady recalls that when Farquhar and Neal received the script, they said they liked it. However, overnight they added a scene wherein Tracy's flamboyance works to semiotically link Omar to gayness because of his relationship to Tracy. Bady recalls, "I protested because I thought they were making fun [of gay people]. They wanted the flaming queen. I protested and protested and Ralph finally said, 'You're not going to win this one.' I should have been fired for how hard I fought to keep Tracy out of that script. To their credit, they did not fire me and Ralph was like, 'I'm calling it, I'm the executive producer, so it's staying in.'"[43] Bady reveals the disciplinary function of network television as it attempts to engage with its workers. Protesting or pushing against dominant ideologies is not rewarded but working within the confines of the system is. Furthermore, as a precariously employed freelance writer on *Moesha*, Bady's feelings about a script that would bear his name could be trumped by those with more industrial power within the writers' room. I suggest Bady attempted to use Stuart Hall's "reversal" transcoding strategy, which seeks to expunge "negative" stereotypes and replace them with a more "positive" image.[44] For Bady, however, Tracy's inclusion undercut that work.

Farquhar saw the addition of Tracy differently while acknowledging that his inclusion was a point of contentiousness in the writers' room. He recalls,

> The one thing we wrestled with was [Omar's] friend [Tracy], who we played in a flamboyant way. Typically, I would not have allowed that if that character were by himself, but because he was also a gay character it seemed OK.... It's a balancing act.... So, it depends on what you need the character for. We needed that character to be [more flamboyant] because in a half hour you have to drive the point home quick. We just needed to have Moesha's reaction and for her to start putting things together in that scene.[45]

Farquhar acknowledges that he, like Bady, is invested in a particular kind of representational politics that recognizes that so-called flamboyant representations had become problematic in the Gay '90s. He also affords flamboyant representations space within *Moesha*'s "Labels" because he can rely on a sense of balance that grants exposure to "both sides" of the gay representational coin. Farquhar *only* allows the "negative" representation of Tracy because its corollary—the "positive" representation—exists in the same space. Simultaneously, Farquhar insinuates that the semiotic efficacy of flamboyant gay characters is suitable for the episodic Black-cast sitcom form, which requires stories and characters to be quickly, readily, and easily identifiable as a "type."[46] Tracy thus takes the "heat" from Moesha for starting the rumor about Omar's sexuality. But more than that, Farquhar inadvertently reveals that both Tracy's and Omar's inclusion in the series is only temporary by suggesting that narrative information about them must be relayed quickly. It seems out of the question that Omar or Tracy might be a part of *Moesha*'s world for more than a single episode, regardless of the complexity of the story the series attempts to tell.

Bady's experience writing "Labels" somewhat mirrors the experience of *All of Us* staff writers and coproducers McKinley and March, who are the credited writers for the episode, "My Two Dads." McKinley recalls of writing the episode, "Scenarios involving that whole family, how they react, those types of things change[d]."[47] I want to draw attention to McKinley's suggestion that the writer's room conversations focused on scenarios about how the family in *All of Us* would react to the inclusion of Black gayness. These kinds of authorial negotiations become important because they set the terms within which Black gayness will appear in the episode(s). For *All of Us*, Black gayness, even in the ideation stage of script development, retains its secondary narrative status.

When March and McKinley worked on TBS's *Are We There Yet?* as coproducers and writers, they still went through the typical writers' room process. Because neither March nor McKinley was the series' executive producer, they had to follow orders and, more generally, the direction the other writers in the writers' room wanted the episode to take. And sometimes the direction dictated by the writers' room and the showrunner does not always net the intended results. As McKinley details, when "the showrunner got [the script for "The Boy Has Style"] and looked at it, he said, 'We can't put this out. I'm a supporter of the gays and I can't have this [episode] coming out.'"[48] The direction that the staff writers and producers suggested McKinley and March take for "The Boy Has Style" received a different reaction when the script was fully written. McKinley and March say they knew the direction from the writers' room would make the script's treatment of homosexuality harsh, but they wrote it following that direction. McKinley says, "When you're a writer you have to follow the [story] outline the room decides; you might not agree with it. I didn't, but the script that we turned in was very harsh, a little harsher."[49] McKinley recalls, "At one point the father was going to come to [Cedric] and say, 'How dare you lead my daughter on?!' We just felt that it was kind of crazy; it was almost bordering on the father almost bashing [Cedric] a little bit."[50] In subsequent drafts, the conversation was softened so that Nick did not appear as hostile toward Cedric's homosexuality—a move that retains the audience's goodwill toward him. Ultimately, the episode was revised to have Nick say that he was fine if Cedric were gay but that Cedric needed to tell his daughter so as not to lead her on; this approach is a degree of shading, but it maintains the spirit of the original idea. More than that, it retains the notion that for *Are We There Yet?*, Cedric's homosexuality is about knowledge production for others—not him.

Weinberger had a different relationship to authorship because he was both the writer and the creator of *Good News*. He says, "I started with the idea that [dealing with a gay parishioner] was an interesting dilemma for a first-time minister in a Black church given what I know about the Black church's point of view regarding gay members or just the gay community. I thought this was an interesting predicament that could be done satirically, but could also make a point, but could also be funny."[51] Weinberger wrote the episode he wanted and, as executive producer, did not have to compromise his vision based on other writers' ideas. However, he was faced with other issues related to authorship and production—finding an actor to play the lead character: "Originally the part was written for Kirk Franklin. He was going to be the star of the show. He objected to the material, and I refused to change it."[52] This power to refuse to make script changes is a power that rested with Weinberger because he wore several hats within the series. As creator, showrunner, and writer, he wielded a kind of power that none of the other writers in this chapter had (it is also worth noting and centering his white maleness within Hollywood).

Weinberger's approach to the difficulties with Franklin was to recast the part rather than make changes. He says that the subject matter of the episode was

> bold enough . . . that Kirk Franklin would choose not to do it because of his religious position, which I guess is a couple of quotations: one in Leviticus and one in either John or Paul's Letters to the Corinthians. . . . We debated the theological grounds for that and went 'round and 'round. I couldn't convince him that Leviticus was wrong and that Jesus never spoke against homosexuality. . . . Had [Jesus] been given that issue, I think he would have sided on compassion and love as opposed to ostracizing somebody because of their sexual orientation. That was an argument that I didn't win with Mr. Franklin. . . . That's how David Ramsey became the [series] lead.[53]

Even after Ramsey was cast instead of Franklin, there were still casting issues for the series because of the subject matter of the pilot. Weinberger wanted the series to feel as real as possible, and to achieve this, he recruited churchgoers from Los Angeles–area churches to work as extras. He recalls,

> At one point one woman objected to the whole idea of the show. When she did, I just made a little speech to everybody expressing my beliefs and what this church [within the series] believed, that this church, at least as long as I was running [the series], it was going to be a forgiving and compassionate one, closer to what I believe Jesus would have said. . . . She was there with her daughter as a matter of fact, and she said to her daughter, "OK, we're leaving." I said that anyone who objects to this should get up and go out. "If the show

is in conflict with your religious convictions, then I think you shouldn't be part of it." That woman was the only one that left out of the two hundred on the show. Once we settled on the principal cast, no one else had any problems with the subject matter.[54]

This power to dismiss cast members and extras is rooted in Weinberger's position within the series. As McKinley, March, Banks-Waddles, and Bady suggested, even if they were unhappy with the direction the writers' room or the showrunner wanted to take, their only form of recourse was to begrudgingly go along with the changes, quit, or be fired.

As the writers and showrunners in this section demonstrate, negotiations over how to get Black gayness representationally "right" is central because, on some level, they understand that they do not have (or will not insist on) the luxury of coming back to these stories to tweak them. The generic closet casts a shadow over these series. To properly "deal with" Black gayness once and for all, they have to do so in ways that carefully think through the inclusion of more "feminine" or "masculine" Black gay characters and the hostility series writers and showrunners produce about Black gayness. As Bady discovered on his "Labels" script and McKinley and March on their "The Boy Has Style" script, sometimes the showrunner simply "pulls rank" and decides that a script should develop in a certain fashion; however, these negotiations are vital to an understanding of the generic closet and the queer politics of the Black-cast sitcom. These culture industry workers are aware that, historically, Black gayness has not been present within the Black-cast sitcom, and they attempt to represent it—even if for only one or two episodes.

COMING OUT OF THE BLACK-CAST SITCOM'S GENERIC CLOSET

For many LGBT individuals, *coming out*—the act of telling family, loved ones, friends, and coworkers about one's sexuality—is an important rite of passage and part of one's identity development. Several psychology and sociology scholars have theorized and tested models to explain gay men's (and sometimes lesbians') processes for making sense of their gayness.[55] The rhetoric behind these models is rooted in gay liberation. To call oneself gay is to be proud and liberated from the homophobic oppression of a heteronormative society. It is equally important to note that most gay identity development models that center the importance of the act of coming out are *white* gay identity development models. When Blackness is factored into the equation, Dorie G. Martinez and Stonie C. Sullivan posit that "the eventual acceptance and integration of one's gay identity may be constructed differently according to social and environmental factors impacting African American gay men and lesbians . . . [and] when there is a strong perception of homophobia emanating from the community to which they feel connected, many African American gay men and lesbians consider themselves to be better off if they do not come out to their families, friends, and community."[56] To avoid negative reactions for spheres of influence, many African Americans do not find that the last phase of most gay identity development models—coming out—essential to their Black gay identity development.

I spend time discussing gay identity development models to underscore that the Black-cast sitcom and its deployment of the generic closet is based on a (partly false) universalist claim that not only flattens gay identity development but does so to ensure three necessities for its narrative world. First, coming out as gay can provide a sense of drama. And as Kristal Brent Zook theorizes, one of the traits of the Black-cast sitcom is its "struggle for drama. Whereas traditional sitcom formats demanded a 'joke per page' . . . [the Black-cast sitcom] resisted such norms by consciously and unconsciously crafting dramatic episodes."[57] Second, it relies on a mostly white claim of the import placed on coming out as a declarative speech act *necessary* for one's identity development. Third, and more germane to this book, the "dramatic" coming-out story line has a clear ending, which helps to reify the Black-cast sitcom's continued deployment of the generic closet. Coming out becomes a point of no return for Black gay characters, a dramatic flourish after which they cannot return lest they create a permanent seismic shift for the series.

Because the Black-cast sitcom assumes heterosexuality as its default position, as a televisual form, it produces (and reproduces) the generic closet, which becomes an organizing logic for Black-cast sitcoms.[58] Unlike white- and multicultural-cast sitcoms, the Black-cast sitcom structures the generic closet as narratively generative for its brief engagement with Black gayness. The generic closet sets up the necessary confession of Black gay identity and its attendant "coming out" within the cycle of detection, discovery/declaration, and discarding.

"Coming-out episodes" are part of knowledge production in that by the end of a half-hour episode, viewers know who is gay and who is not. Once this discovery/declaration occurs, these gay characters, because of their supporting role in the show, ride off into the sunset without allowing viewers to understand what the declaration means. The viewer (usually) knows that the character is gay or lesbian, but they have no concept of what that means for the world the

Fig. 2.2. Toward the end of the *Moesha* episode "Labels," Omar whispers something to his cousin Hakeem that is assumed to be his declaration that he is gay.

other heterosexual characters inhabit. Given this importance (and the possibility for the drama often associated with coming-out stories), it is no surprise that coming-out episodes are among the most frequent episodes that have featured gay characters, particularly in the sitcom, which is often predicated on a "problem of the week" that gets solved within a single twenty-two-minute episode.[59] Nor it is particularly shocking that the coming-out episode remains the conduit through which the Black-cast sitcom chooses to engage with Black gayness.

Bady deviated from most coming-out episodes because the declaration "I'm gay" is never uttered. One of the final scenes in "Labels" shows Omar whispering something to his cousin Hakeem, and Hakeem responding coldly as Moesha recites the lyrics to Edie Brickell's song, "What I Am." What Omar has said remains unknown. Bady recalls, "Everything was very specific about that episode. . . . I remember making all of these impassioned arguments about why we should never hear what Hakeem's cousin says because it really shouldn't matter."[60] As a Black gay man, Bady's steadfastness in maintaining Omar's sexuality as his own, private matter, in some ways, points to how his lived experience as a Black gay man may have shaped the episode he wrote for *Moesha*.

Bady reflects, "The idea that Omar whispers [something] in Hakeem's ear and the audience never hears him say [he's gay] is a mirror reflection of how I was living my life. . . . The idea that I was saying it shouldn't matter meant [Omar did] not acknowledge himself in a very verbal and definitive way."[61] Drawing on his own experiences, Bady seems to be representing a precise version of Black gayness in relation to his understanding of social context and identity. Bady rejected the notion that Omar should demand the world pay attention to his gayness. Rather, Omar's sexuality becomes his own—not out of some "closetedness" but because he wants his sexuality to be private, as it is for most heterosexuals in Western culture. The script for the episode denies the heterosexual characters the opportunity to react to Omar's gayness in fact. They react to the rumor that he *might* be gay. This approach also works as a form of decentering because Omar has no voice, but Moesha's voice speaks the truth for him. Farquhar's insistence on the inclusion of Tracy performs a semiotic queerness that acts as queer labor for heterosexual viewers. I do not mean *queer labor* in the sense that Meg Wesling imagines it, as "the value (both cultural and economic) of the queer [that] opens up ways to think about the labor of sexuality and gender identity beyond what is recognizably queer."[62] Rather, I deploy *queer labor* to suggest that Tracy does the work for viewers (in particular, heterosexual viewers) by drawing on their semiotic knowledge of mediated gayness to be able to quickly read his body as a queer body. Queer labor, as Patrick Mullen argues, "produces and circulates forms of value . . . [and] reveals the social distribution of contemporary power relations."[63] Thus, Tracy's queer labor is useful for *Moesha* so that viewers do not have to perform that detective labor.

On *All of Us*, McKinley and March felt differently than Bady about the declaration of homosexuality in their episode "My Two Dads." The episode deals with series lead Robert's discovery that Earl, the man he knows as his father, is actually his adoptive father and that Luther, his birth father, is gay. McKinley and March are credited with writing the episode, but they are both quick to point out that the story outline was worked out in the writers' room. Unlike Bady's experience on *Moesha*, there was group discussion about the direction of the episode, which was part of a three-episode arc. McKinley notes, "The outline of the entire story was different. We always wanted his father to be gay, but it started in layers. [Robert] finds out that he's adopted and that's where we started. What if he finds out that his father is gay? How does he deal with a new man in his life and the fact that he might not be what he imagined his Dad to be, whatever that means."[64] Interestingly, as with "Labels," Luther never says, "I'm gay." His actions, namely, kissing his boyfriend, perform the function of coming out, redeploying the utility of queer labor in place of a declarative speech act.

McKinley and March were adamant that they wanted no narrative ambiguity. As such, in addition to being seen kissing his boyfriend, Luther is asked by the adoptive father's wife to confirm Luther's gayness. Then Earl asks Luther if he is sure that he is gay. Rather than confirming his sexuality with dialogue, McKinley and March choose to have him "come out" by saying, "Ask my boyfriend." McKinley and March still provide the narrative clarity that has become one of the hallmarks of the coming-out episode, which is concomitantly central to the operation of the generic closet. If there is any ambiguity, the expulsion of these characters for the possibility of being gay might be construed as antigay. The declarative coming out signals not a beginning of a "liberated" life as cast members of a Black-cast sitcom's universe but rather the end of their tenure within it. McKinley underscores that one of the things important to her and March was that they

> didn't want [Robert] to find out [Luther] is gay and that's the reason [Robert] rejects him. We wanted to make it clear that [Robert is] upset [because he finds out] that he's adopted at the last minute. He has to kind of come to terms with the fact that he has a new father *and* he's gay. It was layered on that story. We wanted him to be accepting at the end.... We ... want[ed] him to come to terms and think, "This guy's pretty cool, I want to meet my father." In the last [episode, Robert is] accepting enough for [Luther] to bring his boyfriend [to Thanksgiving dinner].[65]

Tropiano contends that one of the hallmarks of the coming-out episode is that "although hard to accept at first, the character eventually offers his/her support [for the gay character]."[66] Tropiano's racially universalist model was developed before the representational explosion of the (white) Gay '90s, but even as white gayness has moved on to other concerns, Black gayness has remained trapped in this industrial closet. As such, the Black-cast sitcom's deployment of the generic closet is predicated on the mandatory acceptance of Black gayness within the episode. It is part of March and McKinley's insistence that Robert "come to terms" with his father's gayness and allow Luther to "bring his boyfriend" to Thanksgiving dinner. Put simply, "My Two Dads" ceases to be about gayness per se and instead is more concerned with demonstrating the "coolness" of the core cast with respect to the episodic gay narrative "problem." In addition, although sitcoms generally do not have a "memory" in the sense that it is always on a quest to return to stasis, the series could ill-afford to have one of its main characters understood as antigay. *All of Us*'s generic closet, like the generic closets on other Black-cast sitcoms in this book, makes Luther's sexuality not his own. It is a narrative catalyst that underscores homosexuality's relationship to the otherwise heterosexual universe of the series.

When writing "The Boy Has Style," McKinley and March continued insisting on clarity. In particular, McKinley worked under the assumption that homosexuality and identity development are as simple as a speech act. If McKinley, a heterosexual woman, can map gayness onto a potential suitor's body, then he *must* also know and be prepared to disclose his sexuality. Because the televisual understanding of gayness is rooted in a discursively heterosexist standpoint, homosexuality is reduced to a knowingness that can be disclosed rather than one coming into and accepting one's (homo) sexuality. To achieve this goal, McKinley reveals that she worked with the costume designer to ensure that gayness would be grafted onto Cedric's body via costuming. She recalls, "We wanted him to be [visibly] gay, so we put in little traits. . . . We put in a little bit of his wardrobe even though this is a stereotype. He did like to dress. He had some style. It wasn't like obvious, obvious, because we wanted Lindsey to not know."[67] McKinley used fashion as a technology to read gayness onto Cedric's body. Kathryn Bond Stockton contends that "cloth and skin touch on each other's meanings since each is a surface—with intense, complex and variable codings attached to it—that may be the object of prejudice, violence, attraction and invective."[68] Thus, as an episode, "The Boy Has Style" uses the "variable codings" of clothing to create a narrative conflict rooted in homosexuality and a reification of gayness's visual detectability.

The impetus for the episode also has its roots in the societal demand for disclosure. Failure to disclose sexuality that deviates from normative heterosexuality is often considered trickery and dishonesty. Foucault argues "one confesses—or is forced to confess. When it is not spontaneous or dictated by some internal imperative, the confession is wrung from a person by violence or threat; it is driven from its hiding place in the soul, or extracted from the body."[69] The import placed on the declaration of homosexuality structures the episode's development within the writers' room. March recalls that they "chose the dialogue very carefully. . . . The father even said that 'I don't care that you're gay, what I care about is that you are hurting my daughter.' He was cool about it, but he wanted Cedric to tell her that he was gay."[70] In other words, in writing the script, the disclosure of Cedric's homosexuality is what becomes important—even as he is a teenager.

Fig. 2.3. In *Are We There Yet?*, Cedric's pink argyle sweater is supposed to signal his gayness to audiences.

Cedric's declaration is not necessarily rooted in his desire to come out. His sexuality cannot be his own; it must be publicly disclosed. This investment in sexual disclosure is couched within the notion that, according to McKinley, the father was upset that Cedric "was fooling his daughter into thinking that he liked her. He didn't want . . . [his daughter to] think, 'Oh my God! Is there something wrong with me?'"[71] Here, Cedric's coming out ceases to be about *his* sexuality; it is about his sexuality as it relates to *other* characters. The episode's guiding question, then, is not how this character will come to terms with his homosexuality but how his homosexuality will affect the other characters in the series. In fact, what is particularly fascinating is that once Cedric discloses his sexuality to Lindsey, she literally walks him to the door and escorts him out of the series, despite their vow to remain friends.

Let's Stay Together continues an insistence on the declaration of one's "out-ness," which reinforces a reliance on a strict adherence to what Maria San Filipo calls *compulsory monosexuality*—an approach to sexuality that postulates homosexuality and heterosexuality as two fixed points within a binary classificatory system of sexual behaviors and in which one must choose either the same gender or the opposite gender as an object choice, but never both.[72] In fact, Banks-Waddles never considered that Darkanian might be romantically involved with *both* Crystal and his boyfriend Greg. She recalls, "I don't ever

Fig. 2.4. Lindsay discards Cedric after he has declared his homosexuality to her in the *Are We There Yet?* episode "The Boy Has Style."

think we wanted to have him do the down low conversation or make it look like he was having relationships with women, because that's a whole different conversation.... I don't think we ever wanted it to feel like he was deceiving people or deceiving women just by living this double life, just that he was who he was, he only liked men... and because of the industry he was in, he wasn't comfortable saying who he was. We never went down the bisexual route with him."[73] As Banks-Waddles imagines bisexuality, it is first and foremost a "messier" story, and the series was concerned with creating a satisfying story. Banks-Waddles did not "think anybody would've been satisfied with him continuing to live the lie, or having Crystal step forward and lie for him and having him still sort of be in the darkness.... I remember talking about what would be the most satisfying ending for him and having him come out or having him at least acknowledge that, 'This is who I am,' felt like the most satisfying way to wrap up his story."[74] Banks-Waddles's suggestion that Darkanian discontinue living a lie underscores two heterosexist notions about gayness. First, it problematically positions a failure to disclose one's gayness as rooted in deception generally and a deception of women who have the "right" to assume these men are viable sexual and romantic partners. Second, although the episodes decenter Darkanian's homosexuality, they center the insistence that he declare his sexuality. The generic closet demands the disclosure to provide narrative closure—and it suggests that self-disclosure is insufficient. *Any* disclosure of "deviant" sexual orientation must be made to those who want to know. And as Banks-Waddles asserts, coming out is considered stepping into the light after being shrouded in "darkness." Showrunner Edmonds Cofer similarly saw gayness as "a cleaner story" for Darkanian.[75]

Both Edmonds Cofer and Banks-Waddles believed monosexuality was "cleaner" because it narratively evacuates any ambiguity for viewers and settles a narrative "crisis over sexual certainty."[76] Darkanian's failure to come out as gay means that he is attempting to be devious—a common trope deployed to discuss men, particularly Black men, who have sexual relationships with both men and women. Even as the series explores Darkanian's arc over the course of seven episodes, when it comes to sexuality, there is no place for sexual in-betweenness.

The appearance of Black gay characters, however well meaning (and I believe the writers and showrunners in this book are all well-meaning), are discussed and deployed on heteronormativity's terms. As William Henry indicates, when television attempts to engage with homosexuality, it does so from the perspective of heterosexuality and the way *it* deals with homosexuality—not the other way around.[77] Within such an impulse, homosexuality is "rightly" decentered from the main narrative—a decentering that lays bare the politics of the generic closet.

The "Pilot" episode from *Good News* takes a slightly different approach to gayness. In his long career, Weinberger had written gay characters before (he was an uncredited creator of *Brothers* and also wrote a gay character on *The Mary Tyler Moore Show*), but he says "in this case, given the setting of a Black church, it had extra significance because it seemed to be a real issue; it certainly still *is* an issue for me."[78] Ultimately because of his rootedness in "issues television," Weinberger also wrote a coming-out episode wherein David comes out twice—once to the pastor and once to his mother. In both instances, he comes out by specifically uttering, "I'm gay," supporting Joshua Gamson's thesis that within television discourse, homosexuality must be disclosed early and often.[79]

Episodes featuring Black gay characters are inherently predicated on the "surprise" of a character's coming out. However, Weinberger, in some ways, displaces the surprise of coming out. The pastor is undoubtedly surprised by the coming out, but the second coming out is a nonevent because David's mother is unfazed by his admission, which presumably results in humor. Rather than David's mother's being upset that he is gay, she is more disturbed that her son's boyfriend is white. As Weinberger details, casting the boyfriend with a white actor "was the satirical point for [David's mother]—it was far more a problem [but] . . . it was a comic truth as well. She knew he was gay since he was eight years old. . . . So, her outrage . . . that's a comic position, but a true one. 'Why can't you go out and find a gay Black man?' That's a comic point of view, but it's also saying something about her own prejudice and dealing with that."[80] Weinberger perhaps created one of the more progressive Black-cast sitcom episodes to deal with homosexuality in the sense that David's homosexuality is not an issue that the characters within the series have to come to accept—they have to "come to accept" that David's boyfriend is white. Although the episode was ostensibly about David's coming out as gay, Weinberger wanted to downplay any antigay sentiments within the episode (even as he experienced antigay sentiments from an extra and the actor for whom he initially wrote the part). In the process, he ends up decentering David's gayness in lieu of a discussion of interracial relationships.

Coming out within the Black-cast sitcom is imperative, even as identity development models theorize that is not necessarily an important part of being gay for some Black gay men. A failure to come out as gay is construed as being couched in deceit. As Gamson found in the relationship between talk shows and gayness, a formula that can be adapted for Black-cast sitcoms, lying becomes constructed as the "problem"—a problem that the episode is there to correct, "to encourage and facilitate—one might even say enforce—the telling of truths."[81] Indeed, coming out within the Black-cast sitcom *may* be pedagogical in helping to "break down stereotypes by giving gay America a human face" for Black-cast sitcom viewers.[82] Nevertheless, as a *requirement* for Black gay character development within the Black-cast sitcom, it becomes the only way these characters are imagined. *Moesha, Good News, All of Us, Are We There Yet?,* and *Let's Stay Together,* a corpus of Black-cast sitcoms spanning roughly twenty years of television history, could only imagine Black gayness in specific and predetermined ways—as integral parts of reasserting the generic closet. For Omar, Eldridge, Luther, Cedric, and Darkanian, the generic closet is not the beginning of their life as liberated gay subjects. It represents the end of their lives within the series on which they appeared. In other words, the Black-cast sitcom emits a collective shrug about the interior lives of these Black gay characters because the Black-cast sitcom simply goes on to other stories.

QUEER TODAY, GONE TOMORROW

This chapter exposed the conditional terms under which Black gayness has been allowed within the Black-cast sitcom. In the more than twenty years of Black-cast sitcom content, no writers or showrunners have exercised their agency or capital to fight for the ongoing inclusion of Black gay characters. The queer politics of the Black-cast sitcom's writers' room seems to function as what Foucault calls an "internal discourse of the institution," a discursive operation that is "employed to address itself, and which circulate[s] among those who made it function."[83] My extension of Foucault here gestures toward the internal (il)logics of the Black-cast sitcom that ensure that it maintains its norms. Ultimately, the Black-cast sitcom functions within a politics of respectability that props up African American social formations by recognizing, but ultimately expunging, "deviant" sexualities from its narrative universe. The Black-cast sitcom aims to represent "restrained and disciplined behavior" that embodies middle-class, heteronormative ideals and gestures toward Black gayness's engagement as solely responsible for providing information about the core cast.[84] Returning to Edmonds Cofer's suggestion that the characters she wrote were "progressive" in their views toward homosexuality, such tolerance of Black gayness is limited. Its deployment is mostly concerned with Black identity formation dependent on certain bodies "becoming reviled and cast off in order to consolidate the subject . . . while retaining an attraction and repulsion relationship to what is abjected."[85]

In this heteronormative pursuit, the closet and a Black gay character's coming out of it becomes an important and organizing ideological principle around which television writers and showrunners—across race, gender, and sexual orientation—imagine Black gayness within Black-cast sitcoms. As such, the three Ds—detection, discovery/declaration, and discarding—become a kind of three-act structure for the ways these series will ultimately engage with Black gayness. Because of this investment in the three Ds, these writers and producers find the act of coming out of the closet an important and necessary part of the ways they tell Black gay stories; "the closet" contains and constrains how Black gayness can even be imagined.

Those higher on the television food chain affix certain ideologies to their presumed Black viewers that are often out of sync with the actualities of these viewers. When representations of Black gay men make it beyond the pitch, beyond the outline, beyond the script drafts, and are finally broadcast to viewers, it is productive to examine what writers wrote, their authorial intentions, and the struggles between writers and showrunners to get these representations on the air. Because of the few broadly circulated images of Black gay men in television, the writers and showrunners are well aware of the burden these representations must carry. Therefore, even when they are not Black gay men, they exercise caution in attempting to break down long-held tropes about homosexuality generally and Black homosexuality specifically. The TV industry workers in this chapter have certainly not written perfect episodes, but they make Black gayness visible on television—even if only for twenty-two minutes.

NOTES

1. The word *showrunner* and the phrase *executive producer* are used interchangeably throughout this chapter.

2. Raymond Williams, "Base and Superstructure in Marxist Cultural Theory," in *Rethinking Popular Culture: Contemporary Perspectives in Cultural Studies*, ed. Chandra Mukerji and Michael Schudon (Los Angeles: University of California Press, 1991), 410.

3. Alfred L. Martin Jr., "The Queer Business of Casting Gay Characters on US Television," *Communication, Culture, and Critique* 11, no. 2 (2018): 283.

4. Joseph Turow, "Casting for Television: The Anatomy of Social Typing," *Journal of Communication* 28, no. 4 (1978): 18.

5. Felicia Henderson, "The Culture behind Closed Doors: Issues of Gender and Race in the Writers' Room," *Cinema Journal* 50, no. 3 (2011): 146.

6. Horace Newcomb and Robert S. Alley, *The Producer's Medium: Conversations with Creators of American TV* (New York: Oxford University Press, 1983), 16.

7. Alexander Doty, *Making Things Perfectly Queer: Interpreting Mass Culture* (Minneapolis: University of Minnesota Press, 1993), 19.

8. Isaac Julien, "Black Is, Black Ain't: Notes on De-essentializing Black Identities," in *Black Popular Culture*, ed. Gail Dent (Seattle: Bay Press, 1992), 261.

9. See Becker, *Gay TV and Straight America*.

10. Louis Althusser, *Lenin and Philosophy, and Other Essays* (New York: Monthly Review Press, 1972), 175.

11. Ralph Farquhar, interview with author (Denver), June 1, 2016; "breaking a story" is a writers' room process in which the writers brainstorm ideas for script development.

12. Ibid.

13. Vincent Doyle, *Making Out in the Mainstream: GLAAD and the Politics of Respectability* (Montreal: McGill-Queen's University Press, 2016), 52.

14. Shonda Rhimes, "Shonda Rhimes Accepts Golden Gate Award at the #glaadawards," originally aired June 4, 2012, YouTube, 9:13, https://www.youtube.com/watch?v=iHp2WvspFfs&t=331s.

15. Demetrius Bady, interview with author (Austin), February 27, 2013; Farquhar interview.

16. David Colman, "A Night Out with: James Collard; The Corner of Straight and Gay," *New York Times*, July 19, 1998, http://www.nytimes.com/1998/07/19/style/a-night-out-with-james-collard-the-corner-of-straight-and-gay.html.

17. Ed. Weinberger, interview with author (Austin), March 19, 2013.

18. Walters, *Tolerance Trap*, 2.

19. Antonia March, interview with author (Austin), March 18, 2013.

20. Ibid.

21. Foucault, *Discipline and Punish*, 200.

22. Ali LeRoi, interview with author (Denver), March 1, 2017.

23. Ibid.

24. Ibid.

25. Zook, *Color by Fox*, 5.

26. Chambers, *Queer Politics of Television*, 60.

27. Zook, *Color by Fox*, 6.

28. Jacqueline McKinley, interview by author (Austin), tape recording, March 22, 2013.

29. Joyrich, "Epistemology of the Console," 27.

30. Georg Simmel, "Fashion," *International Quarterly* 10, no. 1 (1904): 130–155.

31. A. C. Liang, "The Creation of Coherence in Coming-Out Stories," in *Queerly Phrased: Language, Gender, and Sexuality*, ed. Anna Livia and Kira Hall (New York: Oxford University Press, 1997), 293.

32. Marlon Riggs, "Unleash the Queen," in *Black Popular Culture*, ed. Gail Dent (Seattle: Bay Press, 1992), 101.

33. Generally speaking, episodic series feature episodes with self-contained narratives, whereas serial series build longer, more intricate stories over the course of the episode. No series is purely episodic or serial; however, one narrative form usually prevails in a series.

34. Carla Banks-Waddles, interview with author (New York), September 12, 2015.

35. Jacque Edmonds Cofer, interview with author (New York), March 7, 2016.

36. Ibid.

37. Ibid.

38. Martin, "Generic Closets," 233.

39. Thomas Cripps, *Making Movies Black: The Hollywood Message Movie from World War II to the Civil Rights Era* (New York: Oxford University Press, 1993), ix.

40. Caldwell, *Production Culture*, 199.

41. Jonathan Gray, "When Is the Author?," in *A Companion to Media Authorship*, ed. Jonathan Gray and Derek Johnson (New York: Wiley, 2013), 104.

42. Matthew Tinkcom, *Working Like a Homosexual: Camp, Capital, Cinema* (Durham, NC: Duke University Press, 2002), 10.

43. Bady, interview.

44. Hall, "Spectacle of the Other," 270.

45. Farquhar, interview.

46. Brett Mills, *Television Sitcom* (London: Palgrave Macmillan, 2005), 109.

47. McKinley, interview.

48. Ibid.

49. Ibid.

50. Ibid.

51. Weinberger, interview.

52. Ibid.

53. Ibid.

54. Ibid.

55. Vivienne C. Cass, "Homosexual Identity Formation: Testing a Theoretical Model," *Journal of Sex Research* 20, no. 2 (1984):143–167; Donna J. Johns and Tahira M. Probst, "Sexual Minority Identity Formation in an Adult Population," *Journal of Homosexuality* 47, no. 2 (2004): 81–90; Henry Minton and Gary McDonald, "Homosexual Identity Formation as a Development Process," *Journal of Homosexuality* 9, nos. 2–3 (1984): 91–104; Robert J. Kus, "Stages of Coming Out: An Ethnographic Approach," *Western Journal of Nursing* 7, no. 2 (1985): 177–198; Richard Troiden, "Becoming Homosexual: A Model of Gay Identity Acquisition," *Psychiatry* 42, no. 4 (1979): 362–373; Stephen Brady and Wilma J. Busse, "The Gay Identity Questionnaire: A Brief Measure of Homosexual Identity Formation," *Journal of Homosexuality* 26, no. 4 (1994): 1–22.

56. Martinez and Sullivan, "African American Gay Men and Lesbians," 252.

57. Zook, *Color by Fox*, 9.

58. Joyrich, "Epistemology of the Console," 27.

59. Tropiano, *Prime Time Closet*, 192.

60. Bady, interview.

61. Ibid.

62. Meg Wesling, "Queer Value," *GLQ* 18, no. 1 (2012): 122.

63. Patrick R. Mullen, *The Poor Bugger's Tool: Irish Modernism, Queer Labor, and Postcolonial History* (New York: Oxford University Press, 2012), 20.

64. McKinley, interview.

65. Ibid.

66. Tropiano, *Prime Time Closet*, 192.

67. McKinley, interview.

68. Kathryn Bond Stockton, *Beautiful Bottom, Beautiful Shame: Where "Black" Meets "Queer"* (Durham, NC: Duke University Press, 2006), 40.

69. Foucault, *History of Sexuality*, 59.

70. March, interview.

71. McKinley, interview.

72. Maria San Filippo, *The B Word: Bisexuality in Contemporary Film and Television* (Bloomington: Indiana University Press, 2013), 16.

73. Banks-Waddles, interview.

74. Ibid.

75. Edmonds Cofer, interview.

76. McCune, *Black Masculinity*, 5.

77. Cited in Larry Gross, "Out of the Mainstream: Sexual Minorities and the Mass Media," in *Remote Control: Television, Audiences and Cultural Power*, ed. Ellen Seiter (New York: Routledge, 1991), 138.

78. Ibid.

79. Joshua Gamson, *Freaks Talk Back: Tabloid Talk Shows and Sexual Nonconformity* (Chicago: University of Chicago Press, 1999), 70.

80. Weinberger, interview.

81. Gamson, *Freaks Talk Back*, 70.

82. Patricia Boling, *Privacy and the Politics of Intimate Life* (Ithaca, NY: Cornell University Press, 1996), 135.

83. Foucault, *History of Sexuality*, 28.

84. Ferguson, *Aberrations in Black*, 76.

85. Darieck Scott, *Extravagant Abjection: Blackness, Power, and Sexuality in the African American Literary Imagination* (New York: New York University Press, 2010), 16–17. Emphasis in original.

THREE

—◊—

COMEDY, LAUGHTER, AND
THE GENERIC CLOSET

FOR MANY IDENTITY GROUPS, TO rise out of mediated symbolic annihilation is to be reckoned with and recognized. The first places where Black people appeared on television, particularly as stars of their own shows, was within the sitcom—a space where Black representation has largely remained segregated to this day—with *Beulah* (ABC, 1950–1953) and *Amos 'n' Andy* (CBS, 1951–1953). Gay men and women did not explicitly, episodically appear in sitcoms until the 1970s (largely as part of the sitcom's "turn toward relevance"), although they had been portrayed in other genres of television, particularly medical dramas, before then.[1] Much of the LGBT representational work has been done in the sitcom, including *Soap* (ABC, 1977–1981), *Ellen, Spin City, Will & Grace,* and *Modern Family.* Because sitcoms center humor, they can often address issues of "difference" in a way that privileges the ability to laugh off differences—raising differences but never quite dealing with them—which works to maintain the veneer of narrative neutrality vis-á-vis differences. This chapter emerges from the premise that the laugh track performs additional work to undermine narrative detachment by exploring the Black-cast sitcom's engagement with difference via the laugh track. Throughout this chapter, I argue that the laugh track helps to reconstitute the generic closet.

The sitcom has historically signaled its connection with humor via the laugh track. The laugh track both tethered the sitcom to its theatrical roots and underscored its liveness—presumably, real people were laughing at the comedy as it ensued. Brett Mills argues that the laugh track assists audiences with decoding and universalizing humor by attempting "to close down alternative readings of [a sitcom's] content, by suggesting that if you're not laughing at one of its jokes, then you're the only one."[2] Mills goes on to argue that "the mass of people heard laughing on a sitcom laugh track doesn't just suggest that something is funny; it suggests that something is obviously, clearly, unarguably, unproblematically funny.... Laugh tracks don't include responses from those who *didn't* find a joke funny or were offended or upset by it."[3] The laugh track not only underscores a sense of neutrality in that *everyone* is laughing at a joke but also erases dissent. At the same time, if dissent is made verbally manifest by booing or other audible forms, there are at least three ways to rid such opposition: (1) the person or people can be asked to leave or forcibly removed from set, (2) the scene can be reshot once the dissenter is managed in ways acceptable to the show's producers, or (3) the dissenting voice can be edited out of the version that will be aired for viewers or moved to a more appropriate space. When laughter is heard during a television series, that laughter could have occurred at a different place, could have been sweetened to make a bigger laugh than the audience gave, or could have been created entirely in postproduction.

Laughter (and the laugh track, by extension) is communal and social. Andy Medhurst and Lucy Tuck suggest that the laugh track is "the electronic substitute for collective experience."[4] The laugh track is used to create a sense of ideological community among viewers. Embedded within the idea that everyone is laughing when the laugh track is heard is the notion that laughter informs one about one's own situation and social position. Laughter creates an interior and an exterior with respect to humor—those inside and those outside of the joke. Wylie Sypher argues that "one of the strongest impulses comedy can discharge from the depths of the social self is our hatred of the 'alien' especially when the stranger who is 'different' stirs any unconscious doubt about our own beliefs."[5] This chapter explores the laugh track's positioning of (homo)sexuality as "alien" within the discursive space of the Black-cast sitcom, acknowledging the Althusserian notion that "the existence of ideology and the ... interpellation of individuals as subjects are one and the same thing."[6] The Black-cast sitcom's generic closet at once episodically calls Black gayness out of symbolic annihilation and concomitantly seeks to expunge it from ideals of "authentic" Blackness because it questions the shaky ground on which "Black authenticity"—as always already heterosexual—stands.

There are characters within series whose primary purpose is to provide either comic relief or the impetus for a comedic situation. In the analysis that follows, I posit that the role of the comic is often embodied by Black gay characters in episodes of Black-cast sitcoms, and I explore the ideological and industrial implications of this use of the Black gay body. Gust A. Yep and John P. Elia argue that "because homosexuality is believed to be a threat to hegemonic black masculinity, it is often dismissed, laughed at, and violently rejected."[7]

The notion of laughing at and thereby rejecting Black gayness is paramount to this chapter.

The hegemonic function of the laugh track is central to this chapter for two reasons. First, the audiences of the series in this chapter are understood as being Black viewers. As I detailed in chapter 1, this imagined Blackness shapes the industrial treatment of each series. Second, because the series are understood as being produced for largely Black audiences, the laugh track also exudes Blackness. Carroll Pratt, one of the pioneers of the laugh track, explains how producers of Black-cast sitcoms often wanted "to have a more ethnic sound" that included audiences talking back to actors and other kinds of sonic verbalization.[8] The Black-cast sitcom's laugh track thus signals a specific Black sound that works to create a notion of an invisible Black community laughing at whatever jokes the series has deployed.

Although not specifically discussing the sitcom, Rick Altman points to four important functions of the television soundtrack that are useful in cuing the spaces where humor exists. Three of these functions are useful for my purposes here: Because of how television is watched (often viewers listen to the television from another room or while on social media or otherwise distracted), Altman posits that the "sound track [should provide] sufficient plot or informational continuity even when the image is not visible."[9] In addition, "there must be a sense that *anything really important* will be cued by the sound track . . . [and] the sound itself must provide desired information, events, or emotions from time to time during the flow."[10] In the sitcom, the laugh track aurally signals the comedy if one is listening to rather than watching the screen. For the viewer at home, the laugh track signals that something important is happening. Within the sitcom, import is understood as something funny; what is important for sitcoms is humor and eliciting an emotional response—namely, laughter—in both the studio audience and the audience at home. Throughout this chapter, I draw on and expand a number of humor theories including superiority, incongruity, relief, and surprise, as well as tendentious jokes, nervous laughter, and comedy of recognition. I make the case for the laugh track to be considered as a component of postproduction that performs a hegemonic function in fashioning and refashioning the generic closet.

THE LAUGH TRACK IN AND AS POSTPRODUCTION

The industrial concept of postproduction is generally attached to single-camera series because they are typically shot on location and out of sequential order. Historically, postproduction was not considered important to sitcom production because sitcoms have traditionally been recorded live-to-tape, which suggests the episode is virtually finished at the end of a taping. Often, little consideration is given to postproduction's importance to the multicamera sitcom. The laugh track's absence within many white- and multicultural-cast single-camera series indicates more polysemic ways of understanding and interpreting humor and the industrial segmentation and narrowcasting of white audiences. Contrary to imaginings of Black audiences, the white audience members at whom these laugh-trackless sitcoms are targeted are understood as WELL—wealthy, educated, liberal, and logical (in a riff on Becker's notion of the SLUMPY demographic). Conversely, the laugh track's presence within Black-cast sitcoms attempts to control where humor can be found and where it is not supposed to be found, indicating the industrial understanding of Black audiences for Black-cast sitcoms as BURP: bigoted, uneducated, (overly) religious, and poor(er).

The laugh track is often considered as part of production within the multi-camera series because such series often announce that they are shot in front of a live studio audience. The liveness of laughter within the sitcom generally, and the Black-cast sitcom specifically, suggests an ideological neutrality—that is, the laughter just happens without consideration for what is funny and why it is funny. It just is. If the laugh track is understood as "just" letting the laughs happen as they did at the taping, it absolves the producers and writers from charges that they are encoding particular ideologies and attempting to structure how viewers understand humor within an episode.

While Jeremy Butler recognizes that the laugh track can be sweetened in postproduction, he suggests that the additional laughter and applause are ideologically neutral, subsumed into the notion of sweetening.[11] Embedded within the notion of sweetening is that the laugh track is not only augmented to make something funnier but also can be removed entirely or placed in a different spot. Part of the reason this chapter considers the laugh track as a component of postproduction is that I want to suggest that the laughter/laugh track is neither accidental nor neutral. This is particularly true for the series analyzed in this chapter. *Moesha* and *Good News* were recorded in front of live studio audiences. An analysis of the laugh track in those series might be placed more squarely within the "mob rule" of the in-studio audience. Inversely, the mode of production for *All of Us*, *Let's Stay Together*, and *Are We There Yet?* was altogether different. These series were recorded on soundstages without a live audience, and the laugh track was added in postproduction. The creation of each series' soundtrack in "post" suggests that ideologies about humor can be embedded within the episodes because a sound editor decided precisely where the "humor" within episodes was located. An analysis of laughter and the laugh track in relation to the generic closet is ideologically illuminating and is crucial to understanding the pedagogical and political strategies used to construct, contain, and marginalize Black gayness for an assumed Black heterosexual audience.

ENCODING DEVIANCE IN POSTPRODUCTION ON *ARE WE THERE YET?*

Although shot proscenium-style, *Are We There Yet?* did not include a live studio audience. The audience laughter was simulated in postproduction. Series showrunner Ali LeRoi told me,

> Adding the laugh track in postproduction is a concession that you're making [when not shooting in front of a live studio audience]. You don't want to overdo it, but you kinda know what's supposed to be funny and why. We have an editor and somebody that has worked in multicam before so they understand. When the editor looks at the show, the reality is there's a person who is watching the show without a laugh track and they have to place it. So, you're filtering it through a person who is looking at the show and finding certain things funny. He's putting the laughs at things that he's laughing at. We're not, like, mathematically placing laughs every 3.5 seconds. There's a person sitting there, finding things funny. Finding things funnier than some other things. Even when you're placing a laugh track, there's still a human element to it.[12]

LeRoi tips his hand with respect to the ways humor is subjective in his comment that the sound editor is "putting the laughs at things that he's laughing at." The laughter on the soundtrack is not heard when a group of living, breathing humans think something is funny; rather, it is inserted at spaces where the postproduction crew believes comedy exists.

The episode title, "The Boy Has Style," suggests that its humor operates from the incongruity approach by communicating discord between Black heterosexual masculinity and notions of style and sartorial choices. The episode's title invokes, as Richard Dyer posits, "a certain set of visual and aural signs . . . [that] immediately bespeak homosexuality and connote the qualities associated, stereotypically, with it."[13] At the same time, Mills suggests that such humor "makes clear how important expectations and norms are to humor, for unless a viewer understands the way things are 'meant to be,' incongruity will be unnoticeable and laughter will not occur."[14] Although the word *style* does not necessarily have a connotation rooted in sexuality, the word's ambiguous use here helps to place heterosexuality and homosexuality in tension with one another, which becomes the basis for comedy within the episode.

When Cedric is introduced in the episode, he is costumed in a pink argyle sweater and is carrying a messenger bag. As I discussed in chapter 2, episode writers Jacqueline McKinley and Antonia March participated in costuming the character in specific ways. Because of their involvement in costuming as well as scripting Cedric, his clothing becomes the basis for humor within the episode and the semiotic reading of him as outside of the boundaries of heterosexuality, as demonstrated in the dialogue that follows his departure:

Nick: Did you see how tall that dude [Cedric] was? Oh my God! Yeah.
    [pause] But he seemed nice.
Suzanne: Umhmmm. [affirmative]
Nick: It looks like he likes her.
Suzanne: You're kidding me. [light audience laughter] You didn't see that?
Nick: See what?
Suzanne: Nick. He's gay. [audience laughter]
[Commercial break]

The politics of Black gayness are evident within this short scene. While it mostly works as setup for the scene that follows the commercial break, it also functions to set up the series' rational world and its relationship to gayness. Jerry Palmer suggests that it is possible to distinguish between the butt of a joke and the belief system on which it is predicated.[15] In this brief scene, Black gayness is not necessarily the butt of the joke, so much as it exposes the belief system that Black homosexuality is absurd within the narrative universe of the Black-cast sitcom. After the commercial break, the notion that gayness can be detected by reading the body is the primary way Suzanne has determined Cedric's sexuality.

Nick: How is he gay?
Suzanne: Did you see that sweater and that murse?[16] [audience laughter]
Nick: A sweater and a bag does not make a man gay.
Suzanne: Well, that ensemble [with the French pronunciation] was certainly
    giving it a shot. [audience laughter]
Nick: The boy's a football player.

Aside from demonstrating the first step of the generic closet—detection—this dialogue accomplishes two things. First, it positions homosexuality as something that can be detected via fashion, relying on the historical semiotic utility of clothing and colors to map gayness onto the bodies of gay characters.

For Suzanne, Cedric's pink sweater and "murse" mark gayness in a way that belies any other markers that may prove contrary, like his extracurricular participation on his high school's football team. In essence, football, as an alleged hypermasculine sport, is perceived as being out of sync with homosexuality. Second, the addition of laughter works to identify what is funny—in this case, Cedric's style of dress and its deviation from the series' definition of normative Black men's fashion. Importantly, because the laugh track is understood as group laughter and because it is created in postproduction, the implication that "queer clothing" is funny is encoded within the episode. In other words, as LeRoi's earlier comments attest, producers believe that "everyone" thinks reading clothing for degrees of gayness is funny.

The dialogue continues:

> Nick: You cannot be that tall and be gay. [Laughter]
> Suzanne: I'll call RuPaul and let him know. [Laughter] When Lindsey came downstairs he said, "I love that dress."
> Nick: She looked good in it.
> Suzanne: Exactly, you said she looked good in it. He said I love that dress.

In this dialogue, there is a slippage between ideas about homosexuality and drag in terms of sartorial choices. In one line, Suzanne mentions RuPaul, perhaps the world's most famous drag queen, and in the next line she mentions Cedric's love of Lindsey's dress rather than his admiration of how she looked *in* the dress. Suzanne's connection between gayness and cross-dressing goes unchecked. Her dialogue can also be read as making a connection between gay men's desire for wearing "women's" clothing and Cedric's choice of a sweater in a "woman's" color (e.g., pink). In these cases, comedy is found in the oddness of the hegemonic expectations placed on Black men and masculinity. Mills posits that "the pleasure from laughter . . . comes from the surprise of confounded expectations and laughter is the oral expression of such surprise."[17] In other words, hegemonic Black masculinity and hegemonic femininity in style of dress are incompatible, thus they elicit laughter. The arithmetic that equates masculinity with particular styles of dress results in a "computer error" in this scene. Cedric upends expectations and hegemony requires reconciliation of Cedric's positionality as an "other" in relation to hegemonic Black masculinity.

> Suzanne: It's not an accusation. She's going out with him. I just think she should know.
> Nick: What are you gonna do? I mean you can't just come up to the boy and say, "Hey! Are you gay?" [punctuated with jazz hands] [audience laughter].

Fig. 3.1. Nick uses "jazz hands" to punctuate his use of the word *gay* as he and his wife try to detect Cedric's Black gayness in the *Are We There Yet?* episode "The Boy Has Style."

Suzanne: I don't know. [pause]
Nick: Maybe you should give him a test. See if he likes E. Lynn Harris or
    Cher [audience laughter].
Suzanne: What do you know about E. Lynn Harris?
Nick: Nothing [audience laughter]. I hope Cedric is gay. Then we won't have
    to worry about Lindsey ending up on *16 and Pregnant* [audience laughter].
Suzanne: What do you know about *16 and Pregnant*? [audience laughter].
Nick: Nothing [audience laughter].

This dialogue and its accompanying laugh track are mostly concerned with policing the boundaries of hegemonic masculinity generally and Black masculinity specifically. Certain behaviors and taste cultures are marked as out of bounds. In the dialogue (and the ways the laugh track marks its assent), the connotative meanings attached to E. Lynn Harris, author of several books that explore Black bisexuality and homosexuality, signal gay sensibilities. At the same time, an affinity for Cher and her music work to hitch gayness to whiteness by calling on white gay men's stereotypic affinity for Cher rather than a Black diva like Diana Ross. The semiotic nature of E. Lynn Harris and Cher are such that for a man to enjoy their output is to at least call his sexuality into question and at most label him as gay. In rebuking knowledge of both E. Lynn Harris's novels and Cher, Nick repudiates a connection to semiotic gayness while propping up the hegemonic confines of Black masculinity by excluding Black homosexuality.

As the episode progresses to Lindsey and Cedric's second date, Nick confronts Cedric about his sexuality. Nick begins with a little small talk, asking Cedric, "So, you guys are going to the mall? [audience laughter]. Grab a bite to eat? Watch a movie? Hit the arcade?" Cedric responds, "I mean, I don't know about all that. I'm probably just going to do a little shopping" [audience laughter]. When Nick questions a presumed heterosexual man's proclivity for shopping, Cedric ignores the incredulity and compliments Nick's pink shirt, saying, "I like that shirt man. Where'd you get that?" [audience laughter]. The audience laughter here is again rooted in the incongruence of Black gayness in a Black heterosexual space. Because of television's narrative inner workings, any new, age-appropriate boy should necessarily be understood as a permissible love interest for Lindsey. Similar to the scene that sutures Harris and Cher to potential markers of gay cultures, here shopping fulfills a similar function, as indicated by the laugh track. Taken together, Harris, Cher, and deriving enjoyment from shopping lay significant groundwork for the detection of gayness by viewers (and by those within the series' narrative universe). Because the episode has provided enough "evidence," Nick is free to ask Cedric, "Are you gay?" The question is punctuated by the laugh track and a commercial break, which is deployed to create a sense of drama.

On the one hand, Cedric's sexuality is one of the central questions in the episode, and the answer is presumably about to be revealed. On the other hand, the episode creates a sense of drama from what should otherwise be a private matter: one's sexuality. The laugh track, then, serves two functions. First, following the relief theory of humor, it is meant as a release for pent-up nervous energy.[18] The viewer is meant to care about the question about Cedric's sexuality, not only because they are nosey viewers but also because Cedric's sexuality creates particular expectations for his relationship with Lindsey, one of the series' major characters. The nervous energy released suggests more about the fate of Lindsey's love life than about Cedric's sexuality. Second, the notion that one might be homosexual within a series that otherwise has a possessive investment in heterosexuality seems outside the realm of possibility. Therefore, the comedy ensues from the "felt incongruity between what we know or expect to be the case, and what actually takes place."[19] In this way, the laugh track "textualizes the comic effect and makes it explicit."[20]

After the commercial break, Cedric and Nick have the following conversation:

Nick: So? [pause]

Cedric: Why would you ask me if I was gay?

Nick: Look. You gotta understand something here. Now excuse me if it seems like I'm overreacting a little, but bear with me, OK?

Cedric: OK.

Nick: For the record, I'm a heterosexual man. All right. Now, if someone for some reason asked me if I was gay, what do you think I'd say?

Cedric: I don't think it's any of their business.

Nick: I know. But, if someone whose opinion was important to me asked, I would tell them that I am not gay. Because I would want them to know that I am straight. Because I am. So, with that in mind. [pause]

Cedric: Yeah. I'm gay.

Nick: OK. Thank you.

Cedric: Do you have a problem with it?

Nick: With you being gay?

Cedric: Yeah.

Nick: No. But I do have a problem. Have you told Lindsey?

Cedric: I mean, what difference does it make? We're just friends.

Nick: Come on, man; you know what I mean. She likes you. But you don't like her like that.

Cedric: So. [pause]

Nick: So, in a minute she's going to be asking, "Why doesn't Cedric like me?" She's going to wonder if it's her hair or clothes or if she's not cute enough or smart enough.

Cedric: Yeah, I see what you're saying.

Nick: If you want to be friends, just be friends. But don't half step. Do you like her for who she is?

Cedric: Yeah.

Nick: Then let her like you for you are.

Cedric: Can we still go shopping though? [audience laughter]

Nick: Promise not to buy a shirt like I have on? [audience laughter]

Cedric: I don't know. . . . That's a nice shirt [audience laughter]. What color is that? Mauve? [audience laughter]

This scene is important because not only does it detail the second step involved in the generic closet—discovery/declaration—but the laugh track almost entirely drops out of this scene. On the one hand, little is comic about someone coming out as gay, thus reasserting the significance and seriousness of this stage in many LGBTQ people's lives. On the other hand, it is the heterosexual Nick who educates the homosexual Cedric as he outs him about the heterosexual etiquette of homosexual declaration. Nick does not position Cedric's desire to disclose but instead lectures him about his (and by extension, gay people's) obligations to the heteronormative assumptions of the main characters and the implied audience to come out of the closet and declare his sexuality. The scene forces Cedric to proclaim his sexuality and reifies the notion that to not publicly proclaim one's sexuality is to be dishonest, particularly because homosexuality defies the heteronormative rules the series has set out. Because Cedric has ceased to be a viable romantic option for Lindsey, the script is free to traffic in stereotypes related to his gayness, like a love for shopping, which is ultimately where the audience laughter lies within the end of the scene. Both the characters within the series and the audience consuming it expect the series to confirm their assumptions about sexuality, thus reassuring them that it is not a "gay show" but a heterosexual/ist one. At the same time, while writers March and McKinley suggest they wanted to decouple gayness from notions of femininity, they nevertheless use Cedric's apparent love of shopping and fashion as an avenue from which to draw humor. LeRoi and sound editor Kevin Bowe confirm this humor by the specific placement of the laugh track. Because the series is a Black-cast series, with its attendant ideological underpinnings, *Are We There Yet?* ultimately returns Cedric to the generic closet as a means of reaffirming the series' "coolness" around issues of homosexuality. There is, for the cast generally and for the Black-cast sitcom specifically, nothing wrong with being gay. It simply has no place within the Black-cast sitcom on an ongoing narrative basis.

MOESHA, BLACK MASCULINITY, AND THE LAUGH TRACK

In *Moesha*'s "Labels" episode, the humor and laugh track/audience laughter begin by positioning Omar not necessarily as gay but as different. In the first scene after the opening credits, the episode sets up this difference in relationship to teenage Black masculinity. Before Hakeem, Moesha's friend and neighbor, enters the scene, much of the humor centers on the notion that whenever he visits the Mitchell household, he ravenously eats whatever meal has been prepared. Because the Mitchells are already aware that he will be bringing his cousin Omar, the assumption is that he, too, will have a voracious appetite. Instead, Hakeem's brash personality is contrasted with Omar's politer demeanor. Hakeem quickly seizes on the invitation to join the family for breakfast, telling Omar, "Yeah, grab a plate boy! Don't be shy!" Omar responds, "Thank you. But, I don't want to impose." This utterance stops the Mitchells in their tracks and elicits audience laughter. The humor within this scene is built on the incongruity theory of humor. Incongruity theory hinges on humor arising "from the disparity between the ways in which things are expected to be and how they really are."[21] Incongruity theory is built on the assumption that as humans, we are somewhat like machines: we come to expect particular patterns and when things deviate from that pattern, they are inherently funny, mostly because they shock us with their deviation. By familial relation (and the ways the Mitchells have set viewer expectations), Omar and Hakeem are expected to have similar temperaments. To underscore this strangeness, Frank, Moesha's father, says, "Hakeem, I thought you said this was your cousin," which elicits a second laugh from the audience/laugh track. The third joke in this scene occurs when Omar asks if he can wash his hands before he eats. To further mark Omar's difference onto his body, Moesha's stepmother, Dee, asks Hakeem if he, too, wants to wash his hands before eating (although he is already eating). Hakeem, while licking his fingers, says, "I'm good. I ran [my hands] through the sprinkler before I came over." Taken together, Omar's politeness and manners are juxtaposed against Hakeem's brashness and lack of manners to mark Omar as other. While the particularities of Omar's difference remain unclear, those differences are positioned as ripe sites for laughter.

Furthering Omar's otherness, he tells Dee, "Mrs. Mitchell, in payment for your hospitality, I insist on doing the dishes afterward." This line, which is unlikely considered humorous on its face, is followed by a light giggle from the audience/laugh track. The laughter here is rooted in the incompatibility of Black gayness with the operative norms of the Black-cast sitcom. Building on the politeness and manners Omar has demonstrated, his offer to wash the dishes is also understood as a kind of otherness—one that I argue tethers Omar to the domestic, which is always already understood as feminine (or in Omar's case, he is tied to the "incorrectly feminine"). This tethering sutures Omar to a hermeneutics of suspicion, which Lynne Joyrich describes as an "epistemological exercise" concerned primarily with "solving the mystery of sexual ambiguity and/or identification."[22] Within the hermeneutics of suspicion, well before the end of the episode's first act, viewers are encouraged to become detectives who try to figure out what is "wrong" with Omar.

Omar's difference also stands outside the confines of the kind of hip-hop masculinity that circulated within television discourse on popular series like *Fresh Prince*. Hakeem hews more closely to the ways *Fresh Prince*'s Will mediated televisual Black masculinity in the 1990s, as a safe but still somewhat brash version of urban, teenage Black masculinity. Conversely, Omar is anomalous—good manners and cleanliness were not the order of the day within the hip-hop–infused Black masculinity of 1990s sitcoms.

However, this difference does not preclude "Labels" from positioning Omar as a potential love interest for Moesha. Mills suggests that the sitcom problematically "position[s] heterosexual relationships as not only normal, but desirable."[23] This investment in heterosexuality conditions viewers' expectations and simultaneously begins to construct the generic closet, out of which Black gay characters must emerge to demonstrate their use-value for the series. A handsome, presumably single, age-appropriate boy can be positioned within the realm of romantic possibilities for Moesha. In addition, because Omar does not display any of the semiotic markers that had become shorthand for "detecting" gay characters, it is not possible that his difference can be synthesized within his homosexuality. For many Black viewers, the specter of Antoine Merriweather and Blaine Edwards from In Living Color's "Men On..." sketches served as an image by which gayness could be detected. In the absence of such markers, Omar's body is read as heterosexual and available as a romantic option for Moesha, even in the presence of his positionality as different.

The episode works to exploit viewers' expectations of normativity for comedic purposes. Comedy, as Sypher points out, works to reassure "the majority that its standards are impregnable or that other standards are not 'normal' or 'sane.'"[24] The arithmetic that suggests a "handsome Black man + Moesha = a Black gay character" does not compute, and thus the absurdity prompts the "comedic situation" within Moesha specifically and the Black-cast sitcom in general. When Omar and Moesha go on their date, it is Moesha who acts as the aggressor. She asks him to take her to a movie and suggests that he pay. It is certainly within bounds for a girl to ask a boy on a date. Nevertheless, this feminine aggression seems out of sorts, particularly when considered alongside the ways Omar has been marked as different from Hakeem in the previous scene.

The first act of the episode leaves Omar's presumptive heterosexuality intact. While there are certainly clues that become clearer after his homosexuality has been revealed, there is no overt suggestion that he might be gay. By all appearances, Omar conforms to hegemonic norms of Black masculinity. He accepts Moesha's invitation to go to a movie and agrees to pay for the popcorn and tickets. In addition, after he accepts Moesha's invitation, they hold hands as they leave the coffee shop.

In the next scene, Moesha and Omar are at a restaurant after the movie. This scene continues to build the romantic tension between them, with his suggesting that although Moesha did not like the movie they saw together, he hopes they can see another movie together. But halfway through this scene the laugh track begins to communicate that there is something out of sync with the episode's heteronormative expectations. This becomes particularly important because this scene becomes the episode's "turning point," which, in classical three-act structure, means that the narrative's action shifts "in a new direction."[25] While much work is done within the script (a scene to which writer Demetrius Bady objected, as discussed in chap. 2), the laugh track helps to underscore the oddness of the situation that unfolds.

Omar and Moesha engage in conversation in which Moesha says that she has "never had [a back and forth conversation] with a guy I like before." Omar responds by putting his head down and wringing his hands as if he is grappling with something. While his head is still down, a voice from outside the shot calls Omar's name. Before the camera pans to reveal who has called his name, there is audience laughter and reaction, suggesting that there is something funny outside the frame. The camera finally does a glance-object cut from Omar to Tracy, the person who has called Omar's name. Given Tracy's lisping speech pattern and Moesha's reaction as the camera does a series of shot-reverse shots, which nonverbally communicate that Tracy is supposed to be read as gay, the series positions Tracy as a ripe site for humor. What is fascinating here is that without much dialogue from Tracy, he is perceived as funny and different. Because humor is site-specific, it is important that Tracy is allowed to be perceived as funny within the space of the Black-cast sitcom. For example, if Tracy were in a Black gay-cast sitcom (e.g., *Noah's Arc* [Logo, 2005–2006]), his utterance of Omar's name might not be understood as funny; it might just be a fact. Within *Moesha*, Tracy's Black gay body is read differently.

As the initial laughter dissipates, it immediately begins again as Tracy says to Omar, "I thought that was you. Boy, I know you're not just going to sit there, give me a hug." When the two men embrace, the audience laughter/laugh track grows again. Part of the audience's laughter originates from the "strange" presence of homosexuality within the series. Tracy's presence is marked as comic because, as Critchley suggests, laughter originates from infractions that trouble the "accepted" understanding of a particular worldview.[26] Tracy's flamboyance attempts to trouble the status quo of *Moesha*'s narrative universe.

After Tracy has been semiotically coded as gay, he confirms his gayness by giving Omar his review of the film *Basquiat* (dir. Julian Schnabel, 1996), which he begins by saying, "Two hours in the dark with a man that fine? Ugh, it couldn't be anything but wonderful." The mixture of laughter and hooting from the in-studio audience/laugh track is reminiscent of what Pratt called "strictly black laughs and 'oohs.'"[27] The sound is simultaneously read as confirming the initial reading of Tracy as gay, but it also gestures toward the relief theory of comedy, which suggests that laughter is the release of nervous energy. In this case, it is not just that Tracy is gay but that his gayness expresses some

Fig. 3.2. The camera pans to reveal Tracy's feminized body, which becomes a site for the episode's humor in the "Labels" episode of *Moesha*.

semblance of sexual desire. Reminiscent of the ways Antoine Merriweather and Blaine Edwards reviewed films on *In Living Color,* Tracy confirms his gayness not via a speech act but by expressing his sexual desire for the lead character in *Basquiat.* Particularly within the Gay '90s, acceptable gay characters did not or could not typically express sexual desire. When sexual desire is allowable, it is only within the confines of monogamous homonormative relationships and never as an expression of carnal desire.[28]

When Omar introduces Moesha to Tracy, the series soundtrack proves important. Moesha extends her hand to shake Tracy's hand as she says, "Nice to meet you." Tracy tepidly shakes Moesha's hand and says, "Oh, [pause] you too," before sitting down at the table. The soundtrack offers a mix of laughter and audible indignation. The reaction is immediate and boisterous and signals a shift within the episode's humor. While the laughter elicited by Tracy's presence seemed to be about the incongruity of his presence within the series, the audience, in effect, turns on him after his cold welcome of Moesha. Freud suggests tendentious jokes barely contain, among other things, hostility.[29] Within this scene, Tracy has rejected the series' axial character and has brought his homosexual body into *Moesha*'s narrative universe; as such, it is received aggressively. Importantly, Tracy almost immediately alienates viewer sympathies in part because he embodies what can be read as a displacement of misogynistic attitudes toward Black women onto Black gay men.[30] In the next exchanges, while Moesha, Omar, and Tracy are seated at the table, Moesha is set up to receive all the laughs, while Tracy is positioned as the butt of such jokes.

> Moesha: So. [pause] What's *Basquiat* about?
> Tracy: You've never heard of Jean-Michel Basquiat?
> Moesha: No, that's why I'm asking.
> [audience laughter]
> Omar: He was—[pauses for laughter to subside]. He was this wonderful
>   graffiti artist that rose to prominence in the New York art world.
> Moesha: Oh, that sounds interesting. Maybe we can check it out sometime.
> Omar: Sure, that sounds—
> Tracy: [interrupting Omar] So, Omar. I mean. . . . What have you been up to?
>   You just dropped off the face of the planet.
> Omar: I transferred to Crenshaw [High School].
> Tracy: Crenshaw? Ooh. [pause; audience laughter] Be careful.

In the first instance of laughter, the antagonism toward Tracy continues unabated. The laughter/laugh track signals an alliance with the series' axial character. As the setup for the laughter/laugh track, Tracy "earns" the ire of the in-studio audience/laugh track by interrupting Omar as he is about to agree to a second date with Moesha, again gesturing toward, if not misogyny, antagonism toward women and Moesha. The laugh track returns that hostility to Tracy in a show of solidarity with and for Moesha. In the second instance, Tracy's mannerisms (which hew more closely to behaviors problematically associated with hegemonic femininity) signal an incongruence between the ways a male body generally, and a Black male body specifically, is "supposed" to move through the world. Tracy is simply funny in this moment because he reminds viewers of the semiotic connection between male gayness and femininity. In this way, part of the function of the generic closet is to reify the boundaries of Black masculinity.

An elliptical edit follows, in which time Moesha has left the table. In the time she is gone, it allows Omar and Tracy to have a conversation. Tracy asks Omar, "So. [pause] Everyone's been asking about you. Why are you being so mysterious?" Omar responds, "I'm not being mysterious." While there is no laugh track in this scene, it is significant in that it performs a major narrative function. By Tracy asking Omar about being "mysterious," coupled with Omar and Tracy's seemingly close relationship, Omar's sexuality is narratively called into question, although he has heretofore been positioned as a candidate for a romantic relationship with Moesha. Concomitantly, because of Black masculinity's mediation as antigay, Omar's friendship with Tracy makes him associatively gay and raises narrative hermeneutics of suspicion. Joyrich suggests this suspicion is driven by a heterosexual character's (and viewer's) desire to know another character's sexuality when it deviates from heterosexuality.[31] The beginning of this scene is useful in that it aims to bind Omar to homosexuality by association.

The laughter within the scene creates a binary opposition that suggests the viewer is part of an "us" who believes in both the inappropriateness of "them" appearing within the confines of *Moesha* and the superiority they have over the homosexual "other." Laughter (whether intentional or not) suggests that the one who laughs agrees with and supports the content of a joke. Mills suggests "the laugh track is of significant ideological import because it represents social agreement on appropriate comic targets."[32] Put another way, the laugh track constructs a type of televisual imagined community and those who are outside of it.

As I discussed at length in chapter 2, episode writer Bady did not want this scene in his script, and part of that reason might be that, as he describes it, "While we were taping, that scene got the hugest laugh. It was the biggest laugh of the show, it's what everybody was talking about."[33] According to Bady, not only was there big laughter within the taping of the episode, but he suggests that it was also sweetened in postproduction to ensure that it drove its point home: the presence of a flamboyantly gay character is indisputably funny. Bady understood the laughter as being about the presence of a character that could be easily read as gay. Tracy clearly defies the logics of Black masculinity, which are predicated on performing one's masculinity in hegemonic ways. In other words, the epistemology of Black masculinity is tightly bound to its binary opposite for its hegemonic power. Once Tracy, because of his deviation from the ways "real Black men" act and move through the world, can be undeniably identified through semiotic linkages, he can be positioned as a source of humor within the Black-cast sitcom's universe. It is simultaneously the "surprise" of a Black man behaving in ways inconsistent with the hegemonic scripts of Black masculinity and the "superiority" of heteronormativity that allows marking that surprise as "other." It is important to remember that within "the hugest laugh" to which Bady referred, anyone who recognized Tracy as a part of themselves was rendered invisible and inaudible, including perhaps Black gay queers. The power of the laugh track is in its ability to construct a world in which what is deemed funny is uncontested. And because Tracy is so clearly out of step with the mores of Black masculinity, he can be understood as a universal site of humor.

After Moesha's date with Omar, she discusses her suspicions about Omar's sexuality with her friends Kim and Niecy; although Moesha has asked them to keep it in confidence, they spread the rumor around school that Omar is gay. Moesha's ex-boyfriend Q sees her at her locker, and the use of the laugh track works to uphold the "outsider" status of homosexuality within the series' universe.

> Moesha: What do you want?
> Q: You know, if you really want to make me jealous, you might want to do that with a real man.
> [audience laughter]
> Moesha: What's that supposed to mean?
> Q: It's all over school. Your boy Omar is soft.
> [audience laughter]

The laugh track (and audience laughter) create a semiotic chain between a "real (Black) man" and being "soft," which, in turn, comments on the confines of hegemonic Black masculinity. *Soft*, in this colloquial context, is meant to denote gayness with the assumption that "real Black masculinity" is equated with hardness. As Stuart Hall argues, the ultramasculine performances adopted by some Black men "claim visibility for their hardness only at the expense of . . . the feminization of gay black men."[34] Within *Moesha*'s narrative universe, homosexuality is construed not only as the foreign intruder that must be exposed, disciplined, and discarded but also as entirely out of step with cultural imaginings of Black masculinity. In this way, the joke and the audience's laughter serve a corrective and pedagogical function: homosexuality is not to be tolerated. Moesha suggests that Q "could learn something from Omar about how to be a man." However, because there is no laugh track (or applause) after the line, there is no tacit agreement from the in-studio audience (or via manipulation in postproduction) that would suggest a gay man is capable of teaching a heterosexual man anything about masculinity.

Nevertheless, Omar is not the homosexual other to whom the series directs its ire. It is Tracy. I suggest two reasons for this hostility. First, as I have argued, the series is heavily invested in heteronormativity and Black masculinity. But second, and perhaps more important, as I explored in chapter 2, Bady is heavily invested in transcoding Black gayness to hollow it out from its connection to femininity. Not only does Tracy's gayness fail to conform to gender norms, it

fails to abide by a gay politics of respectability. Such a politic representationally seeks to forward a post-gay rhetoric that suggests those who are gay conform to "proper" behaviors associated with gender normativity in exchange
for admittance into what Gayle Rubin calls the "charmed circle."[35] Extending
Rubin's charmed circle, the only ways "respectable" gay subjects deviate from
heterosexuality (and heteronormativity) is in the gender identity of those to
whom they are attracted.

After Omar (and his cousin Hakeem) confront Moesha about spreading
the rumor that Omar is (not *might be* but *is*) gay, Omar and Moesha have an
altercation that tips the series' hand with respect to how it will engage and deal
with nonnormative sexuality.

> Omar: Mo, why did you do that?
> Moesha: Omar, look....I...I...I didn't say that you were anything. You
> know, I thought you were, and apparently I was mistaken. And I'm sorry. I
> don't know what else to say.
> Omar: Well, you can say that the next time you'll mind your own business
> instead of making up stuff like a stupid schoolgirl.
> Moesha: Hold up. Hold up. Hold up. You know, I didn't make up Tracy.
> Maybe Revlon did, but I didn't.
> [audience laughter]

The laughter in this brief scene underscores that while gayness might be ripe for
the comic, it is a particular kind of gayness. The Gay '90s demonstrated that only
gay characters written within a brand of homonormativity that neatly aligned
their outward gender with societal expectations were granted the space to
demand respect within their televisual universes. Similarly, Candice West and
Don H. Zimmerman suggest that "properly" gendered behaviors are designed
to be so unremarkable that they are "not worthy of more than a passing remark,
because they are seen to be in accord with culturally approved standards."[36]
Because the "new gay" representation did not challenge existing gender binaries, these representations were deemed good and worthy of respect—at least
up to a predetermined limit, usually an episode or two. Because Omar "reads"
as heterosexual, he is granted the leeway to be able to confront Moesha and
suggest that she acted "like a stupid schoolgirl."

However, if one "reads" as gay and looks to be made up by the cosmetics
company Revlon (underscoring Tracy's asynchronicity with hegemonic gender
norms), then jokes are fully within the realm of possibility. In addition, the
jokes gesture toward the slippages between male homosexuality and the desire
to be a woman (or at least feminine). Dyer suggests that when one can be read

as gay, as Tracy can, it "has something to do with not being properly masculine or feminine."[37] Recall that similar slippages occur in "The Boy Has Style"— almost twenty years later. *Moesha*, through its use of humor—whether via the laugh track or actual audience laughter or a combination of both—continues to position the incorrectly feminine Black gay Tracy as open to tendentious forms of laughter. Omar, even as he remains outside of the series' normative realm, is understood as inferior but not an inferiority that necessitates antagonism. The series, then, creates a hierarchy of homosexuality. Femininity in Black gay characters can engender hostility. "Masculine" Black gay characters, like their "feminine" counterparts, are still expunged from the narrative universes of the series but are temporarily tolerable because they "correctly" align their outward gender appearance with their gender performance.

Moesha works within a set of expectations around Black masculinity within televisual spaces. Black maleness is always romantically (and sexually) available to Black women within such spaces. When those expectations are betrayed, there is space for comedy to ensue. Importantly, the laugh track helps to sanction permissible sexualities within the framework of the episode. While gayness is made the object of humor, it is a particular kind of gayness. This humor creates a hierarchy of acceptable gayness, with flamboyant gay men at the bottom of that hierarchy and more homonormative characters, like Omar, slightly above them, although nowhere near the position of the series' heterosexual characters. Jokes are never told about Omar per se; rather, jokes concern the specter of gayness within *Moesha's* heterosexist narrative universe. When jokes are told about specific gay people, it is the gayness that most closely resembles Antoine Merriweather and Blaine Edwards that is constructed as "in bounds" with respect to humor. While *Moesha's* deployment of humor about Black gayness generally remains problematic, most troubling is the way the feminine gay man is singled out for particular derision. Regardless of its more "feminine" or more "masculine" form, Black gayness is ultimately returned to the generic closet lest the series be forced to revise its queer politics.

REACTIONARY HUMOR AND DECENTERED BLACK HOMOSEXUALITY IN *GOOD NEWS*

The *Good News* "Pilot" episode is focused on the new acting pastor's plight in maintaining the church's membership after a beloved pastor has retired. The episode's B-story concerns a young Black gay parishioner, Eldridge, who solicits the pastor's assistance in coming out as gay to his mother. He also wants to invite his new boyfriend to church on Sunday. While the synopsis of the episode's secondary plot seems to center gayness, the script and the laugh track reveal that gayness is, in fact, decentered. About a third of the way through the episode, Eldridge approaches Pastor Randolph to ask for his help. As the pastor attempts to avoid dealing with homosexuality, the laugh track and audience laughter suggest a tacit agreement with Pastor Randolph's desire to evade the topic. After telling Eldridge how much he likes to help young people with their problems, Pastor Randolph says, "Now tell me. What is the problem?" and Eldridge replies, "I'm gay [audience laughter]."

It is important here to acknowledge that the particularities of the laughter and the audience reaction are racialized. The soundtrack sounds Black in its addition of "oohs" to the laughter. Lending credence to my assertion, Weinberger acknowledges, "We were in front of a primarily Black audience for the first two shows."[38] This may seem tertiary, recalling Mills's assertion that the laugh track creates community and Pratt's discussion of the racialization of the Black-cast sitcom's laugh track. However, the audience's reaction to Eldridge's announcement stands in for the notion of a monolithic Black community unused to dealing with the actualities of an announcement of one's sexuality. Much like the Foucauldian notion of the sexual confession, Eldridge's gay subjectivity is undergirded by the admission of his gay "problem."[39] In addition, the scene's humor works within what Simon Critchley calls "comedy of recognition." Such comedy reinforces the status quo and actively refuses to challenge or criticize it.[40] Thus, Eldridge's utterance that he is gay works as a way to "denigrate a certain sector of society" while defining a secondary character by his taboo, shameful, deviant, or problematic sexuality.[41] On the one hand, it is important that *Good News* acknowledged the existence of Black homosexuality as part of the multilayered fabric that is American Blackness. On the other hand, it acknowledges homosexuality only to reinforce its tertiary nature with respect to Black experience and to evacuate it of any power to question the status quo. The scene continues:

> Pastor Randolph: [after a long pause] You know, Eldridge, I'm only the acting pastor [audience laughter]. Maybe you could call [the recently departed] Pastor Douglas [takes Eldridge's arm and attempts to lift him out of the chair].
> [audience laughter]
> Eldridge: I couldn't talk to Pastor Douglas about this. Besides, that's not my problem. You see, for the first time in my life, I met a young man who I like and who likes me.
> Pastor Randolph: Well, Eldridge, tell you what [audience laughter]: I'll pray on it, and you pray on it and come back in a couple of weeks, and maybe we can talk about it [audience laughter].

Eldridge: This can't wait a couple of weeks. And anyway that's not my problem either.

Pastor Randolph: It's not?

Eldridge: I want to bring him to church with me this Sunday.

Pastor Randolph: Well, Eldridge, I can understand two Christian, God-loving *friends* should worship together. It's not like you'll be sitting there holding hands. [pause; leans in to Eldridge] Will you? [audience laughter].

Eldridge: No, sir.

Pastor Randolph: [walking toward his office door to open it to see Eldridge out] Well then, bring him here, and I will do my best to see that he feels welcome.

Eldridge: Thank you, but that's not really the problem either.

Pastor Randolph: Well, we getting any closer to it? [audience laughter]

Eldridge: Well, I want you to help me tell my mother.

Pastor Randolph: [closes door] What part? [audience laughter]

Three things are important to note in this scene and its use of the laugh track. First and foremost, the laughter in the scene is primarily centered on Pastor Randolph's reactions to Eldridge's escalating list of issues with which he is seeking the pastor's help. With the exception of Eldridge announcing that he is gay, all of the laughter comes after one of Pastor Randolph's lines of dialogue. In this way, the laughter works to decenter Eldridge's experiences in favor of a heterocentric positionality that situates gayness as something strange within the narrative universe of *Good News*.

Second, Eldridge is given three opportunities to reveal his problem. Simply put, he wants the pastor's help telling his mother that he is gay and wants to bring his boyfriend to church. However, for comedic purposes, the "problems" are parsed out over the course of the scene. At the same time, Eldridge's problems can be solved only with help from heterosexual characters.

Finally, the scene exposes a key issue when examining Black gay televisual representation. What becomes (and remains) problematic about Black gay representation is that Black gay characters are temporarily accepted into the fold of heteronormative Black-cast sitcom worlds, provided that they do not express sexual desire. Although this prohibition on same-sex intimacy and desire is not specific to Black-cast sitcoms, when coupled with the enduring nature of the generic closet, it takes on a particular valence that speaks to an overarching understanding of Blackness as antigay.[42] Pastor Randolph stands in for a Black public that *might* be comfortable with Black gay people but who are certainly not comfortable with Black gay intimacy. Consequently, when there is a discussion of the possibility that Eldridge might want to hold hands in church with his boyfriend, there is cause for anxiety—or nervous laughter. Critchley suggests part of nervous laughter is rooted in the notion that "we often laugh because we are troubled by what we laugh at, because it somehow frightens us."[43] I suggest the insertion of the laugh track is meant to conjure up feelings of discomfort because same-sex sexuality has not been a part of the narrative universe of Black-cast sitcoms or *Good News* up to this point. While many churches (Black and otherwise) are comfortable with the queer labor that gay congregants provide, they remain uncomfortable with what that sexuality means outside of such labor. Moreover, this laughter engages in the act of allusion. Freud argues that when jokes use allusion, they replace "something small, something remotely related that the listener can construct in his imagination into a full and plain obscenity."[44] In this case, the question about two gay men holding hands suggests sex between two men, which is constructed as wholly out of step with not only the narrative rules of *Good News* but also within hegemonic culture and thus is rendered "obscene" and "other."

The humor within this episode, as in *Moesha*'s "Labels" episode, can be understood as tendentious. The jokes in this scene, as Freud suggests is true of all tendentious jokes, "requires three persons: apart from the one who is telling the joke, it needs a second person who is taken as the object of the hostile aggression . . . and a third person in whom the joke's intention of producing pleasure is fulfilled."[45] Freud suggests there is a symbiotic relationship between the joke teller and the joke receiver (understood here as the audience/laugh track) with the third person as the abject object. For *Good News*, the first position is occupied by the fully heterosexual starring and recurring cast, whereas the second position is occupied by the viewing audience (for whom the laugh track acts as a stand-in), and the third position is occupied by Eldridge, the gay guest star, and by homosexuality generally.

In the next scene, Eldridge discloses his sexuality to his mother, with the help of the pastor.

> Mrs. Dixon: Now, will someone tell me what this is about? I'm on my lunch hour. I haven't been late for work a day in my life, and I'm not going to start today!
> Pastor Randolph: Umm, Mrs. Dixon, your son has something to tell you, and he thought it would be best if he told you here in church with his pastor.
> Eldridge: Well. [pause] I just want to say it's finally time I told you something about myself that I've been afraid to tell you for a long time.
> Mrs. Dixon: Umhmmm. [light audience laughter]
> Eldridge: I'm . . . I'm—[pause]

Fig. 3.3. The reaction from the heterosexual cast of *Good News* on hearing that Eldridge's boyfriend is white.

Pastor Randolph: Remember, speak the truth, and the truth will set you free. [light audience laughter]

Eldridge: I'm gay. [loud male guffaw from laugh track]

Mrs. Dixon: *That's it?* [audience laughter] That's what you drug me down here for? Boy, I knew that even before you did. I knew it when you were nine years old. [audience laughter]

Eldridge: And you're OK with me being—[pause]

Mrs. Dixon: Of course I'm OK.

Eldridge: I love you, Mama.

Mrs. Dixon: I love you too, baby. But I gotta go.

Pastor Randolph: Wait. There's one other thing.

Mrs. Dixon: What's that?

Pastor Randolph: [gestures toward Eldridge]

Eldridge: Well, [pause] I met this young man. And we've been friends now for a couple of months. And [pause] I'd like to bring him to church with me this Sunday.

Mrs. Dixon: Well, bring him. And afterward, we'll go back to the house for my Sunday pot roast dinner. Now, I gotta go. Look at the time!

Eldridge: Ummm. [pause] There is one more thing.

Mrs. Dixon: *Now what?* [audience laughter]

Pastor Randolph: I thought we were done. [light laughter]

Mrs. Dixon: Well, let's hear it.

Eldridge: Well . . . this young man I'm seeing—[pause] he's white. [audience laughter]

[Mrs. Dixon and Pastor Randolph collapse into chairs; audience laughter and fade to commercial break]

At the beginning of the scene, the laugh track gestures toward a nervous form of laughter that suggests the audience is invested in Mrs. Dixon's response to her son's "news" and thus centers heterosexuality—even within a queer story line. In this scene, Mrs. Dixon is the "outsider" in that she is the only one who does not know the reason she has been asked to visit Pastor Randolph's office on her lunch break. There is pent-up energy within the scene, which the relief theory of humor helps to unpack. There is not necessarily a lack of sympathy concerning Eldridge's sexuality (although that might be part of it), but the narrative moves forward in a way that is unfamiliar to the rules and regulations of the Black-cast sitcom. The result of the "actual" release of the pent-up energy is the scene's first "big" laugh after Mrs. Dixon responds to the news with a flippant, "That's it?" The nervousness of the laughter returns when Eldridge explains that there is a third revelation he needs to make and that he, as the homosexual other, is the only one who knows this piece of information. The scene functions with nervousness and nervous laughter as its bookends. Given that the episode goes into commercial break after Eldridge has announced that his boyfriend is white, the suggestion is that the dramatic stakes of the episode have been raised as gay panic gives way to anxieties about miscegenation. In addition, the scene functions as what Palmer calls *perpetia*, the notion that jokes assume the viewer will work within a set of logical assumptions, and humor results from disobeying such logics.[46] The scene ends by upsetting the series' logic in that the audience (and Pastor Randolph) believed they had all the information and just needed to watch it play out. The last bit of humor is derived from the scene's contravention of such logic. The humor was supposed to have occurred (presumably) from watching Mrs. Dixon react to the news that her son has revealed his gayness. Instead, her almost nonreaction releases a pressure valve that is rebuilt through perpetia. After the commercial break, the scene continues:

Mrs. Dixon: I'm sorry. [pause] I didn't hear that. [audience laughter]

Eldridge: I said he's white.

Mrs. Dixon: He's *light*? [audience laughter]

Pastor Randolph: Not light, Mrs. Dixon, what he—

Mrs. Dixon: I heard what he said! [audience laughter] Now. [pause] Just how white is he? [audience laughter]

Eldridge: Very. He's Irish. His name is Daniel O'Connor. [light audience laughter]

Pastor Randolph: Daniel! Good biblical name! [audience laughter]

Eldridge: Mama, I know once you meet him, you'll love him.

Mrs. Dixon: What's the matter with you, boy? There aren't enough nice Black men out there you gotta go find some white boy? [audience laughter and applause]

Pastor Randolph: Please, you just gotta give him a chance to explain.

Mrs. Dixon: [pointing at Pastor] This is all your doing. I knew you were trouble the second I laid eyes on you [audience laughter].

Eldridge: The pastor had nothing to do with this.

Mrs. Dixon: Boy, don't you talk back to me [hits Eldridge with her purse]. See, you need therapy. You done gone crazy [hits Eldridge with her purse] [audience laughter].

[Pastor Randolph attempts to intervene]

Mrs. Dixon: Don't you tell me when to whip my son [hits the pastor with her purse]. I'll whip him now [hits Eldridge with her purse]. I'll whip him on his way home [hits Eldridge with her purse]. And then I'll call the neighbors out and tell them to whip him again [dialogue is punctuated with hitting Eldridge with her purse; then she walks away from Eldridge and the Pastor]. Lord, have mercy. Made me hurt my arm [continuous laughter throughout this dialogue].

Pastor Randolph: Mrs. Dixon, this is a house of God. And anyone, regardless of color or creed, who comes here in good faith, I will not turn away.

Mrs. Dixon: Well, this is my church, too. I grew up in this church. I was married to that boy's father in this church. Lord rest his soul. So, *Acting* Pastor Randolph, come Sunday, oh, come Sunday [light laughter], I'm gonna be sitting in that front pew where I always am. And if that Daniel boy walks in here, I'm walking out [she turns to leave]. And when I do, what's left of your congregation goes with me [she leaves].

Eldridge: She took it a lot better than I thought she would [audience laughter].

The first part of the scene is tightly rooted in racialized humor. Christine Davies posits that jokes dealing with race and ethnicity are not about the groups one despises per se; rather, they are told about groups in close proximity to the joke teller and that live at the margins of their culture.[47] In this case, the jokes are both about whiteness and its concomitant proximity to Blackness and the desire to maintain racial separateness. As I discussed in chapter 2, *Good News* showrunner Weinberger suggested that he wrote the comedy in this scene to be a "satirical point" because Eldridge's mother was less upset that he is gay and more disturbed that his boyfriend, Daniel, is white.[48] Weinberger gestures toward the duality of humor within this scene. He attempts to televisually de-couple homophobia and Blackness, thus representing a progressive approach to gayness; however, he simultaneously continues to forward the notion that racism continues to exist because Black people keep those ideologies alive. Race—or more precisely, an interracial relationship—is made comedic within the episode by displacing the expected homophobia onto the bad object of racial miscegenation while concomitantly tethering Black gayness to white-ness. By placing Daniel within an all-Black community, the episode positions Black communities—represented by Mrs. Dixon—as vehemently opposing the notion of interracial relationships. While Pastor Randolph attempts to work as a mediator, presenting a more moderate view of interracial relation-ships, his role as acting pastor reveals his precarious position when coupled with the way the episode centers Mrs. Dixon. With few exceptions, the audi-ence laughter occurs after Mrs. Dixon's lines, gesturing toward the centering of her comic perspective (and she was the most well-known actor, given her role on Weinberger's similarly church-based series *Amen*). In addition, the laughter implies a tacit agreement of the audience with Mrs. Dixon's outlook. While Weinberger suggests that the joke also tells the viewer something about Mrs. Dixon's prejudices, the laughter suggests that the audience is somewhat ideologically aligned with her. If the laughter/laugh track says something about Mrs. Dixon's prejudices, it also says something about the in-studio audience's prejudices (and, by extension, those of the presumed Black audience at home) about Black gayness and its presence within the episode. Furthermore, the use of Eldridge's relationship with Daniel as the "real" drama of the scene indicates the ways "mainstream black discourse defines black queer identity as untenable to a normalized black identity while . . . connecting it to interracial desire and to whiteness."[49] The episode attempts to decenter homosexuality from the central narrative by cloaking its decentering within interracial relationships, making the episode's real "problem" not *just* Black gayness but rather the opposition to cross-racial gay dating.

Good News works with a specific approach to humor, comedy, and (homo) sexuality. Because the episode never ostensibly centers Eldridge's experiences around his sexuality, the series is well positioned to ensure that Eldridge does not return after the "Pilot" episode. By positioning homosexuality as both strange and inconsequential, the series reifies the failure of homosexuality to exist within the confines of the broader series while binding gayness to anti-Blackness. As Franz Fanon articulates, those Black people who choose white partners hope that the white partner will ensure "that the [Black] partner will achieve denaturalization and (to use a loathsome word) 'deracialization.'"[50] Within deracialization, then, homosexuality is articulated as wholly separate from Blackness because it is so anti-Black that it is "the white man's disease."[51] Consequently, in this theoretical configuration, Black gayness is disconnected from Blackness through its alleged wish to be white. Thus, Eldridge helps increase Black gay visibility, but he does so as a means to shore up the boundaries of authentic Blackness and authentic Black masculinity while reaffirming the utility of the series' generic closet.

THE LAUGH TRACK AND INSIDER/ OUTSIDER HUMOR IN ALL OF US

The fourth season *All of Us* episode "My Two Dads" concerns series star Robert discovering that the man who raised him as his son is not his biological father and that his biological father is gay. In the episode before "My Two Dads," entitled "Like Father, Like Son . . . Like Hell," Robert finds his biological father, Luther (played by Richard Lawson). As Robert and Luther get to know one another, they bond over a mutual love for basketball and Luther reveals that he once played basketball, like his biological son. Sports, as arbiters of hegemonic masculinity, do not cohere with stereotypical gay masculinities. This connection between Luther's love of and participation in basketball, coupled with his failure to display any of the semiotic markers of gayness, removes the possibility of homosexuality from the realm of expected narrative possibilities. When Robert introduces Luther to his friend Dirk, he says, "Yo! [Luther] is mad cool. The weird thing is: he's almost just like me." This line of dialogue becomes the setup for what happens next. Luther's partner Rosie enters their shared home, with a "Hey baby!" followed by a brief kiss. The laugh track begins to work as it does within the superiority tradition of comedy. When the two men kiss, the sound is a mix of laughter and various reaction noises. As with both *Moesha* and *Good News*, the soundtrack is meant to emulate "Black" reactions. Importantly, there is no "oohing" that might suggest that the audience supports the kiss. While part of the laughter may originate as a kind of nervous laughter, it works more closely—as comedy in the superiority tradition does—to "correct mistakes and short-comings, not to foster them."[52] In this instance, I submit that the mistake or shortcoming the episode attempts to correct is homosexuality generally and the display of same-sex intimacy specifically. As I have posited elsewhere with respect to white- and multicultural-cast sitcoms, "The inclusion of [white] LGBT characters comes with conditions: while an argument can be made that gay relationships are treated similarly to their heterosexual

counterparts in terms of storylines, when dealing with . . . same-sex intimate relations, the implicit heteronormativity of televisual spaces becomes clear. Gay
characters are allowed in these spaces but implying sexual intimacy is not."[53]

The last shot in the episode is of Robert and Dirk, thus decentering homosexuality from the narrative stakes in which the episode engages. The viewer
is encouraged to consider how this newly discovered information affects Robert and not the ways homosexuality might function within the narrative universe of the series. In addition, Critchley says humor "is a form of cultural
insider-knowledge, and might, indeed, be said to function like a linguistic de-
fense mechanism . . . [that] endows native speakers with a palpable sense of
their cultural distinctiveness, or even superiority."[54] The laughter as Luther and
his partner kiss confirms the distinctiveness and superiority of the assumed
Black heterosexual viewer. The humor works because, unlike Tracy in *Moesha*'s
"Labels" episode, there have been no semiotic clues that might suggest Luther
is gay. Therefore, the kiss is as much about incongruity theory—the notion that
the audience presumably did not see a same-sex kiss coming—as it is about
homosexuality per se. This kiss, and the audience's reaction to it, is how the
episode concludes, with a "to be continued" slate, leaving the viewer to wait to
find out how the series will grapple with this incongruity.

The next episode, "My Two Dads," begins with an episode recap of "Like
Father, Like Son . . . Like Hell" that again concludes with the kiss between Luther and Rosie. Gesturing toward the potency producers believe exists within
the kiss, the episode's narrative tension, and incongruity theory, the laughter in
the recap remains in the same places it existed in the episode. Of equal importance, and worth remembering, is the notion that *All of Us* is shot on a soundstage without a studio audience. The laughter—its timbre and duration—is
completely created and controlled in postproduction. In this way, the laughter
is not accidental and, in fact, is ideological and political. Palmer argues that
when making someone or something the butt of humor, "it is also a question
of the attributes attached to the butt, of the discourses evoked in the process of
making the butt into a humorous object."[55] Even as the episode writers have a
more progressive agenda, as I detailed in chapter 2, the laugh track ultimately
undermines any gesture toward progressivism. Instead, the soundtrack underscores an ideological and political space that marks the Black-cast sitcom
as a heterosexual-only zone with an investment in the durability of the generic
closet.

The episode prelude of "My Two Dads" devolves into a series of jokes told at
the expense of gayness—jokes that draw heavily on the discomfort associated
with same-sex intimacy and a heterosexist understanding of gay relationships.

to be continued...

Fig. 3.4. and Fig. 3.5. Luther kisses his partner "hello" in *All of Us*, followed by the reaction shot from members of the series' heterosexual cast and a "to be continued" slate.

The jokes' punch lines are accented by the laugh track. Immediately following the previous episode's recap, the first line of dialogue as Robert and his friend Dirk drive back to their home is Dirk's proclamation, "Wow!" which is punctuated by the laugh track. Then, as Dirk recounts that he just saw two gay men kissing "right on the mouth," another round of laughter from the soundtrack can be heard. These recorded reactions to the presence of same-sex intimacy are designed largely to express the absurdity of two Black men kissing "right on the mouth." On their face, neither of these moments can be understood as "jokes" or comic utterances. Rather, they function, as Freud argues, as tendentious jokes do: to exist "simply and solely in the absurd mode of representation, putting what is usually reckoned to be the lesser in the comparative and taking what is regarded as the more important as positive."[56] In this exchange, same-sex intimacy is regarded as absurd because it is deemed to be outside of the bounds of Black heteronormativity.

Shortly after this exchange, Dirk asks if "it makes me gay 'cause I couldn't turn away?" This utterance gives way to laughter that I suggest is rooted in a fear of the homosexual other within. The audiences' laughter suggests that they, too, share this fear. The last joke in the episode's prelude centers gender roles and the ways that a heterosexual understanding of homosexuality (and same-sex relationships) hinges on mapping heterosexist assumptions onto such relationships. Dirk asks, "Which one you think is the chick?" The laugh track suggests agreement with the question being asked while also underscoring that this episode, like the majority of television art, assumes the viewer is heterosexual and has pondered this question with respect to same-sex relationships. The Black gay men in chapter 4 will make similar observations.

The first scene after the episode prelude finds Robert back at home. The audience has insider knowledge about Robert having discovered that his biological father, Luther, is gay, knowledge no one within the series (other than Dirk) ostensibly has. When Bobby Jr., Robert's son, enters the scene with a gallon of milk and says "homo" as he is attempting to pronounce the word *homogenized*, the laugh track is cued, which signals a set of insider knowledge between Robert and the audience, which is "in the know" with respect to why the word *homo* might be funny. Mills's theorization is useful here in that "finding things funny often relies on a number of aspects which are not contained within the actual comic moment itself, and so humor can be seen as a communicative act whose context is vital to its success."[57] The context of this comic moment relies on what the viewer has seen in the previous episode (or the recap) and knows that Luther is a "homo." Without such knowledge, a child uttering "homo" as he attempts to sound out the word *homogenized* ceases to be funny. Furthermore, Mel Watkins suggests that when Black people engage in intraracial humor, this Black humor has a specific target (in comparison to the kind of broad humor used in minstrelsy traditions). He argues, "the speaker usually clearly distinguishes him- or herself from the traits or characteristics being mocked."[58] These jokes suggest that a clear strategy exists to ensure that Black gayness does not belong within the context of the series' narrative universe and Blackness generally.

When Luther arrives, unannounced, at Robert's house, Robert reveals that he has no issue with the "gay thing," partly because he works in television with gay people. At the same time, his description of his alleged "gay friends" can be read as offensive, as he refers to them as "super gay" (small audience laughter), "tiara gay" (bigger audience laughter), and "Judy Garland gay" (biggest audience laughter). Luther represents the "respectable" gay body—a body that does not display the outward markings by which gayness is assumed to be legible including speech patterns, styles of dress, or mannerisms. With Luther present, those who do not fit within the realm of the hegemonically masculine gay man are permissible targets for humor, laughter, and mockery, much like Tracy in *Moesha*'s "Labels" episode. Because "super gay," "tiara gay," and "Judy Garland gay" all seem to refer to a feminized gay man, the laughter works within the superiority theory of humor. It also expresses a corrective function that polices the boundaries within which Black gayness (and Black masculinity by extension) will be temporarily allowed within the heteronormative space of *All of Us*. At the same time, the script's invocation of Judy Garland, like *Good News* and *Are We There Yet?*, works to connect gayness and whiteness. While the "joke" could have named a number of Black divas to whom some Black gay men have affinity, such as Diana Ross (who, like Judy Garland, played Dorothy in the 1978 Black-cast film version of *The Wiz*) or Patti LaBelle, it uses a white gay icon to further tether Black gayness to something that exists outside of the confines of "authentic" Blackness.

Later in the same scene, Luther's presence as a "respectable" gay body becomes explicitly underscored through the use of the laugh track. Robert's adoptive father cannot believe that Luther is gay. He asks his wife, "*He's* gay?" When she confirms, he first asks her, "Are you sure?" which is met with little audience laughter. When she again confirms, he turns to Luther and asks, "Are *you* sure?" which is met with a bigger laugh. Finally, before Earl exits the room to leave Robert and Luther alone to talk, he says, "But he doesn't look gay to me" [audience laughter]. The laugh track suggests an agreement with the line of questioning that Robert's adoptive father is undertaking. Because Luther does not subscribe to how Black gay bodies have historically been mediated, his embodiment of gayness is made problematic and incomprehensible in many ways. In other words, the notion of gaydar is supposed to be infallible for reading gayness onto a body. Gaydar becomes a detection technology; in this case, it has presumably failed, perhaps gesturing toward some progressivism in *All of Us*. On the one hand, Luther troubles Black gayness's historical mediation within television. On the other hand, it is the reason that Luther's body, with its refusal to embody detectable forms of gayness long reified by semiotic associations, must be expunged from the televisual universe of *All of Us*.

All of Us uses the laugh track not only to mark homosexuality as comic but also to delineate between those inside and outside its televisual universe. At the same time, the script is undergirded by a desire to decouple Blackness and gayness while associating gayness and whiteness. Much like *Good News*, *All of Us* uses the laugh track to decenter homosexuality from its narrative while suggesting that homosexuality generally, and Black homosexuality specifically, are unwelcome within the series.

LET'S STAY TOGETHER AND TWO-FACED HUMOR

While the Black gay character Darkanian appears in six episodes over two seasons of *Let's Stay Together*, the analysis of the laugh track in this chapter focuses on two of those episodes. This focus is important because over the course of the first four episodes, Darkanian is assumed to be heterosexual through both his actions and his romantic pursuit and coupling with series regular Crystal. The humor in which the episodes traffic is particularly important and ripe for analysis because, like *Are We There Yet?* and *All of Us*, it is created entirely in postproduction. This postproduction of laughter implies its falsity, divorced from the liveness of a studio audience whose members are (presumably) free to laugh when they see fit and free from the ideological underpinnings of laughter. By placing the laughter in postproduction, the series' producers are free to encode humor at the places *they* see fit, choosing not to amplify (or even to remove) laughter in places where an actual audience found humor.

In one of the first scenes in which Darkanian appears within the series in the episode "Leave Me Alone," he is positioned as a womanizer, wooing Crystal through a series of sexually charged advances that attempts to center his claim to masculinity. Such a claim is short-circuited by the laugh track. While his first line of dialogue, "Yo Kita! You ready to have my baby yet?" is meant to reassert his heterosexuality, the laughter that immediately follows the line undercuts the virility of such a question. The insertion of the laughter could suggest that the line is genuinely funny as a first line of dialogue to introduce a new character;

however, I argue that it begins to lay the groundwork for a hermeneutics of suspicion about Darkanian's "true" sexuality. Darkanian's bravura display of masculinity suggests that a woman's (in this case, Kita's) vagina is literally and figuratively the portal through which his heterosexuality can be validated. As Larry Gross details, queers are socialized into heteronormative culture.[59] They generally—and Darkanian, specifically—understand that a boisterous display of Black masculinity, rooted in heteronormative gestures toward coupling or mating rituals, can prop up their performative "passing" as heterosexual. The laugh track works to weaken any claim Darkanian might have to hegemonic Black masculinity and instead positions his display as comical.

When Darkanian is "outed" as gay in the episode, "Wait . . . What?," the series engages in what I have elsewhere called *two-faced humor*, building on Freud's theorization of tendentious jokes. "While Freud's triumvirate includes a third person who is responsible for producing the 'pleasure' of the joke, two-faced humor is explicit in its operation as a somewhat covert form of humor in that its humor is deployed when the abject person/object is removed from the situation in which the joke is told."[60] Two-faced humor is also "rooted in popular vernacular, where referring to someone as 'two-faced' means they display duplicitous behavior," thus the abject object of the joke "is imagined as outside of the intended audience for the joke."[61]

In the specificity of *Let's Stay Together*, the two-faced jokes originate from an antigay stance that I suggest is rooted in the imagination of its Black audience. Darkanian's homosexuality is revealed not by his own admission but instead by his having a boyfriend in a scene from the "Wait . . . What?" episode.

> Crystal: Um, sir, where did you get that key?
> Greg: From Darkanian.
> Crystal: Oh, OK. I'm Crystal, Darkanian's girlfriend.
> Greg: Oh, so you're Crystal. I've heard so much about you. I'm Greg—[pause] Darkanian's boyfriend. [soundtrack reaction and laughter]
> Crystal: Say what now? [commercial break]

The laughter on the soundtrack gestures toward the incompatibility of Darkanian having a boyfriend because in the previous episodes he has been solidly positioned as a love interest for Crystal. The humor works because Greg's introduction defies not only the expectations associated with the ways Black men should be mediated but also the logics of Darkanian's very existence within the series. While the laughter reveals the "absurdity" of homosexuality within the series, it is also two-faced humor—directed at Darkanian and his (homo)sexuality—outside the scene but within the narrative universe of the series. As a narrative interloper who has been passing as a heterosexual man, the two-faced humor in this scene works to abject Darkanian from notions of Black masculinity. Importantly, part of the two-faced nature of the humor in this scene is that Darkanian does not appear in either the scene or the episode. In other words, revelations about his homosexuality are entirely in the hands of characters other than him. His sexuality is no longer his story to tell but rather a topic that can be revealed and laughed at and about without his presence.

In "Game Over," the last episode in which Darkanian appears, he has agreed to use his celebrity as a football player in a mayoral campaign ad to help Jamal, one of the series' main characters, get elected. The ad shoot takes place in an Atlanta gym and features extras who play basketball while Jamal pitches why Atlanta residents should vote for him. This episode's import lies in two areas. First, its title can be read as the end of Darkanian's passing as heterosexual while simultaneously suggesting that Darkanian's use-value for the series is "game over." Second, and most important for this chapter, the use of the laugh track reveals the series' ideological stance. A scene near the middle of the episode begins to tip the series' hand around the ways humor and the laugh track work. Greg, Darkanian's boyfriend, is on set and is hit when an extra wildly throws a basketball. Darkanian rushes to Greg's side:

> Darkanian: Baby, are you OK?
> Greg: I'm OK, honey.
> Director: Did they just call each other baby and honey? [audience laughter]

The laugh track laughter grows as the camera pans around the scene to show extras taking cell phone footage of Darkanian's and Greg's expressions of care for one another. The laughter signals an "inside joke" in the sense that the audience already knows Darkanian is gay. Part of the humor originates from laughing at the director (the only white person in the episode) discovering that Darkanian and Greg are a romantic couple when the audience already knows that Crystal and Darkanian's relationship is a facade.

At the same time, the laughter within the scene can also be theorized within the relief theory of comedy. Heretofore, Darkanian and Greg have only announced their relationship but have not necessarily expressed affection toward one another. That this is the last episode on which both Darkanian and Greg appear is important. While Quinn Miller rightly suggests that "comedy conventions allow secondary characters to deviate from norms in ways that main characters seldom do," the laugh track works to discipline such deviations.[62] In forcing audiences to reckon with their relationship, Darkanian and Greg must be disciplined and expunged from the Black-cast sitcom universe. This

Fig. 3.6. Darkanian holds a press conference in which he comes out while his "beard" Crystal and his boyfriend look on, signaling "Game Over" for his tenure within *Let's Stay Together.*

temporary moment of affection sets into motion their expulsion from the series. The laughter signals, in part, that Darkanian and Greg's relationship is absurd within the context of the series' normative universe and that it is, in fact, game over for their tenure in the series.

Finally, Darkanian holds a press conference in which he declares his gayness. After the outing in the previous scene, which is played for laughs, Darkanian's coming out is treated as a somber affair. His confession is treated simultaneously as his own declaration but also a call to arms for others to be unafraid of the consequences of coming out as gay. Darkanian says, "I was worried that if I revealed the truth, it would take away from the athlete that I am. But speaking the truth is making me the man that I want to be. And I want anyone who is living in fear of a bully, or your family, or of anyone else, that it's all right to love who you love. And who you love shouldn't stop you from being anything you want to be in life including a hard-nosed, head-knocking, game-changing championship running back. Any questions?" The scene concludes with series regulars suggesting that they are proud of Darkanian for coming out; however, after he has delivered his version of an "It Gets Better" speech, he is no longer useful to the series. The monologue serves as Darkanian's "farewell" speech, a speech in which he has not only confessed his "sin" of poisoning the series with his deviant sexuality but uses his confession as a "lesson" to viewers about tolerance, even if the series will not tolerate a recurring Black gay character. That Darkanian's speech concludes with silence and not laughter (or applause) displays the animosity with which homosexuality is met in the episodes. Darkanian is not welcome in the series because he troubles the binary ways sexuality exists and operates culturally. After the series forces him to "pick a side," he is expunged because he reveals the ways heterosexuality is a hegemonic construct and not one based in the myriad ways sexuality functions in the world.

At the same time, because the series' narrative universe expunges Darkanian, and because this is the most contemporary series discussed in this book, the series uses paratexts to create an extratextual engagement with Black gayness. In this way, the series presumably treats Darkanian as it does for narrative reasons, not for ideological ones. As I have detailed elsewhere, BET created online paratexts including "a slideshow of past and present NFL players who would support Darkanian's fictional coming-out, based on their past as LGBT rights supporters."[63] In addition to the slideshow, the production included a letter from Crystal to Darkanian that reads as follows:

Dear Darkanian . . .

You may never read this, but given the complex nature of our relationship, I thought it would be in my interest to compile a list of football players (and ex-football players), who would support you if you came out no matter what team you play for (no pun intended).

Sincerely,
Crystal[64]

Presumably, the series producers knew it had acted hostilely toward Darkanian. Its use of paratexts (which rely on fans of the series engaging with such paratexts) attempts to have it both ways. On the one hand, it textually seeks to rid itself of Darkanian. On the other hand, it paratextually repositions itself as progressive by demonstrating the core cast's "coolness" with respect to Black gayness generally, and Darkanian and Greg specifically, while still making no space for them to exist within the fabric of the series.

Within *Let's Stay Together*'s Black heteronormative narrative space, the laugh track marks Darkanian as an abject other, even as the actors within the scenes and series maintain a somewhat neutral position about the presence of homosexuality. This neutrality is achieved by the very ways the laugh track functions. Even as the actors retain a semblance of being "in the scene" and not reacting to the news that Darkanian's homosexuality has "invaded" their space, the laugh track does that heavy ideological lifting for them. Without the cast having to necessarily remark on the series' understanding of the absurdist nature of same-sex relationships, the laugh track can do that work.

ENCODING BLACK QUEENS

This chapter demonstrated the importance of the laugh track as an element of postproduction aesthetics that is also an ideological tool for Black-cast sitcoms. Although only two of the series in this book were shot in front of a live studio audience, the laugh track suggests a rootedness in the traditional conventions of the genre and provides a way to encode where humor exists within an episode. The laugh track also performs the role of creating community—a community that excludes Black gay people—and sometimes the separation is inhospitable, whereas at other times the separation is simply rooted in difference.

There is no single way Black-cast sitcoms make Black gayness comic. However, they rely heavily on humor theories—superiority, incongruity, surprise, relief, and two-faced humor—and expand these theories in new ways to delimit the boundaries of (hetero)normative Blackness. In particular, by creating the laugh track entirely in postproduction, *All of Us*, *Let's Stay Together*, and *Are We There Yet?* rely on the laugh track as an electronic substitute for the audience. At the same time, these series create a soundtrack in postproduction that is at odds with the ideological way the writers and showrunners (discussed in chap. 2) suggest they see the place of Black gayness within their respective series and episodes. While both Jacque Edmonds Cofer and Carla Banks-Waddles make no mention of animosity toward Black gay men specifically or gayness generally, *Let's Stay Together*'s deployment of two-faced humor calls their ideological stances into question.

Taken together, these series cannot be pinned down for a particular approach to humor—they shift their shape depending on the objectives the episode's writers, showrunners, and networks hope to convey. But these series always decenter, marginalize, or objectify Black gayness in the service of the same heteronormative Black domestic ideals, through the ideological machinations of the laugh track. Humor and the laugh track come together to make Black gayness not only strange but comical in the Black-cast sitcom's narrative universes. The laugh track and humor converge to suggest that these story worlds are a "heterosexuals only" universe. The actors who play the parts are heterosexuals pretending to be gay (or they are at least not openly gay), which insulates producers from dealing with "real" Black gay men in gay guest-starring roles, who might object to the tenor of the humor within the episodes. Without an authentic "outsider," the narrative is free to engage in humor rooted in humor theories.[65] Casting presumably heterosexual actors as Black gay characters within episodes maintains the social contract needed for humor to exist.

The laugh track also serves a socialization function. When paired with Black gayness in the Black-cast sitcom, the laugh track (and laughter) creates the boundaries and the terms within which Black gayness can exist in the Black-cast sitcom's diegesis. While Black gay male characters are (begrudgingly) accepted into the narrative fold on *Moesha, Good News, All of Us, Are We There Yet?*, and *Let's Stay Together*, they are discarded just as quickly. Gayness is ejected from the (hetero)normative universe of the series because it is connected with deceit and belies expectations of heterosexual(ist) romantic pairings. However, even though *Good News* and *Are We There Yet?* are more narratively welcoming of the gay "intruder," these characters are never heard from again because after they have come out and demonstrated the "enlightened" ways of the core cast, their comedic function has been exhausted. Similar to Gross's assertion that gay characters are "defined by their 'problem'" and confined to the "problem-of-the-week," Omar, Tracy, Eldridge, Luther, Roosevelt, Cedric, and Darkanian remain trapped in the Black-cast sitcom's closet.[66] Simultaneously, when Black gay characters are trotted out, it is to be laughed at and positioned as the homosexual, abject, comedic "other." Collectively, through humor, the Black-cast sitcom continues to build, rebuild, and renovate the generic closet for Black gayness.

NOTES

1. Gitlin, *Inside Prime Time*.
2. Mills, *Television Sitcom*, 51.
3. Brett Mills, *The Sitcom* (Edinburgh: Edinburgh University Press, 2009), 81.
4. Andy Medhurst and Lucy Tuck, "Stereotyping and the Situation Comedy," in *Television Sitcom Comedy*, ed. Jim Cook (London: British Film Institute, 1982), 45.
5. Wylie Sypher, "The Meanings of Comedy," in *Comedy*, ed. Wylie Sypher (New York: Doubleday, 1956), 242.
6. Althusser, *Lenin and Philosophy*, 175.
7. Yep and Elia, "Queering/Quaring Blackness," 35.
8. Robert Kubey, *Creating Television: Conversations with the People behind 50 Years of American TV* (New York: Routledge, 2009), 115.
9. Rick Altman, "Television/Sound," in *Studies in Entertainment: Critical Approaches to Mass Culture*, ed. Tania Modleski (Bloomington: Indiana University Press, 1986), 42.
10. Ibid., 42–43. Emphasis in original.
11. Jeremy Butler, *Television: Critical Methods and Applications* (New York: Routledge, 2012), 221.

12. LeRoi, interview.

13. Richard Dyer, "Stereotyping," in *Media and Cultural Studies: Keyworks,* ed. Meenakshi Gigi Durham and Douglas M. Kellner (New York: Wiley-Blackwell, 2012), 278.

14. Mills, *The Sitcom,* 83.

15. Jerry Palmer, *The Logic of the Absurd* (London: British Film Institute, 1987), 177.

16. *Murse* is a colloquial reference to a messenger bag, which is created from the contraction of the phrase *man's purse.*

17. Mills, *The Sitcom,* 82.

18. Critchley, *On Humor,* 3.

19. Ibid., 3.

20. Antonio Savorelli, *Beyond Sitcom: New Directions in American Television* (Jefferson, NC: McFarland, 2010), 23.

21. Mills, *The Sitcom,* 83.

22. Joyrich, "Epistemology of the Console," 29.

23. Mills, *Television Sitcom,* 120.

24. Sypher, "Meanings of Comedy," 244.

25. Seger, *Making a Good Script Great,* 28.

26. Critchley, *On Humor,* 56–57.

27. Kubey, *Creating Television,* 115.

28. Alfred L. Martin Jr., "It's (Not) in His Kiss," *Popular Communication* 12, no. 3 (2014): 156.

29. Sigmund Freud, "The Joke and Its Relation to the Unconscious," in *Standard Edition of the Complete Works of Sigmund Freud,* vol. 8, ed. James Strachey (London: Vintage, 2001), 87.

30. Johnson, "Specter of the Black Fag," 226.

31. Joyrich, "Epistemology of the Console," 28.

32. Mills, *The Sitcom,* 80.

33. Bady, interview.

34. Hall, "What Is This 'Black,'" 292.

35. Gayle S. Rubin, "Thinking Sex: Notes for a Radical Theory of the Politics of Sexuality," in *The Lesbian and Gay Studies Reader,* ed. Henry Ablove, Michèle Aina Barale, and David M. Halperin (New York: Routledge, 1993), 13.

36. Candace West and Don H. Zimmerman, "Doing Gender," *Gender and Society* 1, no. 2 (1987): 136.

37. Richard Dyer, *The Culture of Queers* (Routledge: New York, 2001), 97.

38. Weinberger, interview.

39. Foucault, *History of Sexuality.,* 39.

40. Critchley, *On Humor,* 11.

41. Ibid., 12.

42. Martin, "It's (Not) in His Kiss," 156.

43. Critchley, *On Humor*, 56–57.

44. Freud, *The Joke and Its Relation to the Unconscious*, 97.

45. Ibid., 97.

46. Palmer, *Logic of the Absurd*, 41.

47. Christine Davies, *Ethnic Humor around the World* (Bloomington: Indiana University Press, 1996).

48. Weinberger interview.

49. Stephanie K. Dunning, *Queer in Black and White: Interraciality, Same Sex Desire, and Contemporary African American Culture* (Bloomington: University of Indiana Press, 2009), 4.

50. Franz Fanon, *Black Skin, White Masks* (New York: Grove Press, 1952), 53.

51. See Eldridge Cleaver, *Soul on Ice* (New York: Delta Books, 1991).

52. John Morreall, *Comic Relief: A Comprehensive Philosophy of Humor* (New York: Wiley-Blackwell Publishing, 2009), 8.

53. Martin, "It's (Not) in His Kiss," 163–164.

54. Morreall, *Comic Relief*, 68–69.

55. Palmer, *Logic of the Absurd*, 177.

56. Freud, *The Joke and Its Relation to the Unconscious*, 89.

57. Mills, *The Sitcom*, 15–16.

58. Mel Watkins, *On the Real Side: A History of African American Comedy from Slavery to Chris Rock* (Chicago: Lawrence Hill Books, 1994), 131.

59. Larry Gross, "Out of the Mainstream: Sexual Minorities and the Mass Media," in *Remote Control: Television, Audiences, and Cultural Power*, ed. Ellen Seiter, Hans Borchers, Gabrielle Kreutzner, and Eva-Maria Warth (New York: Routledge, 1991), 139.

60. Alfred L. Martin Jr., "The Tweet Has Two Faces: Two-Faced Humor, Black Masculinity and RompHim," *Journal of Cinema and Media Studies* 58, no. 3 (2019): 161.

61. Ibid.

62. Quinn Miller, "*The Dick Van Dyke Show*: Queer Meanings," in *How to Watch Television*, 1st ed., ed. Ethan Thompson and Jason Mittell (New York: New York University Press, 2013), 113.

63. Martin, "Generic Closets," 230–231.

64. "Football Players Who Would Support Darkanian Coming Out," BET .com, April 2013, https://www.bet.com/shows/lets-stay-together/photos1 /photos-old/2013/04/football-players-who-would-support-darkanian.html.

65. See Martin, "Queer Business of Casting."

66. Gross, "Out of the Mainstream," 138.

FOUR

—ฑพ—

BLACK QUEENS SPEAK

The Generic Closet, Black-Cast Sitcoms, and Reception Practices

IN MANY WAYS, THIS BOOK has been about Black gayness. Through discussions of the industrial imaginations of (monolithically constructed) Black audiences, the politics of the writers' room, and the ideological power of the laugh track, Black gayness has been the *object* of information but not the *subject* of information.[1] This chapter seeks to shift Black gayness from object to subject while moving from production-related practices to meaning-making ones. Along the way, I want to answer Dwight McBride's question "Can the Queen Speak?" with a resounding "Yaaassss Qwain!" by centering twenty Black gay men's voices in a discussion about their relationship to Black gay representation within the Black-cast sitcom.[2]

This discussion carries import because media does not simply do things to people, contrary to the "hypodermic needle" models of media effects. As Janet Staiger neatly synthesizes, this line of media effects research has largely been driven by "fears of effects, especially couched in language about unformed, ill-formed, or weak minds."[3] Rather, the people who sit in front of their televisions, computers, tablets, and smartphones consuming content are engaging with media images and making meaning from the images that flash across their screens. John Fiske notes that when researchers understand viewers as active, it allows for the recognition that "the social subject has a history, lives in a particular social formation . . . and is constituted by a complex cultural history that is both social and textual."[4] David Morley adds, "The audience must be conceived of as composed of clusters of socially situated individual readers, whose individual readings will be framed by shared cultural formations and practices pre-existent to the individual."[5] Morley's theorization centers the importance of axes of identity in structuring how meaning is made. He proposes that studying the reception practices of those who are raced, gendered, classed, sexually oriented, and aged has value as a means to understand how their axes of identity shape how they make meaning. This chapter answers that call.

I acknowledge that privileging the voices of Black gay men is a political act. I deliberately chose to engage with Black gay men's reception practices and to do so without the inclination to "validate" their observations by comparing them with a "control" group. To do so, to my mind, would keep Black gay men's voices as subaltern rather than lifting and centering them. It is also an epistemological intervention into Black gayness and television audiences. In this chapter, I seek to understand the ways Black gay men make meaning from the images of Black gayness within *Moesha, Good News, All of Us, Are We There Yet?,* and *Let's Stay Together.* I also endeavor to explore these Black gay men's contestation of industrially produced knowledges about Black gayness.

The Black gay queen is infrequently allowed out of his subaltern position within both Blackness and white gayness. This is underscored by the scant research on the reception practices of Black gay audiences. Scholars like William G. Hawkeswood and E. Patrick Johnson explored Black gay men's interior lives, but the focus of their work is not on media.[6] Essex Hemphill's study of Black gay men and lesbians in Philadelphia and Washington, DC, is the only small-scale study of Black gay men and their reception practices, focusing specifically on Fox's *In Living Color* and the "Men On . . ." sketches.[7] Hemphill found that for every person like Anthony Owens, who enjoyed the show because "it's a parody . . . [and it] should be taken as such," there were those who were troubled by "Men On . . . ," like famed filmmaker Marlon Riggs, who thought it "justifie[d] all of the very traditional beliefs about black gay sexuality."[8] Put simply, Hemphill's interviews revealed that Black gay men have a negotiated relationship to the Black gay images in the "Men On . . ." sketches. I build on Hemphill's study by addressing several texts. Rather than focusing on a close reading of the representations, the Black gay men I interviewed consider structures related to representational practices—namely, the generic closet. This chapter also builds on Alexander Doty's theorization that "the queerness of mass culture develops in . . . historically specific cultural readings and uses of texts by self-identified gays, lesbians, bisexuals and queers" by engaging the reception practices of Black gay men.[9]

Studying Black gay audiences also builds on the scant but important literature that includes work on Black audiences and fandoms, including my own as well as that of Jacqueline Bobo, Robin R. Means Coleman, Rebecca Wanzo, and Kristen Warner. It also builds on white gay male audience studies, including those by Michael DeAngelis, Richard Dyer, Brett Farmer, Frederik Dhaenens, and Larry Gross.[10] While this body of work is methodologically varied, from interviews and focus groups to theorizations and examinations of fan-produced material, it confirms that media texts are read in multivalent and polysemic ways. However, within the contours of these variant readings, each scholar reinforces the import of critical engagement with "real" minority audiences to understand their reception practices.

METHODOLOGY

A more in-depth discussion of methodology is necessary to situate the work I undertake in this chapter. I conducted individual, in-depth interviews with twenty self-identified Black gay men. Justin Lewis writes that part of the methodological value of the in-depth, one-on-one interview is its ability to allow "us to explore a particular reading in some detail. It also gives us the opportunity to develop and clarify points without pausing to consider the effects of a particular set of group dynamics in the formulation of that reading. We do not, for instance, have to worry that our interviewee is finding it difficult to get a word in edgeways."[11] This was beneficial in my interviews; however, I also chose individual rather than group interviews because I wanted to ensure these men had a safe space to discuss not only these episodes but also their own biographies. All of the Black gay men I interviewed had self-identified as gay, but not all were out to everyone in their lives. Group interviews might have "outed" them to members of the group or, through social associations that those within the group might have, to others to whom the Black gay men were not out.

To guide the interview, I used an instrument (see app. C) that was divided into three broad categories: (1) background and demographic information, (2) experience with their own coming out, and (3) Black gay characters in Black-cast sitcoms. The interview instrument served only as a guide, as the interviews were semistructured. Although I had prepared questions, the interview proceeded more like a conversation, which allowed us to dig deeper into particular topics that either of us found fascinating. I regularly told interviewees, "I also want you to feel free to just ramble on if you need to ramble on to get to what you need to say."[12] Although the interview was semistructured, I covered all topics within the interview script, although often not in exactly the order in which the questions are listed.

I began the recruitment process through two Black gay men and two Black heterosexual women who functioned as key informants to recruit participants for the study. This particular method was used because I wanted to attempt to gather Black gay men whose social formation differed from mine, particularly with respect to education and income level. Participation in the project was limited by two criteria: (1) the men must identify as Black and gay, and (2) they must have passing knowledge of *Moesha*, *Good News*, *All of Us*, *Are We There Yet?*, and *Let's Stay Together*. Through these two avenues, my sample size reached ten participants (eight Black gay men in addition to the two who served as key contacts). Each man was asked to contact others who might participate in the study (purposeful snowball sampling), ultimately resulting in a sample of twenty men. Coleman explains purposive snowball sampling as choosing participants "who can aid in securing maximum information, rather than generalizable findings."[13] This chapter follows Clifford Geertz's work in which he argues that reception studies work that does not seek to be generalizable across all populations "begins with a set of (presumptive) signifiers and attempts to place them within an intelligible frame. . . . In the study of culture, the signifiers are . . . symbolic acts or clusters of symbolic acts, and the aim is . . . analysis of social discourse. But the way in which theory is used—to ferret out the unapparent import of things—is the same."[14] This chapter continues to use the generic closet as a theoretical framework to understand these Black gay men's responses to *Moesha*, *Good News*, *All of Us*, *Are We There Yet?*, and *Let's Stay Together*. In so doing, following Sut Jhally and Justin Lewis's assertion, I use my "knowledge and skill" to make sense of what the men told me "rather than accept all testimony at face value."[15] In the discussion that follows, I attempt to present these Black gay men's voices while offering my own analysis.

The interviews were tape-recorded and transcribed following the interview. Seven interviewees were contacted for follow-up interviews to provide clarification and to respond to criticisms and counterpoints raised by other interviewees. Before the interviews, each interviewee was asked to watch *Moesha*'s "Labels," *Good News*'s "Pilot," *All of Us*'s "Like Father, Like Son, Like Hell" and "My Two Dads," and the *Are We There Yet?* episode "The Boy Has Style."[16] The episodes were provided to respondents via Google Drive, and the respondents were asked to take notes while watching.

My aim is to present these twenty Black gay men's voices as authentically as possible. As a scholar, I am selective about which quotes I pull from each man, but I have not "cleaned up" their speech. I have included colloquialisms to maintain the veracity of what the men said. In addition, the use of ellipses in this chapter denotes a pause in the men's speech, not an omission of words. On the rare instance that words are omitted, that will be designated by a square-bracketed set of ellipses.

The next section provides background on the men I interviewed. I include some interview extracts in these brief biographies of their thoughts on the

Black-cast sitcom generally, their experiences coming out as gay, and their thoughts on the state of Black gay representation. My hope is that these briefs help to humanize the men I interviewed so that they are not cardboard cutouts but are real people.[17]

THE BLACK GAY MEN

Before introducing the twenty Black gay men I interviewed, I would be remiss if I did not acknowledge that I am, in many ways, the twenty-first Black gay man in this chapter. Researchers cannot claim to be completely absent from their work. But I want to be reflexive about my positionality as a Black gay male scholar who has interacted with the same images as the men I interviewed. We differ based on educational attainment and socioeconomic status, among other axes of identity, but being Black, gay, and male also creates shared identity categories. I also want to acknowledge that my similar subject position with the men I interviewed (at least for race, gender, and sexuality) likely aided in the type of information I was able to glean through the interviews.[18] Concurrently, although commonalities exist between me and these Black gay men, as a scholar studying Black gay men, I remain what Patricia Hill Collins calls an "outsider within"—I am both one of the tribe and apart from it.[19]

The men in this chapter range in age from twenty-seven to sixty-three, with an average age of 45.3 years old. They have annual household incomes ranging from less than $10,000 to more than $100,000 per year, although the highest concentration of respondents earns more than $100,000 per year. The men are mostly a college-educated group, with thirteen respondents having completed a bachelor's degree and five men having completed a master's degree. To protect the men's anonymity, I refer to them using pseudonyms.

Eli was born in 1974. He holds two bachelor's degrees and earns between $40,000 and $59,999 per year. He is married to his partner and identifies as a Democrat. Eli defines a Black-cast sitcom as a series that "deals with racial issues, but not necessarily only Black [issues]."[20] However, he says on the rare occasion that the Black-cast sitcom engages with Black gayness, its engagement is "not so [good] most of the time."[21]

Thomas was born in 1961 and lives with his partner. He identifies as a Democrat, has a master's degree, and makes more than $100,000 per annum. Thomas has come out as gay to most but not all of his family members. He expressed a vexed relationship to watching Black gay representations. He says, "To be completely honest, all of those sitcoms I felt extremely uncomfortable watching them. Talking about gayness within Black culture is not always positive, and

so I felt in all of those episodes extremely uncomfortable watching them . . .
I felt myself sort of just on edge wondering where the story line was going to
ultimately go . . . I wasn't quite sure how the subject matter was going to be
represented."[22]

Derek earned a bachelor's degree, and his salary is between $75,000 and
$99,999 per year. The Democrat lives with his husband and was born in 1974.
Derek expresses a belief that Black gay characters within television fit into "one
of two categories. They're either the homo thug or really sassy queens. The
glaring exception I have is [Carter Heywood] from *Spin City*. He was kind of
a professional Black man who just happened to be gay. Yeah, there were some
sassy moments that he had, but he was not, I don't believe, a sassy character. I
think that's kind of weird that it came from a white space on this show that was
trying to appeal to middle America."[23]

Colin identifies as a Democrat and was born in 1967. He makes more than
$100,000 per year and hold a master's degree. Colin admits that he "sometimes
feel[s] a little bothered by the over-the-top stereotypical portrayal of someone
who is gay."[24] He lives with his partner but has not come out to his family members or in his workplace. Colin uses "the term *gay* more often than anything else,"
to describe himself but says "in my normal discussion I don't identify as a gay
person. I think I identify as someone who just loves someone who happens to be
of the same sex."[25] Although he has not made a public declaration of his gayness,
he is "certain that [his family] know[s] he is gay but simply have not asked."[26]

Ralph was born in 1985, is a Democratic-leaning voter, and holds a bachelor's
degree. At the time of our interview, he was single and earned between $25,000
and $39,999 per year. He expresses the belief that "half the time [Black gayness
is] never represented in [Black-cast] sitcoms. Not as a recurring character. It's
mentioned here and there, but never like a constant character that someone can
identify with . . . they're not part of the main cast of the characters."[27]

Paul was born in 1956 and completed two years of college. He makes between
$40,000 and $59,999 per year and is a single Democratic-leaning voter. He was
born and raised in the southern United States and was raised within the Southern Baptist Church. This upbringing, Paul says, meant that within his family
"there was a lot of denial and there were a lot of people accepting [gayness], but
not really talking about it. It sort of led me to this place where I didn't really talk
about it. And I didn't feel like I was hiding, but I realized that I was [gay], but I
wasn't really talking about it."[28]

Kenneth is single and holds a bachelor's degree. Born in 1969, Kenneth earns
more than $100,000 per year and identifies as a Democrat. Kenneth classi-
fies most representations of Black gay characters within Black-cast sitcoms as

flamboyant. He says, "I don't like how it always has to be a flamboyant character. I consider myself to be a very masculine, educated African American man, and you don't even have to be educated. You don't have to have a college degree to be a successful gay Black man, but the flamboyantness [*sic*], whether you're successful or not, I struggle with that one. Because to me it's not a true representation of gay Black men."[29]

Dave was born in 1966 and earns between $75,000 and $99,999 per year. He completed his undergraduate studies, identifies as a Democrat, and was single at the time of our interview. Dave, who is not out to everyone he knows, says "I mean, I'm a private person. But, like, if you ask me? Yeah, I'll tell you, you know?"[30] Dave expresses his belief that Black gayness is presented in ways designed to be "so shocking that people will turn away and say, 'OK I can't look at this!' You know, even if they don't [turn away], on the inside they don't feel comfortable. I don't see many Black gay characters that are like me; that are not out and not flamboyant, just you know, living everyday life, going to an everyday job, having, you know, everyday family, extended family, etcetera."[31]

Charles was born in 1987 and is partnered. He holds a master's degree and makes between $25,000 and $39,999 per year. He identifies as a Democrat. Charles broadly understands a Black-cast sitcom as a series that has "members of the cast who identify, or the audience identifies as being Black or African American. I would also include a Black sitcom being one that speaks about issues specific to the Black community. And also, how the Black community is kind of interwoven and integrated in American society. So, kind of being able to touch on things that we, as Black people, talk about amongst our own families. And kind of being able to see bits and pieces of your own family in those people as well."[32]

Andrew earns between $60,000 and $74,999 per year. He was born in 1992 and was single at the time of our interview. He holds a bachelor's degree. For Andrew, Black gayness is portrayed within television broadly as "more of a sidekick, funny role. We are never usually like . . . the serious ones. We're usually always the funny ones, the over the top [ones]. You know? Comic relief." He continues, "Although I am happy that there are more people on TV that represent at least a portion of who I am, I feel like it gives those who aren't as educated or diverse in their friends category the wrong idea. There's a lot of people I know who, when I first meet them and stuff, they don't realize that I happen to be gay until like, after I'll say something like, 'Oh yeah, that guy's hot,' or something like that. After that time, I think it's this expectation like, 'Oh snap, so you like going shopping?' Although some of that may be true, that's an assumption based off what you see on TV."[33]

Cory was born in 1966. He earned two master's degrees and makes between $60,000 and $74,999. He politically identifies as progressive and is partnered, although the two do not cohabitate. While he identifies as gay, he expresses a desire to just be Cory. He remembers, "my mother saying about six years ago, she actually asked me if I was going to ever get married to man, woman, whatever and she said something that sticks in my mind. She's like, 'You're not gay, straight. You're just Cory.' I'm sorry, I almost cried because that struck [...] home because it just makes sense for me. I'm just Cory and those things, my color, my sexuality, are just an aspect of me. I don't try to deny them. They are a part of me."[34]

Alex was born in 1965, earned a master's degree, and was single at the time of our interview. He identifies as a Democrat and earns between $25,000 and $39,999 per year. He has come out as gay to his only brother but says he never came out to his mother because "she was really homophobic, and I sort of left [home]. When I was seventeen, I just left and then we have a really weird relationship and now, in the last fourteen years she's been sick, like mentally, so by the time I felt really free about [telling her I am gay] she got sick."[35]

Robert earns between $10,000 and $24,999 and holds a bachelor's degree. He identifies politically as an independent and was born in 1991. At the time of our interview, he was single. Robert says,

> [I] had a lot of fears coming out to my mom. I definitely thought that she was going to kick me out [of the house]. That didn't happen but her reaction wasn't really good. It was very much she didn't accept me being gay. She thought that I was going to have a hard life. She basically said that she wouldn't really acknowledge the fact that I was gay unless I brought home a boyfriend. Even now there'll be times when I'm hanging out with a girl and she'll be like, 'Oh do you guys like each other?' It's like, 'No, I don't because I like guys.' She told me this story about how she used to have a friend when she was still a hairdresser and apparently, he was a gay guy, but he had told her that he really didn't want to be gay and that it had been really hard for him. I guess eventually he started trying to date women again. I think that shaped her view of gay men that she thinks that we all just hate being gay and that we want to be with women.[36]

Frank was born in 1959, holds a bachelor's degree and earns between $40,000 and $59,999 per year. He politically identifies as independent and was single at the time of our interview. Frank said that Black gay representation continues to fit within what he calls "the tragic characters. We're still the things that aren't generally spoken about. If we're spoken about, it's not in necessarily a good light, or we're confused or ostracized."[37]

Anthony was born in 1992 and is currently dating rather than in a long-term relationship. The Democrat makes less than $10,000 per year and is a high school graduate, enrolled in college at the time of our interview. Anthony said he first realized his attraction to men while watching the cartoon *Johnny Bravo* (Cartoon Network, 1997–2004). He said, "I remember looking back at it and I thought the show was absolutely stupid as a kid, but there was something that just kept me watching it, and I guess it was just because there was a muscular guy. I usually like more muscular guys, so generally speaking, I mean, I guess he was on the tall side. I generally like tall guys. I don't really go for a specific race or anything. I'm pretty open with that."[38]

Greg earns between $40,000 and $59,999 per year and holds a bachelor's degree. He identifies as a Democrat, was born in 1968, and was single at the time of our interview. Greg came out as gay at nineteen. He reports that the person to whom he came out was "a guy I was trying to come on to."[39] The two ended up briefly dating, and thereafter Greg came out as gay to all of his family and friends.

Raphael was born in 1975, earns between $60,000 and $74,999 per year, and is partnered. He holds a master's degree and politically identifies as independent. Raphael considers himself a TV buff and watches a lot of Black-cast television. He reports that "Black sitcoms were such a big part of my life growing up. In the '80s, I watched lots of re-runs of 1970s sitcoms like *What's Happening!!* [ABC, 1976–1979] and stuff with my sisters and brothers. [Black sitcoms] always make me think of family because they were the one time my family generally agreed on what we would watch on TV."[40]

William was born in 1972, holds a master's degree, and earns more than $100,000 per year. He identifies as a Democrat and was single at the time of our interview. William realized he was gay when he was about eight years old, although he could not "put a name to it" then.[41] He recalls, "I knew something was different then, you know? But I actually knew what gay was and that I was gay and told someone when I was sixteen. I told a fellow [news]paper carrier. He wasn't even like a good friend or anything. We just happened to be—I don't know. We were hanging out, but I was like . . . He had invited me to play basketball or something at some point and I generally was awful with sports and things like that and we happened to be talking in his basement afterward or something and I just felt like telling him. I thought he was cute so—I didn't actually tell him he was cute—but I thought he was cute and as part of that I told him I was gay."[42]

Michael was born in 1969 and at the time of our interview was working on a master's degree. He is in a cohabitating relationship and earns more than

$100,000 per year. He most closely identifies with the principles of the Democratic party. When Michael thinks of Black-cast sitcoms, he thinks of characters who "are exaggerations of real people, not real per se. They are either way far to the left or way far to the right and they don't necessarily appeal to me because I don't identify with them because, in most cases, they feel like they're written by white people for Black people."[43]

Samuel was born in 1976 and has earned a master's degree. He is currently partnered, although they do not live together. His annual income is between $40,000 and $59,999 per year. He generally does not identify with a political party but currently identifies as Democrat because of his affection for President Barack Obama. Samuel told me that the series *In Living Color* "really contributed a lot to what [I thought] Black gays were like. I was like [in] middle school or something when that used to come on. And that was how I thought all Black gay men were. I was really young, so I didn't think about myself being gay, because I hadn't done anything [sexually]. But seeing [Antoine Merriweather and Blaine Edwards] I will say, in terms of what I thought gay men were like, that was the image that was in my head."[44]

My discussions with these twenty Black gay men are largely structured around the generic closet. The first section focuses on these Black gay men's understanding of semiotics and gay-by-association as a technique to detect Black gayness within the heteronormative tele-universe of the Black-cast sitcom. In the following section, the men explore the ways coming out is always understood as central to the narrative discovery/declaration of Black gayness. Within the discussion, the men also illuminate the ways they see the last step of the generic closet, discarding, as a device to structure Black gay characters' existence within the Black-cast sitcom, which is always already decentered (explored in the fourth section). The fifth section examines these Black gay men's discussion of humor and the laugh track to position Black gayness as an abject object within the "mainstream" heterosexual worlds these Black gay characters episodically inhabit. Finally, the Black gay men discuss how they would produce Black gayness outside the confines of the Black-cast sitcom's generic closet.

DETECTING GAYNESS FOR THE GENERIC CLOSET

One way controlling images of Black gayness suture gayness and femininity is through the use of semiotics. Cobb and Coleman suggest that controlling images of Black gay men urge viewers "to believe that the presence of purportedly queer behaviors such as dramatic outbursts, effeminate mannerisms, and outlandish dress must necessarily correspond to a gay identity, even where the man in question has not made such an identity claim for himself. Further, heavily imbuing the performance of gay identities with such exaggeration asserts the visible, detectable nature of gay Black men, thereby controlling the definition and reception of Black men's sexualities."[45] In this section, I wish to explore Cobb and Coleman's concept of the interconnectivity of controlling images and reception, alongside a discussion of the power of semiotics. The Black gay men I interviewed understand how episodes of Black-cast sitcoms deploy semiotic gayness as a way to detect gayness on the bodies of "suspect" characters. First, semiotic gayness draws on costuming to signal gayness (alongside stereotypic behaviors and demeanors). Second, after drawing on those first signals, semiotic gayness is used to question the sexuality of the person associating with an "obviously" gay person. In a semiotic sense, a failure to conform to gender performativity can lead one who is reading clothes as a sign to make certain assumptions about another's sexuality. Black gay men understand these two manifestations of semiotic gayness within Black gay representation as a technology to detect Black gayness for the otherwise heterosexual cast of Black-cast sitcoms.

For Andrew, this worked within *Moesha*'s "Labels" episode, in which he noticed that Omar was wearing an earring. He recalls, "When I saw Omar, I was like, 'Oh snap!' When you wear an earring on your right it usually means . . . that you're letting other people know that you're gay."[46] The subtlety with which *Moesha* utilizes this trope makes gayness legible on Omar's body. In addition, UrbanDictionary.com has two terms that codify Andrew's reading of Omar. One is *gay ear*, defined as "the ear that most homosexuals tend to get pierced more often than the left ear," and the other is the *right earring rule*, which declares that "any male [who] wears an earring in his right ear is deemed gay."[47] Sartorial choices are thus understood as a meaningful (and reliable) technology to detect gayness.

On the one hand, some of the men, like Andrew, use these semiotic clues to detect queer bodies. On the other hand, this semiotic gayness can be used as a kind of queer detection device within the narrative of Black-cast sitcoms, and some of the Black gay men found such a deployment problematic. For example, Frank objects to the use of gaydar as a means of detecting Black gayness within "The Boy Has Style" because such a detection relied on a connectivity to sartorial choices and stereotype. He laments, "Because he has a murse or because he dresses this way, [Suzanne, the mother] assumed he was gay." He further suggests that because of her use of gaydar, he "was offended by [Suzanne] . . . I thought some of the things that she said to out Cedric as gay were over the top."[48] As I detailed in chapter 2, cowriter Jacqueline McKinley suggested that Cedric's wardrobe was a vital part of laying the narrative crumbs that ultimately lead the series' heterosexual cast to "detect" Cedric as a Black gay man. Alex also objects to the use of narrative gaydar in "The Boy Has Style," suggesting that "I don't like that whole 'I can clock people' . . . I mean, it had to be something more than just the fact that he had on a bag that didn't look that feminine to me and then, you know, a weirdly colored sweater and then yeah, he's gay; and then he turned out to be, which is a confirmation of that whole [notion of gaydar]."[49] Alex zeroed in on the problematic use of gaydar as a detection device *outside* of gay communities. His comments indicate that he would have preferred those codes be used not as a narrative detection device but as a way to demonstrate that stereotypes are not always a reliable method of detecting sexuality. Alex heatedly asserts, "You can't always do it like that. So, for every straight guy that desires to wear something in a different color or likes fashion, you're boxing him in and you're saying, you're gay."[50] Problematically within *Are We There Yet?*, the use of gaydar was positioned as infallible and absolute, particularly when clothing or costuming was used as the primary means of detecting gayness. This narrative gaydar works not only to detect (and ultimately expunge) the Black gay body from within the Black-cast sitcom but also to discipline sartorial norms for Black heterosexual men.

Anthony suggested that he did not necessarily pick up on the "clues" that were being set up for Cedric's detection as gay: "I didn't realize where this story line was going until [Suzanne] was like 'Oh, he's totally gay,' and I was like 'Wait, oh!' Because I didn't catch it myself, I didn't notice the messenger bag and I didn't even notice that as being anything out of the ordinary. I was like, 'Oh, well he's in school and he's wearing pink, OK whatever.'"[51] Anthony points to the arbitrariness and unreliability of "reading" gayness onto bodies. Problematically, however, the episodes that use gaydar position the practice as flawless. This positions reading gaydar as a practice for heterosexuals such that the "clues" are illegible to some Black gay men in the Black-cast sitcom's detective game.

The semiotic chain between sartorial choice and gayness is also used to determine that previously "undetected" gay characters, like Omar in *Moesha*'s "Labels" episode, can be detected because of their association with semiotically gay characters. For example, as Ralph says, "There's the suspicion once someone gets around . . . you didn't know until [Tracy] showed up . . . It was almost like guilt by association."[52] He continued by connecting Tracy and Omar with his own personal story of being understood as gay by association with a gay person. "I started hanging out with a gay guy who was totally open and when I came out, even my best friend said, 'Well, I kind of figured it out when you started hanging out with so-and-so a lot more, you never done that before, and I just put two and two together.'"[53] Kenneth had a similar reading of Tracy: "It wasn't really until Tracy came into the picture . . . Moesha just automatically assumed Omar was [gay] as well [because of his friendship with Tracy] . . . to me it was gay by association, even though she didn't really know that he was gay or not."[54]

Cory says, "Once Tracy came into the picture on *Moesha*, I figured that Omar eventually was gonna have to come out."[55] The episode reifies the notion that Black heterosexual men and Black gay men are not supposed to be friends or friendly, lest the connection call the heterosexual man's sexuality into question. While the episode teaches that knowledge, Charles explains, "Just because he had this gay friend, that shouldn't automatically make [Omar] gay."[56] Similarly, Cory disliked the mediated notion that Black gay men and Black heterosexual men cannot or should not be friends: "It was literally a big assumption. And that becomes more of an assumption when you have a lot of straight people who have a lot of gay friends and more and more straight people have gay friends. You can't make the assumption that this person's gay because of their friends."[57] In this way, the Black gay body also functions as a disciplinary body for Black masculinity by assuming that a Black heterosexual man is semiotically gay should he have a friendship with a gay man, Black or otherwise raced. Furthermore, Frank contends that "a lot of people might look at [the friendship between Tracy and Omar] as guilty by association, but that still doesn't necessarily define who and what you are and what you think about that person, or even if you are like that person. You could be straight and still defend or want to be friends with somebody that's not."[58] The men in this study not only disliked Omar being made gay by his association with Tracy but also expressed anger that such a narrative stance is pedagogical with respect to how friend groups operate. For them, the episode espoused an ideology that Black gay people should only have other Black gay people as friends and, conversely, that Black heterosexual men should only have Black heterosexual friends.

Samuel summarizes the narrative utility of Tracy and his introduction into the script: "Tracy was something of a plot device to move that story and to out Omar. Tracy drove the plot along in terms of Moesha telling her friends she thought Omar was gay. Through their friendship, Omar was considered gay by association."[59] Similarly, Charles suggests that "it was like they purposely juxtaposed these two parts [to present] Black gay men as a spectrum. We have this guy who's not really detectable. Could pass [as heterosexual] . . . And then you have Tracy, I was like, 'Oh, he's absolutely gay.' But the fact that they were friends . . . didn't naturally make me assume that [Omar] was gay. Although, I think that's what they wanted me to think."[60]

In the same vein, Ralph suggests that this semiotic gayness makes for a narrative detection game. He says of "Labels," "No one really knew for sure, but then you start hanging around people who are openly gay at that age, then it's like OK. The rumors start, 'Maybe he is, and we don't know. He's not saying anything.' Then . . . everyone wants to figure it out 'cause it's a puzzle . . . you *have* to know 'cause everyone needs to know everything."[61] This desire to know who is gay (and who is not) drives the Black-cast sitcom's engagement with Black gayness. It works (presumably) not only for heterosexual viewers but also for gay men because, as Gross observes, minority audiences often internalize the codes and conventions of majoritarian culture.[62]

Cory also observes semiotic gayness within *All of Us*, arguing that the only reason Luther was given a partner (Roosevelt) was as a "vehicle for the father to come out . . . [the partner] became just basically like an ornament on a tree."[63] In other words, Roosevelt had no real place within the scripts for "My Two Dads." or "Like Father, Like Son . . . Like Hell." Instead, his import lies in his ability to complete the semiotic chain for (presumably) Black heterosexual viewers.

The Black gay men in this study understand that the key within the Black-cast sitcom family is to expose deviance from heteronormativity by associating "obviously gay" characters with not-so-obviously gay characters, to ensure that the latter can be ferreted out and detected. Equally critical is that these Black gay men understand that Black-cast sitcoms are not necessarily for them. They are not part of the imagined audience, and they understand that the role of Black gay characters within each series is to be detectable as gay for the presumed heterosexual audience. The ability to detect gayness completes the crucial first step in constructing and, for them, deconstructing the Black-cast sitcom's generic closet.

DISCOVERING, DECLARING, AND DISCARDING BLACK GAY CHARACTERS

In each of the episodes discussed in this book, the Black gay characters had to come out as gay—regardless of whether or not they were comfortable with their own sexuality. It became, and has remained, an implicit part of the "contract" for Black gay characters granted tenure within the narrative confines of the Black-cast sitcom. As Joshua Gamson argues about talk shows, "homosexuality . . . is the love that is required to speak its name as quickly, clearly, and continuously as possible" because of its deviation from hegemonic normativity.[64] The same is true for Black gay characters within the Black-cast sitcom. As I will explore later in this chapter, and also as explored in chapter 2, the "coming out" within these episodes is never for the Black gay characters themselves; rather, its primary goal is knowledge production about Black gayness and then demonstrating the "coolness" of the series' core cast.

Colin expresses how coming out becomes tethered to external articulations within television discourse on *Moesha*. He comments, "I think Omar was just not self-disclosing, because he didn't shy away from engaging with Tracy when he approached him, whereas if he was [closeted] he may not have acted like he even knew him or distance himself from him, or not go out with him afterward."[65] Colin relied on two discursive sets in his reading of Omar. He articulated a kind of semiotic gayness that suggested that, because of the ways Black masculinity is mediated, only a Black gay man would not shy away from the more flamboyant Tracy. At the same time, Colin's reading suggested that Omar is already gay to himself, and as such, what is read as the coming out at the end of the episode is not a kind of liberation for Omar. It is more a mechanism for *Moesha*'s heterosexual cast rather than a political act showing that a person is proud and liberated from the oppression of homophobia within a heteronormative society.

Ralph conveys a similar reading of *Moesha*:

> Omar was somewhat out, but he didn't want anyone really to know, and then he happened to be around [Tracy]. He knew who he really was, but he really wasn't ready to accept it and let other people know that part of him. 'Cause especially when it comes to family, you kind of go, 'I'm not going to risk it yet.' Because you don't want the rejection, especially at that age. You're not out of the house, you don't want to cause any kind of trouble 'cause you hear the horror stories. Once you say you're gay, you're out of the house, no matter what. So, you keep it hidden as long as you can.[66]

Here, Ralph spoke to the calculated risks associated with coming out, particularly, as was the case in *Moesha*, when the character coming out as gay is a teenager. For Omar, then, Ralph reads him as not necessarily hiding but as a character concerned with his own well-being. In this way, Moesha telling her friends of her suspicion about Omar's homosexuality reads as potentially putting Omar's home life in jeopardy.

With *Moesha*, most of the men in this study continuously return to the notion that Omar's coming out was involuntary. Charles says, "Omar was pushed out of the closet, so to speak. It's not like, I wake up and, 'Hey, I'm gay!' one day.

That's not how it works. . . . It's more of a journey getting to the point where you can actually verbalize it. That moment where Omar tells Hakeem, you couldn't hear it. Like, he couldn't actually say it out loud. We did not hear him say, 'I'm gay.'"[67] Charles's reading is significant for at least three reasons. First, he cor-roborated the other men's reading that Omar is not yet ready to come out as gay but is forced to do so. Second, while the act of coming out is certainly an important rite of passage, it remains a development that, as Charles surmised, does not hatch as fully formed. In fact, several scholars have formulated iden-tity development models to explain the ways gay men (and sometimes lesbi-ans) make sense of their homosexuality. However, as I discussed in chapter 2, when factoring in race, some scholars found that the coming-out speech act is unnecessary for some Black gay men, for myriad reasons including the main-tenance of kinship networks and the perception of anti-gayness within imme-diate communities.[68] Third, and more importantly, Charles read the episode's coming-out imperative in contrast to Omar's self-proclamation of gayness. While Charles and the other men in this study read Omar's whispering to his cousin Hakeem as a coming out, he simultaneously reads the whispered com-ing out as rooted in Omar's unpreparedness to make a loud, verbal speech act.

Like "Labels" episode writer Bady, Andrew expresses the belief that "when it comes to coming out, I feel like that is something that you personally have to decide when you're ready to do it and who you do it to. To me, you don't have to broadcast your sexuality to the world. My brother, who's straight, doesn't have to walk around and let everybody know, 'Hey, I like to have sex with women.' So I don't feel, for the sake of equality, that's what gay people should have to do either."[69] Andrew read Omar, and disclosures of sexuality, more generally, as private affairs that should involve only the people who are engaging in sexual relationships with one another. Rather, Andrew noted the ways the insistence on a sexual confession is rooted in heterosexist knowledge production.

Thomas underscored this approach in *All of Us*: "Looking at the two men who at least appeared to be living together, I get the feeling that they were somewhat out already and it was a matter of coming out to the biological son."[70] While one can certainly argue that coming out as gay to one's biological son is critical, in *All of Us* it becomes the raison d'être for Luther's tenure within the series. Thomas continues, "In *Are We There Yet?*, he may have been out in some settings but not completely out."[71] Perhaps Thomas's reading is informed by his own coming-out story. He is openly gay in most aspects of his life but has not come out as gay to all of his family members because, he says, "I have an uncle who is very conservative."[72]

Kenneth goes further than Thomas and says Cedric "was so confident when he first came over. He didn't seem to be nervous. Then when Terry Crews asked him if he was gay, he was like, 'Yeah, I'm gay.' To him it was like what's the big deal?"[73] Kenneth underscores how homosexuality within these episodes is a matter of a failure to disclose, not necessarily because the men are trying to be devious. As the Black gay men I interviewed read these episodes, the Black gay characters are forced to confess their homosexuality.

The Black gay men in this chapter reported that they believed the Black gay characters could presumably be brought back as part of the series' casts. Ed. Weinberger suggested he could not think of any other gay stories for *Good News*, and Ralph Farquhar asserted that *Moesha* had done "the gay story." Nevertheless, the interviewees regaled me with stories in which Black gay characters could be integrated within the series. Charles offered that within *Good News*, he "felt like that character would be a part of the cast. I felt like that wasn't just gonna end there. Like, I felt like we would see more of him down the road."[74] Derek says, "I definitely felt like Eldridge would come back. I guess for comedic effect for the mother to try to be accepting but still have her comments on the side."[75] Derek's observation is important to parse; his understanding of the Black-cast sitcom's engagement with Black gayness is through comedic modes, and by extension, the generic closet. In particular, Derek suggests that Black gayness, as a long-term narrative proposition, is to provide the "setup" for jokes. Because Eldridge is the son of one of the series' regulars, and there is no mention of his visiting from out of town, Charles's and Derek's observations would seem within the realm of narrative possibility, although for Weinberger, that was not the way he wrote Eldridge.

Unlike Farquhar, Greg articulated *Moesha* stories that could continue to include Omar. He says, "Maybe we could have seen some more of that character and got Moesha to like him so it wasn't a big deal that he was gay. Why just stop at *that* particular point, we could have gone a little bit further with it? Within that same episode, or somewhere else along the way. Maybe he wants to be a brain surgeon or something, and she says, 'Wow, I thought all you cared about was fashion.'"[76] Greg indicated that Omar lacked a sense of character development outside of being gay. In other words, Omar was a gay teenager. Outside of his gayness, he had no character traits that might prove worthy of exploration; perhaps that is why Farquhar thought there were no more stories for the character.

The producers and writers for *All of Us* suggested that the series was canceled before they had a chance to write more stories that included Luther. However, Ralph expresses that "the dad in *All of Us* could definitely come back.

There could even be an episode where he says, 'Hey I'm getting married' and maybe asks his son to be a groomsman at his wedding."[77] To Andrew, Luther's exclusion after the two episodes in which he appears is strange because "his biological father seemed to be very much like him, which was another thing that I appreciate 'cause it was the fact that it gave dimension to being gay. It was like although he was just like you, he just has a different [sexual] orientation."[78]

Ralph is not at a loss for story ideas that could have kept Darkanian as part of the narrative fabric of *Let's Stay Together*. He suggests a story line: "How does society take an athlete getting married, while he's still in his professional career? The team dynamics, introducing him to the wives of the other players. How does his partner fit into the professional realm that he's in? Does he still stand in the background, down on the sideline or in the regular stand? Or is he going to be allowed into the press box with all the other wives and girlfriends of the professional athletes?"[79] Andrew adds, "One thing I really liked and I wish they would have continued on, was the fact that they were showing that gay relationships can be successful and it's not just about sex. It's legit. 'Hey, I have true feelings for you just like a heterosexual man and a heterosexual woman do.'"[80] Robert assumed that Darkanian and Greg "were actually regulars on the show after that point . . . I guess the episode ["Game Over"] when they're shooting the commercial, he accidentally outs himself on camera. That actually seemed to me like they were being introduced to be more regular characters on the show."[81] In Robert's reception, Darkanian's "outing" seems generative of story lines rather than the conclusion of his narrative arc. Again, this perspective demonstrates the disjuncture between how Black-cast sitcom production understands Black gayness within the context of a series versus the ways Black gay men read such characterizations. These Black gay men become not just consumers but producers within their reception practices. They express a desire to captain the ship that will navigate the ways Black gay stories will and can be told within the Black-cast sitcom.

Once (homo)sexuality is declared within the episode(s), it can be discarded. Although that discarding is somewhat expected, the Black gay men in this study were still disappointed by it. Cory says,

> I didn't think Omar [on *Moesha*] would come back. I just didn't. Eldridge in *Good News*, I didn't think he would come back. I definitely don't think his boyfriend would be back after that episode. Luther [on *All of Us*] may come back but the boyfriend probably wouldn't. He was just an extra. . . . They might refer back to him, but they would not bring him back. In *Are We There Yet?*, Cedric won't come back and the reason why I would say that is because

the girl is [. . .] looking to have her first boyfriend. . . . That's what you're going to see and that's the only reason that you won't see him. I don't think they really gave him enough depth to think, OK, we want to see this character again, . . . *Good News?* I don't think you'll see those two again ever. When [Black-cast sitcoms] delve into [Black gay] characters a little bit more, when they put more depth into a character where you can connect with them more, I think that it is likely that they'll bring them back for more episodes, but they're not if they're just bringing them in to talk about a theme or a story.[82]

The ways Cory read these Black gay characters is fascinating because it is less about the characters than it is about the Black-cast sitcom industry. First, he implicitly refers to a sense that while Black gay characters might be permissible within a Black-cast sitcom in the future, he simultaneously expresses his perception that Black gay couples are not. In this way, while Cory thought *Good News* might explore the possibility of bringing Eldridge back for subsequent episodes, there was no way he could imagine his boyfriend being brought back. At the same time, when he imagines a televisual world in which Luther is part of *All of Us* on an ongoing basis, he believes that audiences might know that Luther is partnered but that his partner would never emerge again. Second, and perhaps more importantly, Cory argued that the Black gay characters within these series lack depth, partly because they are introduced as a means to address other issues (a topic I explore more deeply in the next section of this chapter). In other words, Cory read these characters as simply gay. As an audience member, he knew little about these characters other than their sexuality. Alex articulates, "None of these people were regular characters. They're on for the purpose of being gay for this episode. So, what I want is a character that's on all the time that's gay and he could be closeted for a little while, he could do anything, you know. [. . .] This person was on this show just because he was gay and he's not going to be back."[83] Furthermore, Paul says, "I thought it would be great to see these characters, see what their lives were like in their own homes. I think that would be really brilliant. You don't really see that on TV."[84]

The easy discarding of Black gay characters is underscored by Eli, who says, "Fans would be like, 'Oh, OK.' Then next week the show doesn't have anything to do with Black gayness."[85] Or, as Colin says, "I felt like we've wrapped this particular issue up in thirty minutes, and then there'll be some other topic for the series next week."[86] Eli's and Colin's expectations of the Black-cast sitcom's engagement with Black gayness recall Sara Ahmed's theorization about inclusion. She argues that inclusion can "be read as a technology of governance: not only as a way of bringing those who have been recognized as strangers . . .

but also of making strangers into subjects, those who in being included are also willing to consent to the terms of inclusion."[87] In other words, the Black gay men I interviewed are well aware of the rules of their inclusion—even if it means that part of those rules includes their ultimate banishment from the Black-cast sitcom's tele-universe. Andrew speaks to this set of rules of inclusion by offering the caveat, "Of course, this is regular TV on a national network. They can't be too risqué 'cause ratings may go down and you don't want kids to be seeing this 'cause this might have an adverse effect on them and all the other BS people throw out there for why we can't show or face real life problems that are affecting our community."[88] While Derek says Darkanian's story would make an interesting arc on *Let's Stay Together*, he ultimately concluded that the Black-cast sitcom is disinterested in "normal guys being gay. Even though he was kind of thuggy and he's a football player, I don't think they would be into that kind of character being gay. I just don't think Black audiences would be into it at this time."[89] Greg adds, "I think that Black audiences have been brainwashed—and all people of color for that matter—to believe that [being gay is] not OK. And that's why TV shows and writers are scared to address those issues. And when they do, they'll go back to stereotypical stuff, and that'll be it."[90] These Black gay men reveal that Black gay characters' long-term inclusion in the Black-cast sitcom is a chicken-or-egg situation. On the one hand, these men suggest that the television industry remains conservative about Black LGBT issues on television. Andrew noted that the differences among broadcast, basic cable, and premium cable networks may hold the key to unlocking Black gay representation. On the other hand, the interviewees also articulated that Black-cast sitcom audiences are too conservative to be counted on to continuously and fannishly watch a series that regularly includes Black gay characters. Similar to a television industry executive's imagination of Black (heterosexual) audiences, many of the Black gay men in this chapter project these same configurations onto Black audiences.

These men remain disappointed in the representational parameters industrially placed around Black gayness. As Charles summarizes, "I think that's why I was a bit disappointed about [the "Labels" episode of *Moesha*], 'cause I felt like they were just gonna leave it there. Like, this conversation wasn't gonna come back up."[91] Samuel observes that within *Good News*, he "thought Eldridge might have been part of the series and that might have come up again. Guess that was his shot. I think it sucks, but then too it was at a time when homosexuality wasn't as accepted in the mainstream media as it is today. Now it's almost used as a tool to boost ratings and things."[92] Samuel's suggestion that represented homosexuality is contemporarily different than it was at the dawn of the Gay '90s is true, demonstrating his critical stance as a television viewer. However, the outlook has not changed for Black gayness within the Black-cast sitcom in the same ways as it has for white and Black gay characters within white- and multicultural-cast sitcoms.

Coming out, then, retains its import not as a device for these Black gay viewers but for the needs of the generic closet. Omar, Eldridge, Luther, Cedric, and Darkanian are introduced so that their gayness can be detected, discovered/ declared, and discarded. The writers and producers could generally not see a narrative way forward for their respective Black gay characters. However, the Black gay men I interviewed were not at a loss for ways these Black gay characters could be included in the series on which they appeared. In this sense, the men appear to understand that they are not the intended audience for these representations. This notion of Black gayness being decentralized from the Black-cast sitcoms on which they appear is the focus of the next section.

DECENTERING BLACK GAYNESS IN RECEPTION

As I discussed in chapters 2 and 3, homosexuality is decentered within the production and postproduction phases of the creation of Black-cast sitcom episodes with Black gay characters. Such encoding of Black gayness as secondary could be observed in *Moesha, Good News, All of Us, Let's Stay Together*, and *Are We There Yet?*, and the Black gay men in this study also decoded images of Black gay men in that vein.[93] As will become clear throughout this section, the Black gay men in this study voiced (and lamented) the marginality of their stories within Black-cast sitcoms. Although the narrative effectiveness of such decentering can be debated, the fact remains that Black gayness is made secondary within the narrative universes of these series.

Part of this problematic can be located within two schemata laid out by Isaac Julien and Kobena Mercer with respect to Blackness. I adapt their theorizations here to discuss Black gayness within the Black-cast sitcom. First, they observe that individual subjectivity is denied because Black gay characters are often "positioned as a mouthpiece, a ventriloquist for an entire social category which is seen to be 'typified' by its representative. . . . Secondly, where minority subjects are framed and contained by the monologic terms of 'majority discourse,' the fixity of boundary relations between center and margin . . . returns the speaking subject to the ideologically appointed place of the stereotype."[94] Julien and Mercer's observations are easily transferrable to a discussion of Black gayness within the Black-cast sitcom, particularly because this discursive move is observed by many of the Black gay men in this study.

Certainly, Black gay characters are not always stereotyped as flamboyant. But the fact remains that the function of Black gay characters is to come out as gay, to demonstrate the central cast's hipness with respect to Black gayness, and then to leave the series and never return. This section details some of the Black gay men's responses to this stereotypic use of Black gayness as a conduit to reinforce Black gayness as always secondary to the central concerns of the series discussed in this book.

The decentering of Omar is evident in what the Black gay men in this chapter read as the scene in which Omar comes out as gay. Alex notes, "He's so much not part of that story that you hear the main character reading a screwed-up song while what should be the main action is going on in silence. . . . To me, if Hakeem walked away from his cousin because he's gay, he was rewarded at the end of the episode and made to seem like a hero because he got his friend back."[95] The "screwed-up song" to which Alex refers is Edie Brickell's "What I Am." Moesha recites the lyrics of the song while Omar whispers in his cousin's ear (a whispering that is largely read as Omar telling his cousin that he is gay). For Alex, the absence of the speech act—the audible declaration of Omar's membership in the tribe called "homosexual"—is problematic and results in his reading that gayness is not truly what the episode wants to explore. In the silence that follows what is read as Omar's coming out, Hakeem walks away and is, in Alex's reception of the scene, rewarded by being reunited with Moesha. Alex's reading of Hakeem as "winning" at the end of the episode also speaks to the narrative necessities of the Black-cast sitcom to always re-center heterosexuality and to re-center the main characters and their relationship with viewers and fans of the series. Moesha, as a series composed of individual episodes, is more concerned with returning itself to stasis and not irrevocably changing the main characters or fans' relationship to them. Thus, Omar is expendable because the imagined Black viewers of the series have no relationship to him, and Hakeem and Moesha's relationship is one of the things that presumably keeps them tuning in weekly.

Moesha was most problematic for Derek because he anticipated that after Omar came out to his cousin that "they would go more into Hakeem's reaction" to actually engage with conversations about Black homosexuality.[96] Derek expressed that he hoped for a kind of engagement that at least suggested what Omar whispered to his cousin. Instead, the episode ends with Moesha in voiceover saying, "Dear Diary. Today I got my friend back," as Hakeem walks onto Moesha's porch.

Charles summarizes Moesha's decentering of Black gayness and Omar by suggesting that "Everything was kind of in relation to Moesha, or her friends . . . and not necessarily how [Omar] interacted with other people . . . It sort of almost wasn't really about him, although, it was about him. It was more like other people's perception . . . So, whether it was Moesha and her friends, or Moesha and her mom, they were kind of the hub of having the conversation, expressing and talking about [Black gayness]."[97] Charles's comments recall Michel Foucault's theorization that the gay "other" is an "object of information" about sexualities and their deviance from what is understood as "normal."[98] Charles's reading of heterosexuality as the "hub" of discussions about sexuality within *Moesha* underscores Black queer characters' exclusion from producing knowledge about homosexuality within the Black-cast sitcom; knowledge is produced *about* them. There is never an attempt to relate narratives from the perspective of the Black gay "other." Rather, he is always providing information about the hegemonic confines of "authentic" Blackness and Black masculinity.

Andrew indicates that the end of the episode does not provide a satisfying end to Omar's narrative. He says,

> I feel like that ending was so abrupt. Does Hakeem accept his cousin after coming out or is he just like, "Hey Moesha, I'm sorry I was mad at you when I'm actually mad at my cousin because he lied to me all this time." The ending was just like, "Hey Moesha, thanks for telling me the truth because now I know you weren't just lying to me so you're my true friend." That's a nice ending in terms of friendship, but what does that do with your relationship with your cousin? Are you still mad at him? Are you all talking through it? Do you not hang out with him no more because [of] the way it looks? [. . .] I feel like production felt like they hit their quota in terms of . . . Every sitcom seems to have their gay episode . . . I feel like they are just trying to check that box like . . . In addition to that, I feel like [in that episode] the producers wanted to focus more on the friendship of Moesha and Hakeem.[99]

Andrew underscores the work *Moesha*'s narrative engages to re-center "universal" themes like friendship—in this case, *heterosexual* friendship. In Andrew's reading of the conclusion of "Labels," Omar is narratively discarded in the interest of Moesha and Hakeem's friendship. Despite episode writer Demetrius Bady's suggestion that the absence of Omar's coming-out speech act meant that he was maintaining his sexuality for himself, Andrew read this as opening the door to discard his narrative.

Because Black queerness is decentered (and its corollary means that Black heterosexuality is centered), not only are Black heterosexual characters allowed to produce knowledge about Black homosexuality but some of the Black gay men in this study perceive that centering as being concerned with the teleology of *Moesha*'s recurring characters. Ralph suggests that the "Labels'" ending was written as such because

> The writers didn't want to put a main character into a light that would affect how you perceive him for the rest of the show. Because if you see, at the conclusion, Hakeem being very inclusive and saying, "I appreciate you" and stuff like that, that makes that character, in some people's eyes, a weaker character.... You're not really a man. Or if you say, "No, I'm not going to like my cousin anymore," you get the opposite. You get people going, "He's insensitive, he's not really a cool person." [...] I think the writers are trying to get to a point where if the characters are deep enough, viewers can draw their own conclusion on how Hakeem would really take it.[100]

Two points are worth exploring within Ralph's reading. First, he works within a hegemonic understanding of the discursive functions of Black masculinity. Herman Gray theorizes that popular culture's construction of Black masculinity is exemplified by "drugs, sexism, pleasure, excess, nihilism, defiance, pride and the cool pose of disengagement," which are all part of the "style, personality, vision and practice of an assertive heterosexual black masculinity."[101] Gray's theorization of the mass-mediated imagination of Black masculinity coincides with Ralph's observation of Black masculinity, in which heterosexuality and homosexuality do not and cannot televisually coexist. Because of Black masculinity's mediation within popular culture, the kind of semiotic gayness to which the Black gay men referred earlier in this chapter recurs and suggests that acceptance of homosexuality is connected to a loss of the credentials associated with "authentic" Black masculinity. Second, Ralph's ascription of viewer reading position is important. On the one hand, the assumption that viewers can decode messages about Black gayness within *Moesha* without a heavy hand is laudable. On the other hand, in so doing, Ralph positions *Moesha*'s producers and writers as being cognizant of the long-term effects any positionality with respect to Black gayness might have on the male characters within the series, in this case, Hakeem. The narrative necessity of maintaining Hakeem's claim to Black masculinity outweighs the episode's need to provide a welcoming environment for Black gayness.

As discussed in chapter 2, *Good News* also decenters gayness within the production process. However, within the reception process, some Black gay men were uncomfortable with the decentering, even as they understood its attempts to neutralize Black gayness as an "issue." Ralph encapsulates the tension that emerges in the reception of *Good News* by these Black gay men:

> What was great about the episode was that the mother was like, "I knew your entire life [that you were gay]. I knew before you even knew." The extreme part came when, "I'm dating a white guy who happens to be Irish who wants to come visit the church." And that's when it was like, OK, so you're totally fine with your son being gay, but then it comes into a whole different realm when his boyfriend is white. [...] I don't think the episode was geared more towards a parent's love for their gay son, it was more towards, here is the interracial relationship that's going to be more in your face, and how can you deal with it? I think that's what the episode was trying to deal with more.... It focused a lot more on the interracial relationship aspect of it. Here's your son, he's gay. But the first gay encounter he's going to bring is this really white guy that your friends will turn their heads to, and talk about within the church.... So, this is really what it boils down to: it's fine that he's gay, but it's bad that he's dating someone outside of the race.[102]

Ralph decoded the episode's quick disposal of gayness as a ploy to recalibrate the narrative focus onto one of the main (heterosexual) character's feelings. In particular, Ralph was troubled by what, to him, felt like a false sense of where the narrative led him to believe it would go. He continues, "The thing that got me was still, OK we got the gay character out the way, and the mom's accepting of it, but she—and even the preacher had this, 'Oh my god' moment about him dating someone who is white. So, the episode really was halfway about building up to this gay character coming out. But it was really more about how do you receive the love of someone who's not raised in the church."[103] While Thomas felt similarly, he understood the quick resolution of the "gay issue" to be "refreshing and unexpected" even as he recognized that in doing so, the narrative failed to focus on the gay character and his feelings.[104]

Colin was similarly mixed in his reception of *Good News*, partly because the episode's narrative thrust was aligned with the heterosexual members of the cast:

> I had a lot of mixed feelings about *Good News*. I felt it focused a little bit too much on the new minister and trying to work his way in with the congregation. And just knowing what the message for the episode was supposed to be about, I think I would have liked to have seen more of the focus on that. But I kind of get that the whole point was that the church had a new minister with a new mindset, and we're going to get past the hatred and the bigotry and the "old-school" way of thinking [...] and this was a story to draw from as an example of that.[105]

Colin's comments represent the ways Black gayness is often decentered within narratives on Black-cast sitcoms. In his estimation, gayness stands in for a broader set of ideological issues within the series writ large. The episodic appearance of Black gayness, then, represents a sense of progressiveness that seeks to break the (fictional) semiotic chain that links conservative ways of thinking, Black gayness, and religiosity.

While recognizing this progressive stance, the episode does so by quickly resolving gayness. William says, "Eldridge says he's gay, and they go right through that and the mother has more of a problem with [his boyfriend] being white . . . Actually, at that point, I was like that was just playing for laughs here, playing for what they think the audience will understand or something."[106] William's comment emphasizes an imagined audience member and, by extension, an audience whose cognitive registers are predictable with respect to humor and comedy. He surmises that the reason Eldridge's story (and Black gayness, more broadly) is obscured lies in its inability to conform to (an imagined) audience member's expectations—expectations that he, as a Black gay man, does not share.

Thomas also recognizes the ways dominant ideologies about Black gayness are related to Black churches. He expresses, "Having this immediate acceptance about the character's sexual orientation was a bit of a surprise. So, I kept thinking, OK, so that's not a problem. So, what *is* the problem?"[107] Thomas clearly understands the Black-cast sitcom's narrative function and how Black gayness has been presented within them. Because sitcom episodes always have a "problem" that needs to be solved within a single episode, he automatically assumed that gayness would be the problem of the week.

Concomitantly, Alex, who is in an interracial relationship himself, finds the move from coming-out to cross-racial dating unfulfilling because the episode's story ended with "another moment when you've got singing and all this stuff going on and you totally lost sight of Eldridge. He wasn't an active participant in that scene. You hear singing and you have to see the story in kind of pantomime. So, you have to guess what the characters are saying and nobody's talking."[108] The scene to which Alex refers is the last scene of the episode when Eldridge's mother finally meets his white boyfriend, Daniel. Similar to how *Moesha*'s "Labels" episode handled its "big scene," *Good News* does not use dialogue to convey the story; instead, the main action is acted out over gospel music. For Alex, this use of music (and the absence of dialogue) works as a tool to remove Eldridge's agential positionality from the episode. He continues, "You decided to not have words and you decided to pull the focus of that story with other stuff."[109] Michael similarly says, "They didn't characterize Eldridge very well,

at all. He was just kind of a backdrop for the other story."[110] Michael's suc-
cinct observation gets to the heart of the Black-cast sitcom's engagement with
Black gayness. The genre gestures toward including Black gayness, but it is only
imagined as a conduit for other "mainstream" stories that deal with the series'
otherwise heterosexual cast.

For many Black gay men in this study, the Black-cast sitcom rarely engages
with the *fact of Black gayness*. Here, I borrow from and extend Franz Fanon's
"fact of blackness," in which he argues, "As long as the black man is among his
own, he will have no occasion, except in minor internal conflicts, to experience
his being through others."[111] The fact of Black gayness inverts the fact of Blackness and forces dominant Black scripts to reckon with a major conflict—one
that challenges the monolithic imagination of Black masculinity. In so doing,
the Black-cast sitcom, as an imagined vanguard of Black masculinity, fails to
fully explore the pink elephant in the room—the Black gay man. As such, the
Black gay man can be temporarily permitted into the space but cannot be understood as a primary focus.

The Black gay men in this chapter read *All of Us* as reiterating this epistemological decentering. Thomas observes that "it was more surface . . . So, there's
no conversation about being gay, but we're more focused on how [the news]
impacts [Robert]."[112] Similarly, Alex says that "the fact that he was gay, it was
a plot point, you know? The story didn't start on it. The story you know hinted
on it at the end and then it went boom! to other things."[113] Colin argues that
"from my perspective, the gay dad part of the story was not really the focus . . .
it seemed like the focus was more around [Robert] being abandoned [by his
biological father]. [. . .] The gay part of it was shocking but [Robert] quickly
accepted that, and then it went into what it is to be a dad and to be a man."[114]
Thomas and Colin read the pair of *All of Us* episodes as forgoing the particular
for the universal. The assumptive stance of the series is that Black gayness is too
specific for its viewership, thus it focuses on the universal themes of fatherhood
and Black manhood.

The episodes deploy Black gayness to demonstrate the intra-series lib-
eralness of its main cast, leading Colin to remark on the speed with which
Robert accepts Luther's gayness. The position of Black gayness within the *All
of Us* episodes is best described as tolerance—the series does not fully embrace Black gayness but allows it to exist within the series for a short period
of time.[115] At the same time, this acceptance is ultimately concerned with
producing knowledge about the main heterosexual cast; once the episodes
produce that knowledge, Black gayness can be expunged from *All of Us*'s
narrative universe.

Thomas, Alex, and Colin read the *All of Us* episodes similarly, whereas Andrew approves of the script's lack of dwelling on Luther's gayness. "I feel everybody wasn't hung up so much on the fact that he was gay. It was like that few minutes and then it was done."[116] Andrew seems to be subscribing to a post-gay logic that longs to see Black gay images on television but does not want Black gayness to seem strange or different. In heralding the "few minutes" the series dwells on Luther's gayness, Andrew (unlike the other Black gay men I interviewed) seemed to find the deemphasis pleasurable because it diminished its difference. Similar to Gray's argument that assimilationist television discourses construct televisual worlds in which differences are marginalized "in the interest of shared and universal similarity," Andrew notes that he prefers a televisual space in which gayness is flattened in the interest of downplaying (homo)sexual difference as a strategy to gain acceptance into the Black-cast sitcom's televisual world.[117]

Within "The Boy Has Style," Dave similarly appreciates how gayness was made unimportant within the episode. He says that Terry Cruz's Nick "talking to Cedric really redeemed it for me. And it really put the focus on what was important here. Not that this man is gay, but the fact that he could hurt your daughter ... that should have showed people that watched that that's not a good lie to tell. [...] It's a lie about who you are, and that's what I got from that [...]. And I thought it was done responsibly."[118] What is important about Andrew's and Dave's readings of the secondary nature of Black gayness is that Andrew, in many ways, empathized (and perhaps sympathized) with the episode's heterocentric stance. Gross argues that "those of us who belong to a minority group may nevertheless have absorbed the values of the dominant culture, even if these exclude or diminish us."[119] In this instance, Andrew understands Cedric's failure to disclose his sexuality as deceitful. His reading re-centers heterosexuality and privileges Nick's attempt to protect his daughter over Cedric's agency to have his sexuality be his own—despite other heterosexual expectations.

Conversely, Charles finds the centering of the needs and desires of the heterosexual characters problematic: He says,

> I had a problem with them telling him, "You need to tell my daughter that you're gay, because she likes you." I don't feel like he should have to tell her that just because she likes him. What he can tell her is, "I'm not interested in you," but why does he have to come out of the closet in order to curb her? If he's not interested in her, he doesn't have interest in her. His reasons why are his reasons. But all she needs to know is he don't like her like that. ... I mean if she asked why, I guess he can tell her. But, to lead with, "You need to tell my daughter that you're gay," I was kind of like, "Um, yeah, I don't know about that."[120]

Charles expresses a belief that one's sexuality is a private matter that does not have to be disclosed for someone else's benefit. And in some ways, Charles suggests that "they pushed Cedric out the closet" because it ultimately worked to recalibrate the episode's focus so that homosexuality was transformed into a conversation about Lindsey's (misplaced or misconstrued) feelings.[121]

Andrew sums up his reading of all of the episodes in this book when he says, "I feel like these episodes didn't really touch on the sexuality. I feel like a lot of them had multiple areas they were hitting. They weren't 'The Gay Episode,' they were like, 'The Episode that We Sprinkled Gay On.'"[122] This notion of "sprinkling gay on" an episode is picked up by Paul, who says that the episodes were "brought in for shock value . . . let's introduce this gay story so that everybody can go, 'Oh.'"[123] Both Andrew and Charles acknowledge the notion of progressivity inherent, particularly in the Gay '90s, in adding gay characters to a series for an episode or so to seem hip and edgy. However, within Black-cast sitcoms, this hipness and edginess was limited. Black gay characters can be part of *Moesha, Good News, All of Us, Let's Stay Together,* and *Are We There Yet?* for an episode or two, but they can never be understood as an ongoing fixture of the Black-cast sitcom.

LAUGHING AT AND WITH BLACK QUEENS

As I discussed in chapter 3, the laugh track works as an ideological tool that highlights who and what is funny. I brought my own theoretical understanding of humor and the laugh track to that chapter. In this section, I highlight how several Black gay men in this study discussed the problematic use of humor and the laugh track in the episodes they watched. Paul said that all of the Black-cast sitcoms in this book were a combination of laughing at and laughing with the Black gay characters "because of the strangeness of being gay in that situation. I think there was a nervous laughter at sort of the exotic nature of it."[124] I connect Paul's comments with Simon Critchley's observation that the things we laugh at barely disguise that we are troubled by the thing at which we laugh.[125] Homosexuality's "exotic" positionality makes it a permissible site for laughter.

Alex suggests that the use of laugh tracks for shows that are not funny, particularly in relationship to Black gay characters, was troubling. For Black-cast sitcoms more broadly, he complains that "they're not really funny . . . and they have these horrific laugh tracks."[126] Robert addresses the laugh track and its stakes more directly. He says, "The laugh track tells you that this is a joke and that you should laugh at it just like the audience in the laugh track. . . . When the audience reacts, like, 'Oh, my God,' it's telling the audience that they should also be shocked that this person is gay."[127]

Colin reads Tracy as having been "introduced for humor, sort of to poke fun at the stereotypical flamboyant gay person that, when I think at the time, for that period, when people thought of gay people that's how they thought they looked and acted and dressed."[128] Greg observes this as well. He says the laugh track was meant to ridicule Tracy, a ridiculing that was made particularly obvious in the scene in which Moesha and Omar meet Tracy.[129] He continues, "The audience's response [to Tracy] is what killed the episode for me. . . . I really liked that episode. The only problem I had was with the live audience and the laughing and their reaction."[130] Similarly, Dave describes the laugh track within "Labels" as telling "the audience that [gayness] is not at all cool."[131] He says the laugh track was designed to mark gayness as something that exists outside of hegemonic constructions of Black masculinity.

Greg makes an important distinction between the laugh track and in-studio laughter when he deduces that *Moesha* used "real" laughter versus a laugh track and that he finds the laughter disrespectful. He suggests that the laughter was in some ways premature and that the story was not allowed to develop before the audience laughter instructed the at-home audience how to decode the episode: "It was like you have to wait to see where we're going with all of this before you turn your nose up at it."[132] In his suggestion that the laugh track was "real," Greg "blames" the laughter of a presumed Black audience for an antigay stance versus having held a belief that the laugh track was or could be positioned in postproduction. Greg implicitly critiques the presumed Black heterosexual in-studio audience. Whether his understanding of their laughter is real or imagined, his interpretation implies that the imagined Black audience is always already antigay. He more explicitly states his distaste for the ways "Labels" positioned Black gayness. Historical Black gay mediation has conditioned Greg's expectation that most Black gay characters will be more flamboyant because TV makers "still have an obligation to make audiences laugh. But I hated that they chose to have the same old stereotypically loud person [Tracy]. I recognize this is still a business. This is a comedy that has to make people laugh, but it's unfortunate that's the way they chose to do it."[133]

Thomas describes some jokes, particularly those related to gender binaries within relationships, as disconcerting. Within *All of Us*, he observes, "The thing that sort of keeps coming to mind were that there were stereotypical jokes about gay men. 'Who's the man? Who's the woman?' Like, why do they always go there?"[134] For Thomas, the jokes within *All of Us* worked to map heterosexist logics onto queer relationships, ultimately suggesting that one partner must always perform a prescribed or preassigned sexual role. At the same time, Thomas's flagging of the gendered joke in *All of Us* speaks to the problematic cultural ways the receptive partner is understood as the one assuming the "woman's" role in queer relationships. Here, Thomas's reading is (intentionally or not) informed by Alan Sinfield's theorization of the "classic inversion model of the 'passive' male homosexual; he wants to be female and his desire, like that conventionally expected in a woman, is for a man."[135] The joke turns on "conventional" heterosexist "wisdom" about homosexuality and, as such, functions as two-faced humor that, importantly, does not include a gay person either within the scene or within production (with enough agency and power in production to speak up about the joke) to refute the reductive nature of the joke.[136] Part of what makes this joke permissible is that the "joke" is presumably "among friends," clearly articulating its two-facedness.

As the Black gay men demonstrate, when viewing images that are designed to represent one's identity group, the laugh track is difficult to ignore. In the episodes they watched, the respondents felt the laugh track was used as a device to make fun of Black gayness and position it as a thing that exists outside of hegemonic understandings of Blackness generally and Black masculinity specifically. At the same time, it works as a tool to make Black gayness secondary—an act of decentering. Like an audible controlling image, the Black gay men discussed the laugh track as simultaneously hailing them and then holding them up as abject objects of derision and humor.

PRODUCING BLACK GAY CHARACTERS
OUTSIDE THE GENERIC CLOSET

Many of the Black gay men interviewed in this chapter find the Black-cast sitcom's representations of Black gay men lacking. However, each of the study participants offered ideas for changing Black gay representation to make it feel more representative, inclusive, and fair to them. Their suggestions for "fixing" Black gay televisual representation are often fraught with contradictions, inadvertently underscoring the difficulty associated with getting representation "right." To create a Black gay character that would meet Michael's expectations, he suggests that the character should "have gay friends, live a gay lifestyle, but still have a circle of friends some that know and some that don't know because they don't need to. But I also think that if they really wanted to expound on relationships where you have to actually tell a person that you're gay, just make sure that it's the right relationship and it's a relationship that you think that you want to maintain or move to another level, and that's why you're telling them."[137] Ultimately, Michael argues that a Black gay character should be as fully developed as any other character a writer might write, echoing what Mary Beltrán calls "meaningful diversity." For Beltrán, four questions help to determine if representations are meaningful or if they are simply filling a quota for diverse representation: "1) Are the characters of color fully realized individuals? 2) Do the writers and producers appear knowledgeable about and interested in the worlds and perspectives of the non-white characters? 3) Does the diversity of the cast appear natural? 4) Do the . . . producers exploit the natural diversity of a story's setting or subject matter?"[138]

William articulates that the key to better Black gay representation is more representations within the same series. He says, "If you get to have only one Black gay character in your sitcom, I suspect there are more of us out there who don't fit that stereotype than do."[139] Cory adds that he would like to see a broader spectrum of Black gay characters within a single series. "You have the so-called 'hood rat' out there and then you have people who claim to be 'the intelligentsia' and they're smarter than everybody and they're better than everybody and they set themselves apart. So you have the entire spectrum of society in gay people and I'd like to see that on a TV show."[140] By presenting more Black gay characters (quantitatively speaking) within the same series, there is a greater likelihood that those viewers of the show would see a broader view of Black gayness. In other words, as some respondents in this study suggested, nothing is explicitly problematic with effeminate Black gay characters; rather, there are issues with characterizations being presented as the *only* way Black gayness can be mediated. This stance is similar to Farquhar's rationale for including Tracy in the "Labels" episode.

Samuel communicates that writers and producers of Black-cast sitcoms "need to represent gays in a broader sense."[141] He points to *Teen Wolf* (MTV, 2011–2017) as a series that broadly mirrors the way that he'd like to see Black gay men represented: "The show's very, very diverse. . . . There are gay couples and things like that and they reoccur on the show. [Writers on] Black sitcoms should watch how they integrate that into just the daily lives of these characters. . . . [The episodes] still have humor, and it seems seamless to me."[142] For Samuel, Black-cast sitcoms need to take the emphasis off coming-out narratives. Using *Teen Wolf* as an exemplar, Samuel says the series does not feature "plot twists that focus on [the main character] being gay . . . You just have this person who fits seamlessly in this world. They aren't making his gayness a big deal . . . But then too, it's a white show." Samuel observes an industrial difference between white- and Black-cast television's relationship to gayness and to what he perceives as the limitations of genre and target audience. He implicitly suggests that white gayness is more easily situated within white televisual worlds than Black ones. I argue that part of this exclusion of Black gayness from Black narrative worlds and formats is rooted in a reluctance to include Black gayness as a normative part of Blackness and, by extension, the imagination of Black audiences. In other words, because the television industry understands Black gayness as existing outside of hegemonic Blackness, it can be excluded from "authentically" Black-cast sitcoms.

Alex adds,

I think that I would actually like to see gay characters like on *Downton Abbey* [PBS, 2010–2015], where they actually have characters and you know them and then all of a sudden, you say, "Oh, they're gay," and you didn't know at the beginning. I find that really fascinating. I want to see regular Black gay characters and make them part of the story line. When I was watching these shows [in the study] I thought, "I would try to have an actually funny show with Black gay characters as part of the story line." Not just in one episode and then put away.[143]

Alex suggests a post-gay approach to gay representation would be useful in the Black-cast sitcom. He calls for television sitcoms in which Black gayness is a minor part of the story line. In other words, there is no need for an "official" coming-out episode; rather, viewers learn that the character is gay through exposition. In addition, to find a representation that can be used as a model for the Black-cast sitcom's engagement with Black gayness, Alex must turn not only to a different genre (the historical period drama) but also to whiteness.

Colin similarly cedes comedy to heteronormativity and focuses on drama as the space for more nuanced and developed Black gay characters:

My concern is with comedy, while you can still get some points across and you have the messages embedded between the laughter, I think you just get more engrossed and more involved, and it feels more believable, and it's more memorable when it's embedded in a serious format, or a drama, a genre that is taken seriously. It's receiving recognition or Emmys, and it's well written, and it's well acted, and you've got respected actors and actresses who are being a part of the series and the drama and dealing with real issues and problems and drawing attention to abuse or intolerance or hatred, or whatever. Whereas a comedy's shorter period of time doesn't allow you to get as engrossed in the story lines, because it's typically going to have the happy ending, and because it's designed to make you laugh.[144]

Colin's critique of Black gay representation hinges not only on genre but notions of quality. His assumption is that drama can do things that the sitcom cannot in terms of storytelling, which involves story line developments that are assumed to be more complex. He implicitly argues that to tell Black gay stories, it is necessary to tell them in a complex manner. Colin's comments also echo "quality TV" discourses, which cite acting, cinematography, and, increasingly, network brand, to explain drama's "better" ability to develop and represent Black gay characters. For example, Black-cast dramas such as *The Haves and the Have Nots* (OWN, 2013–present) and *Empire* (Fox, 2015–2020) include costarring Black gay characters whose gayness ultimately becomes secondary to their character's development. Ultimately, he contends that comedy generally and the Black-cast sitcom specifically are unable to articulate a complex portrait of Black gayness, even as they do a more thorough job with Black heterosexual characters.

Taken together, the Black gay men in this chapter have articulated two broad ways they hope Black gayness develops within the Black-cast sitcom. First, writers and producers should reject the gay tokenism that has become a pervasive representational strategy, in which a single Black gay character is called on to represent all Black gayness within a series or episode. These single characters carry the burden of representation, whereby they must embody all that viewers know about Black gayness. As the men in this study have illuminated, when there is a single Black gay character, it is nearly impossible for the character to be all things to all people. Second, addressing the burden of representation that single Black gay characters are called on to carry, the men in this study argue that more representations are needed to allow the spectrum of Black gayness to be mass-mediated. About half of the men in this study cited the Logo series *Noah's Arc* (Logo, 2005–2006) as a model that adequately demonstrated a fuller spectrum of Black gayness on television. The half-hour dramedy followed the lives and loves of four Black gay men in Los Angeles. The series featured characters who spoke to the myriad ways Black gayness can exist, from hegemonically masculine characters to the effete. The men in this study suggest that if there are multiple Black gay characters, it becomes more difficult to find the use of stereotypes problematic.

RECEPTION INSIDE THE GENERIC CLOSET

The Black gay men I interviewed do not have the language of the "generic closet" to articulate and shape their discussions of Black gay representation. But the fact remains that they see Black gay representation as a game of detection, discovery/declaration, and discarding. As a three-step process, the use of subtle clues, which are often manifest through sartorial choices like color combinations and earrings, jump start the "game" of detecting Black gayness, These series deploy semiotics to lay the foundations for these characters being construed as "not quite right." Part of the efficacy of the generic closet is that it positions Black gayness as an "issue of the week" that, once detected, can be used as a form of knowledge production for the cast and, by extension, the at-home audience. Coming out becomes a demanded and necessary speech act that is often out of sync with how these Black gay men come to understand their own sexuality. Seven of the men in this study are not out to everyone in their lives, but that does not preclude them from identifying themselves as Black gay men. However, coming out to literally anyone—a cousin, a schoolmate, the church pastor, a parent, an adult child, or a schoolmate's family—is necessary for the generic closet's functioning. The interviewees share that coming out within the context of *Moesha, Good News, All of Us, Let's Stay Together,* and *Are We There Yet?* is an act for others, not for the Black gay characters.

Finally, once the Black gay character has come out, his utility within the series has been exhausted. The men read this discarding as not only an act of constituting and reconstituting the generic closet but as a way to decenter gayness. Within the act of decentering Black gayness, the men in this chapter demonstrate an understanding that the Black-cast sitcom is not telling these Black gay stories "for them" but for an imagined Black heterosexual audience.

Relatedly, the secondary nature of gayness is deployed as comic—Black gayness can be hailed and then held up as a space within which the series can find humor. They read the laugh track and the humor within the episodes as working against the ways they decoded the episodes. More than that, the men in this chapter expressed an oppositional reading of the laugh track. The laugh track was instructing laughter, but the instruction was not for them. For these Black gay men, the laugh track is presumed to represent Black heterosexual audiences that are always already hostile to the presence of Black gayness within the series. Crucially, because each series uses a laugh track, five of the Black gay men noted that these series' humor is almost entirely manufactured. In other words, jokes that are not necessarily funny can be forced to be "funny" through the use of the laugh track. And while the laugh track is meant to be a device for creating community, the Black gay men here find that it isolates and decenters their story.

They still hope for more representations that feature Black gayness as a component of the Black gay character's otherwise intersectional identity. This chapter demonstrates their ability to develop scenarios that would keep Black gayness as a part of Black-cast sitcoms. They suggest they want more Black gay characters within the Black-cast sitcom to lessen the burden of representation that single Black gay characters are asked to carry. It is not that any single representation is false but rather that one Black gay representation has to be all things to all (Black queer) people. Ultimately, the Black gay men in this study read episodes of *Moesha, Good News, All of Us, Let's Stay Together,* and *Are We There Yet?* in multivalent ways, but one thing is clear: they read these Black gay representations within the language of the generic closet.

NOTES

1. Foucault, *Discipline and Punish,* 200.

2. Dwight A. McBride, "Can the Queer Speak? Racial Essentialism, Sexuality and the Problem of Authority," in *The Black Studies Reader,* ed. Jacqueline Bobo, Cynthia Hudley, and Claudine Michel (New York: Routledge, 2004).

3. Janet Staiger, *Media Reception Studies* (New York: New York University Press, 2005), 165.

4. John Fiske, *Television Culture* (New York: Routledge, 2006), 62.

5. David Morley, *Television, Audiences, and Cultural Studies* (New York: Routledge, 1992), 54.

6. Hawkeswood, *One of the Children.*

7. Essex Hemphill, "In Living Color: Toms, Coons, Mammies, Faggots, and Bucks," in *Out in Culture: Gay, Lesbian, and Queer Essays on Popular Culture,* ed. Corey K. Creekmur and Alexander Doty (Durham, NC: Duke University Press, 1995).

8. Alan Bell, quoted in Hemphill, "In Living Color," 393, 392.

9. Doty, *Making Things Perfectly Queer,* xi.

10. Jacqueline Bobo, *Black Women as Cultural Readers* (New York: Columbia University Press, 1995); Michael DeAngelis, *Gay Fandom and Crossover Stardom: James Dean, Mel Gibson, and Keanu Reeves* (Durham, NC: Duke University Press, 2001); Frederick Dhaenens, "Gay Representation, Queer Resistance, and the Small Screen: A Reception Study of Gay Representations among Flemish Fans of Contemporary Television Fiction," Working Papers Film and TV Studies WP2011/1 (2011), https://www.ugent.be/ps/communicatiewetenschappen/cims /en/publications/working-papers/gay-representation-queer-resistance.htm; Richard Dyer, *Heavenly Bodies: Film Stars and Society* (London: Routledge, 2003); Brett Farmer, *Spectacular Passions: Cinema, Fantasy, Gay Male Spectatorship* (Durham, NC: Duke University Press, 2000); Gross, "Out of the Mainstream"; Alfred L. Martin Jr., "Fandom while Black: Misty Copeland, Black Panther, Tyler Perry, and the Contours of US Black Fandoms," *International Journal of Cultural Studies* 22, no. 6 (2019): 737–753; Coleman, *African American Viewers*; Rebecca Wanzo, "African American Acafandom and Other Strangers: New Genealogies of Fan Studies," *Transformative Works and Cultures* 20 (2015),

https://journal.transformativeworks.org/index.php/twc/article/view/699/538;
Kristen Warner, "ABC's *Scandal* and Black Women's Fandom," in *Cupcakes, Pinterest, and Ladyporn: Feminized Popular Culture in the Early Twenty-First Century*, ed. Elana Levine (Champaign: University of Illinois Press, 2015).

11. Lewis, *Ideological Octopus*, 89.

12. Eli, interview with author (Denver), February 20, 2017.

13. Coleman, *African American Viewers*, 269.

14. Clifford Geertz, *The Interpretation of Cultures* (New York: Basic Books, 2000), 26.

15. Jhally and Lewis, *Enlightened Racism*, 9.

16. Because "My Two Dads" was pt. 2 of a two-part episode, I asked the respondents in this study to watch both parts.

17. Gitlin, *Inside Prime Time*, 203.

18. See Michael C. LaSala, "When Interviewing 'Family': Maximizing the Insider Advantage in the Qualitative Study of Lesbians and Gay Men," *Journal of Gay and Lesbian Social Services* 15, nos. 1–2 (2003): 17; Alford A. Young Jr., "Coming Out from under the Ethnographic Interview," in *Workshop on Interdisciplinary Standards for Systematic Qualitative Research*, ed. Michèle Lamont and Patricia White (Washington, DC: National Science Foundation, 2008), 172.

19. Patricia Hill Collins, "Learning from the Outsider Within: The Sociological Significance of Black Feminist Thought," *Social Problems* 33, no. 6 (1986): s14.

20. Eli, interview.

21. Ibid.

22. Thomas, interview with author (Austin), September 20, 2014.

23. Derek, interview with author (Denver), January 12, 2017.

24. Colin, interview with author (Austin), October 29, 2014.

25. Ibid.

26. Ibid.

27. Ralph, interview with author (Austin), September 21, 2014.

28. Paul, interview with author (New York), June 22, 2016.

29. Kenneth, interview with author (Denver), October 12, 2016.

30. Dave, interview with author (Austin), December 2, 2013.

31. Ibid.

32. Charles, interview with author (Austin), February 15, 2014.

33. Andrew, interview with author (Austin), January 20, 2014.

34. Cory, interview with author (Austin), December 21, 2013.

35. Alex, interview with author (Austin), December 27, 2013.

36. Robert, interview with author (New York), June 6, 2016.

37. Frank, interview with author (Denver), August 15, 2017.

38. Anthony, interview with author (Austin), November 25, 2013.

39. Greg, interview with author (Austin), November 12, 2013.

40. Raphael, interview with author (New York), April 4, 2016.

41. William, interview with author (Austin), December 18, 2013.

42. Ibid.

43. Michael, interview with author (Austin), May 15, 2013.

44. Samuel, interview with author (New York), May 3, 2016.

45. Cobb and Coleman, "Two Snaps and a Twist," 86.

46. Andrew, interview.

47. UrbanDictionary.com, s.v. "Gay Ear," http://www.urbandictionary.com
/define.php?term=Gay%20Ear; UrbanDictionary.com, s.v. "Right Earring Rule,"
http://www.urbandictionary.com/define.php?term=Right%20Earring%20Rule.

48. Frank, interview.

49. Alex, interview. *Clock* is a colloquial term meant to signify the ways that
one detects another's sexuality.

50. Ibid.

51. Anthony, interview.

52. Ralph, interview.

53. Ibid.

54. Kenneth, interview.

55. Cory, interview.

56. Charles, interview.

57. Cory, interview.

58. Frank, interview.

59. Samuel, interview.

60. Charles, interview.

61. Ralph, interview.

62. Gross, "Out of the Mainstream," 139.

63. Cory, interview.

64. Gamson, *Freaks Talk Back*, 70.

65. Colin, interview.

66. Ralph, interview.

67. Charles, interview.

68. Martinez and Sullivan, "African American Gay Men and Lesbians," 252.

69. Andrew, interview.

70. Thomas, interview.

71. Ibid.

72. Ibid.

73. Kenneth, interview.

74. Charles, interview.

75. Derek, interview.

76. Greg, interview.

77. Ralph, interview.

78. Andrew, interview.

79. Ralph, interview.

80. Andrew, interview.

81. Robert, interview.

82. Cory, interview.

83. Alex, interview.

84. Paul, interview.

85. Eli, interview.

86. Colin, interview.

87. Sara Ahmed, *On Being Included: Racism and Diversity in Institutional Life* (Durham, NC: Duke University Press, 2012), 163.

88. Andrew, interview.

89. Derek, interview.

90. Greg, interview.

91. Charles, interview.

92. Samuel, interview.

93. Stuart Hall, "Encoding/Decoding," in *Culture, Media, Language: Working Papers in Cultural Studies, 1972–79,* ed. Stuart Hall, Dorothy Hobson, AnColin Lowe, and Paul Willis (London: Routledge, 1991), 136–138.

94. Isaac Julien and Kobena Mercer, "Introduction: De Margin and De Centre," *Screen* 29, no. 4 (1988): 4.

95. Alex, interview.

96. Derek, interview.

97. Charles, interview.

98. Foucault, *Discipline and Punish*, 200.

99. Andrew, interview.

100. Ralph, interview.

101. Herman Gray, "Black Masculinity and Visual Culture," *Callaloo* 18, no. 2 (1995): 401.

102. Ralph, interview.

103. Ibid.

104. Thomas, interview.

105. Colin, interview.

106. William, interview.

107. Thomas, interview.

108. Alex, interview.

109. Ibid.

110. Michael, interview.

111. Fanon, *Black Skin, White Masks*, 82.

112. Thomas, interview.

113. Alex, interview.

114. Colin, interview.

115. Walters, *Tolerance Trap*, 2.

116. Andrew, interview.

117. Gray, *Watching Race*, 85.

118. Dave, interview.

119. Gross, "Out of the Mainstream," 139.

120. Charles, interview.

121. Ibid.

122. Andrew, interview.

123. Paul, interview.

124. Ibid.

125. Critchley, *On Humor*, 56–57.

126. Alex, interview.

127. Robert, interview.

128. Colin, interview.

129. Greg, interview.

130. Ibid.

131. Dave, interview.

132. Greg, interview.

133. Ibid.

134. Thomas, interview.

135. Alan Sinfield, *On Sexuality and Power* (New York: Columbia University Press, 2004), 18.

136. Martin, "The Tweet Has Two Faces," 161.

137. Michael, interview.

138. Mary C. Beltrán, "Meaningful Diversity: Exploring Questions of Equitable Representation on Diverse Ensemble Shows," *Flow* 12, no. 7 (2010), http://flowtv.org/2010/08/meaningful-diversity/.

139. William, interview.

140. Cory, interview.

141. Samuel, interview.

142. Ibid.

143. Alex, interview.

144. Colin, interview.

—◆◆◆—

CONCLUSION

Trapped in the Black-Cast Sitcom's Generic Closet

THE BLACK SPACES UPN, TBS, and BET carved out for Black-cast sitcoms throughout the 1990s, 2000s, and 2010s were constructions for a particular imagining of Black audiences not as a set of "real" people but as a demographic profile that could be used to sell these viewers to advertisers. In particular, as I detailed in chapter 1, these networks invented an antigay Black viewer based on an imagination of Blackness as (over)religious and organized around hip-hop sensibilities, specifically hip-hop masculinities. This view is particularly problematic because industrial decision makers are overwhelmingly white. As the authors of the 2014 *Hollywood Diversity Report* underscore, "historically, there has been a dearth of gender, racial and ethnic diversity in film and television—both in front of and behind the camera."[1] This lack of diversity suggests (other than a real problem with Hollywood's employment practices and pipelines) that Black viewers are imagined in a way that may be out of step with how they exist in fact. These viewers are likely wholly different than the cardboard cutouts that industry executives imagine. As Larry Gross suggests, "when groups or perspectives attain visibility, the manner of that representation will itself reflect the biases and interests of those elites who define the public agenda. And these elites are (mostly) white, (mostly) middle-age, (mostly) male, middle and upper-middle class, and entirely heterosexual (at least in public)."[2] Because there are few people of color among the ranks of those making programming decisions, ideas about Blackness and its alleged antigay ideology can proliferate unchecked.

These constructions of Blackness, as I've argued throughout *The Generic Closet*, work discursively to represent a unique set of representational practices for Black-cast sitcoms—strategies different from Black gayness within white- and multicultural-cast sitcoms like *Spin City, Brooklyn Nine-Nine, Don't Trust the B**** in Apartment 23, Sirens,* and *The Unbreakable Kimmy Schmidt* (Netflix, 2015–2019). These white- and multicultural-cast series have historically engaged Black gay representation because, as Ron Becker argues, white audiences are constructed as liberal consumers of "edgy" content.[3]

A detour to a Facebook conversation I had a few years ago about *Empire* is instructive. A Black heterosexual man who is a friend of a Facebook friend objected to the Black gay content on *Empire*, specifically a kiss that series regular Jamal shared with a suitor. Although he was quick to suggest that his objection was not about an antigay stance, I think that was part of it. He asserted that Fox, as a major broadcast network, was not the place for such content. Instead this content should be mediated on premium subscription cable channels, like HBO, Showtime, and Cinemax. For this man, Black gay content belongs in spaces that are behind a paywall so that, presumably, he does not have to see it in what he deems a "safe space." Series like *Empire* and *The Have and the Have Nots* are not necessarily for Black heterosexual men but rather for Black women who are BLAMPs. Although *Empire* is founded on the logics of hip-hop commodification and its attendant (monolithically and stereotypically understood) anti-gayness, it is not generically bound by the same logics as the Black-cast sitcom, which imagines its audience as the proverbial "every(Black)body."

Concomitantly, the Black-cast sitcom fixes its mode of address on safety. As I have argued throughout *The Generic Closet*, the Black-cast sitcom cannot afford to repeatedly broadcast "risky" content because of its precariousness within industrial discourses. As a consumer category, Blackness is only as valuable to television networks as advertisers deem it, and any ratings softness could mean cancellation for a Black-cast sitcom. Unlike "quality" white demographics, which can save a low-rated series like *30 Rock* (NBC, 2006–2013), Black fervor has not yet saved any television series. The series *Underground* (WGN America, 2016–2017) is a prime example. As I have discussed elsewhere, fans of the slavery-focused drama began a campaign, encouraged by series executive producer John Legend, "for black-focused networks like OWN and BET, or streaming platforms like Hulu to pick up the show" after it was canceled by WGN America for low ratings.[4] In an interview, Oprah Winfrey said that the OWN Network could not afford to pick up *Underground* because "It costs twice as much to make as [OWN Black-cast drama] *Queen Sugar*," pointing to the cost associated with producing Black-cast quality TV content vis-à-vis what advertisers will pay to reach those viewers.[5] She continues, "As a matter of fact, my dear friend John Legend called me personally and asked me about it, but we'd already been talking about how we could make it work, but it's, like, $5 million an episode, so we can't afford it. It's not cheap."[6] *Underground*'s second season ratings were also less than stellar, having "averaged a .02 rating among adults 18–49 and 567,000 viewers for initial airings, down from 993,000 in season one."[7] Those numbers are paltry at best but particularly abysmal when considering the value television channels and networks place on so-called "blue chip demographics." As Robert Thompson details, these blue chip demographics comprise "upscale, well-educated, urban-dwelling young viewers advertisers so desire to reach [and] tend to make up a much larger percentage of the audience for [quality TV] shows than other kinds of programs."[8] Thompson does not name the whiteness of the imagination of blue chip demographics, and that distinction is important. Because of networks' sporadic engagement with Blackness, its use-value is similarly temporary. In other words, for networks like WGN America, Fox, UPN, The WB, The CW, and TBS, Blackness becomes what Jennifer Fuller theorizes as "a method of cultivating brand identities with transracial appeal."[9] The transracial appeal Fuller highlights is important because it gestures toward the preciousness of Blackness as a brand strategy. Networks can pivot from (and to) brand strategies at will, leaving Blackness for the far more lucrative "transracial" (which really means white) audience.

UPN's and TBS's turns to Blackness, and even BET's turn to Black scripted fare, might be temporary. But these turns also provided opportunities for Black writers and showrunners to mediate stories that spoke to Black viewers between the mid-1990s and the mid-2010s. In this way, the Black-cast sitcom functioned (and continues to function) as a Black public that discursively stands in for a monolithic notion of Blackness. The mythology that Black people are antigay (and more antigay than their white counterparts) is overlaid onto the Black-cast sitcom as a Black public. This configuration of the Black-cast sitcom as Black public dictates the ways the generic closet functions to contain "black gayness into specific coming out episodes/story arcs before discarding [Black gay] characters for other 'mainstream' stories."[10]

In *The Generic Closet*, I set out to make Black gayness in Black-cast sitcoms legible. When I have talked about this project, so few people, even those who consider themselves fans of Black-cast sitcoms, remember Black gayness within such series because its appearance is fleeting. But this book is not just about legibility—that would, in some ways, entail asking how Black gay characters appear across Black-cast sitcoms. In *The Generic Closet*, I attempted to answer the *how* and *why* questions in a way that would shift from the representational to the industrial. The generic closet, as a concept, points out how *Good News, Moesha, All of Us, Let's Stay Together*, and *Are We There Yet?* use single episodes or short arcs to hail Black gayness to come out, but such a coming out exhausts the narrative utility of Black homosexuality. Although Eldridge was the teenage son of one of the series' main characters, he appears only in the pilot and is never mentioned again (although the series lasted only one season, with twenty-two episodes). When asked, Weinberger says,

> It wasn't a decision to exclude him. It wasn't the intention of the show to deal with gay issues in church or to deal with his issues in the church. Given the other characters, this was not either strongly delineated or a strong enough character to pursue. I thought we pretty much covered . . . you can obviously do far more stories with him, but considering the actors we had to serve, we just . . . really didn't have a need for that character, and he didn't really fit in. He was, no pun intended, really not a comedic character. He was a nice guy, and that was the point of the first episode. . . . He didn't have a comic characteristic and I didn't want that. As we got into the series, the story simply evolved around the other characters. Nobody sat down and said, "OK let's not do gay anymore." I couldn't think of any more stories with him. I didn't really choose to pursue it.[11]

Weinberger suggests that (at least for him) there is no utility for gay characters once they have performed the narrative function of coming out. Homosexuality did not fit into the fabric of his show outside of creating the episodic narrative problem. Homosexuality only has a place within *Good News* as a "very special episode." At the same time, Weinberger's comments can be viewed through Darieck Scott's theorization of abjection, which "emphasizes the processes of exclusion and boundary-setting."[12] For Weinberger, and, by extension, for *Good News*, there are clear boundaries (even if they are not articulated) around what is permissible within the series and what Weinberger, as executive producer, will allow. Furthermore, Weinberger contends,

> I went on to other stories, which were guns, contraception, and a few other issues that I thought were interesting for the church or for this minister to deal with. I think it was just my inability or failure to find another gay issue that I wanted to deal with. And I didn't really have the actor to do it. That was really a small part, and he did it really well, but it wasn't a continuing role. He was never hired as an ongoing member of the ensemble. It wasn't like we sat down and said . . . we had no network comments that said, "OK, no more gay characters or gay shows." That was never an issue. It was really once in and out. I thought it was a very good pilot story. I thought it pointed out some of the things that I thought were interesting. I thought it made a very good first

show in a way of introducing the characters. To make gay or lesbian themes part of the series, that was never the intention . . . I guess if I had another year to go and I was able to find another story to deal with, I would have done it.[13]

Weinberg never answers why the character he wrote could not have returned to the series (versus writing a new character). To suggest that he did not have the actor to play a Black gay character is to suggest that there were no new issues that could have been brought up for the same character, particularly considering that he was a child of one of the main characters. In addition, Dwain Perry, the actor who played Eldridge, might have been available if Weinberger wanted to create additional story lines with the character; according to IMDB.com, Perry did not have his next role until two years after *Good News* had ended. Ultimately, Weinberger concedes that the lack of ongoing Black gay characters was rooted in his own lack of imagination to create and develop new stories for gay characters within the series that do not deal with coming out.

The same industrial (il)logic permeated Bady's experiences on *Moesha*. He says,

> I would try to bring Omar back. What was so fascinating is with the amount of respect that they gave to that script by not changing it and re-writing it, I didn't realize the way most Black writers in particular think about the subject of gay characters as, "We did that story." That's what they would always say. . . . What was interesting is I would always think, you know, being gay isn't a story. It doesn't begin and end with the opening credits and the last journal entry [as it did with the "Labels" episode]. I could never convince them that there was a life for the character beyond that particular story. I never won. It was always, "We already did that story." It was as if gayness in and of itself was a special interest story, an after-school special, but there was no life beyond that. There was no complexity.[14]

Bady implicitly articulates the constricting nature of the generic closet for Black-cast sitcom narratives. Within the Black-cast sitcom, the entirety of Black gayness is reduced to a "story" that has a distinctive three-act structure (a.k.a. the generic closet). For the genre, the question remains, if a Black gay character is not coming out, what possible utility could he have for a series?

McKinley and March's experiences on *All of Us* and *Are We There Yet?* differed slightly. In both series, they suggest they wanted the gay characters to return to the series, but industrial factors made that difficult. In the case of *All of Us*, March contends, "Absolutely we wanted to bring [Luther] and his boyfriend back. We just couldn't, the show had ended."[15] Given the organizing logic of the generic closet, McKinley and March's reason for excluding Luther from further episodes is likely a defensive truth or a ready-made decision that shields them from actually having to acknowledge that the generic closet precluded them from continuing the story.[16]

While the series' cancellation was the reason suggested for the exclusion of Luther and Rosie on *All of Us*, McKinley and March give the syndication schedule as the reason for Cedric's failure to return. McKinley recalls that there was not even a discussion of bringing the character back. Because of the production schedule of *Are We There Yet?* in which one hundred episodes of the series were written and filmed in a short period of time, there were few recurring characters within the series. March recalls,

> We would have loved for the character to come back but *Are We There Yet?* was made for syndication, so you can't really do continuous episodes. You can't have arcs. They have to be episodes that can stand alone. If you tune in [you have to] know who those characters are and know that there will be a beginning and end. I don't have to wait to see what happens next week. It's just because they don't know how they will run them. It was unfortunate because we had a lot of characters we would have loved to bring back.[17]

March slips from a specific discussion of the exclusion of Cedric to a broader discussion of the inability of minor recurring characters within a made-for-syndication Black-cast sitcom, thus inadvertently reinforcing that the generic closet is not wholly representational but industrial. Put another way, the decision to exclude Cedric is not about excluding Black gayness but conforming to the needs of a syndicated series and stripping as a programming strategy. More broadly, though, March attempts to absolve the production staff and the television industry more broadly from charges of homophobia and excluding Black gayness. March is unwilling (or perhaps unable) to suggest that Black gayness was wholly excluded from returning to the series; rather, that there were no recurring characters in the series because of how its production (and syndication) cycle operates. However, March's assertion is undercut because several minor heterosexual characters reappear in some of the series' one-hundred-episode run, including a character described as "Nick's football buddy," who appears in three episodes, and Curtis, who plays one of Lindsey's friends and appears in six episodes. March employs what I have elsewhere called *subterfuge*, which wallows in the "commercial ambivalences about the business of television."[18] In its initial theorization, the term referred to casting practices as a component of media industries work. I extend it to demonstrate how March implicitly denies that the business of television, the syndication market, and *Are We There Yet?*'s Blackness converge to shape the generic closet.

Audiences can be "trusted" to remember "regular" recurring characters when the series is aired out of order. Cedric could never be understood as a "regular" character within the fabric of the series.

Edmonds Cofer suggests that although Darkanian's arc stretches across seven episodes, it was never central to the story *Let's Stay Together* was telling. She says, "The main reason [Darkanian and his boyfriend were secondary characters] was because it really was Crystal's story. If Darkanian is her side character, then the boyfriend is a side to the side character."[19] And although Darkanian and Crystal vow to remain friends, Darkanian is never seen or discussed within the series again, although the series functions as a serial narrative versus a purely episodic one—a hallmark of many sitcoms. Put another way, *Let's Stay Together* (and its viewers) have a memory that carries across episodes and seasons.

As my analyses of *Moesha, Good News, All of Us, Let's Stay Together,* and *Are We There Yet?* demonstrated, the trap is that Black gay characters are hailed to perform the three-act structure of the generic closet. They are called on to be detected and discovered and to declare their homosexuality before being discarded. As the Black gay men I interviewed in chapter 4 observed, that role works to decenter Black gayness. As the television writers and showrunners discussed in chapter 2, Black gay story lines are imagined and written only within the generic closet, scripting Black gayness's central concern as the maintenance of narrative stasis and heteronormativity within the series. By decentering gayness, the act of coming out is positioned as a cause-effect chain rooted in heterocentric reactions to homosexuality. These characters' gayness ceases to be about them but rather about the information they provide: *Moesha* asks, "Is Omar gay?," while *Good News* asks, "How will Eldridge's mother react to his homosexuality?" *All of Us* ponders whether or not Robert will accept his birth father's gayness, and, like *Moesha, Are We There Yet?* wonders, "Is Cedric gay?" *Let's Stay Together* centrally asks, "How long will Darkanian be able to conceal his homosexuality?" These questions have little to do with Omar, Eldridge, Luther, Cedric, or Darkanian because the characters are written, and read, as objects of information and never the subject of information.[20] Viewers discover that these Black characters are gay, and their gayness becomes the only information revealed about them. That small piece of information (and often the speculation about such information) sets off a narrative chain of events that often occurs when these Black gay characters are not on screen. They are talked about, but they are not often allowed to engage in those conversations. When Black gay characters are not performing the coming-out function, they are held up as abject others to be ridiculed and, in the process, to reify Black masculinity. These characters demonstrate what happens when one transgresses the (artificial) lines of authentic Blackness.

The use of the laugh track and humor, as I argued in chapter 3, helps not only to position Black gay characters as permissible sites for jokes but also to clearly position Black gayness as outside of and unwelcome within the heterocentric Black-cast sitcom. The instructive possibilities of the laugh track are particularly important for two reasons. First, the Black gay men in chapter 4 noticed the laugh track, which underscores the ways that they read the whole text, not just the narrative. Second, because the Black-cast sitcom largely retains its use of the laugh track (often wholly created in postproduction on series that do not film in front of a live studio audience), it can help to structure meaning for viewers. As some of the respondents emphasized in chapter 4, the laugh track was deemed "disrespectful" in its engagement with Black gayness, demonstrating the ideological power the laugh track wields. It grants permission to laugh at (or with) certain characters. Although there are similarities in the engagement of white-cast sitcoms with Black gay characters, white- and multicultural-cast series have historically engaged more deeply with Black gay characters (although not necessarily their Blackness), given their status as costars or series regulars. However, Black gayness in Black-cast sitcoms is treated differently.

THE POST-GAY REPRESENTATION TRAP

Importantly, from a Black-cast sitcom production and reception perspective, Black gay representation is bound up in post-gay rhetoric, which is a reflection of a politics of "normal" that seeks to flatten gayness. In some ways, post-gay rhetoric owes much of its currency to the work of GLAAD and other gay rights advocacy organizations that fought (and continue to fight) against so-called negative stereotypes in media. However, this rhetoric has been picked up and recirculated by gay men and lesbians themselves. In October 2013, on an episode of *Oprah's Next Chapter* that focused on "Gay Hollywood," Winfrey hosted producer and actor Dan Bucatinsky, Jesse Tyler Ferguson from *Modern Family*, and comedian Wanda Sykes. In the episode, Bucatinsky suggests that what he most enjoys about Shonda Rhimes is that she writes gay characters who "just happen to be" gay. However, in suggesting that these gay characters "just happen to be," he ignores the cultural specificity of gayness in favor of flattening differences because in his worldview, *difference* seems to be a dirty word. Bucatinsky seemingly adopts Eve Sedgwick's "universalizing view" in his suggestion that sexuality is less important than a kind of overarching humanism.[21] In the process of flattening gayness to make it palatable for both heterosexual and "respectable" gay viewers, gayness fails to maintain its cultural specificity.

From a production perspective, as I demonstrated in chapter 2, the drive to reconfigure the meanings attached to Black gayness is ensnared in a post-gay rhetoric that narrowly defines the parameters within which "positive" representations can exist, becoming a new form of hegemony. Using this logic, there can be only a certain number of ways to be a Black gay character on television, and those include being "normal." Put another way, these characters have to be masculine and either happily single (and celibate) or partnered or married and having (or thinking about having) children. A rejection of the Black queer feminine body exists in Black-cast sitcom production (on the rare occasion that Black gay bodies exist), as exemplified by the ways Demetrius Bady fought to keep a flamboyantly gay character out of his script and by Jackie McKinley and Antonia March's attempt to include Black gay characters who are just "regular" in their scripts. I am not suggesting that their motives are entirely problematic. Quite the contrary, I believe they are honestly attempting to do something different with Black gay representation. However historicized, notions of negative stereotypes have resulted in a narrow framework within which "good Black gay televisual subjects" can be imagined. The writers and Black gay men in the real world are still reacting to and against the still-potent controlling image of Black gay men presented in *In Living Color*'s "Men On . . ." sketches.

The Black-cast sitcom does not wholly disallow gayness from its collective narrative universes—just *Black* gayness. Filipino actor Alec Mapa played series regular Adam Benet, an openly gay assistant on *Half & Half* (UPN, 2002–2006). And white actor Peter Oldring played Fabian on *Love That Girl* (TVOne, 2010–2014). Weinberger hypothesizes that because these gay characters are not Black,

> they could be allowed to be as stereotypical without alienating the Black
> audience. . . . I have a feeling that if they tried to make those characters Black,
> they wouldn't have been able to get on the air. . . . They're afraid that if you
> show [Black gay] people, the audience won't accept them. You can do a Black
> man in a dress playing a woman, like Martin [Lawrence in *Big Mama's House*]
> or Tyler Perry playing Madea, and they love that, but if you do a plain [Black]
> gay character, you would have a problem getting past the network. They're
> afraid of what their audience is going to say."[22]

Weinberger suggests that the Black-cast sitcom functions as a carrier of a set of discourses about Blackness (whether real or imagined). The ease with which white or Filipino gay characters can be included in the Black-cast sitcom reveals that it is not necessarily an aversion to gayness that plagues Black-cast sitcoms. It is an aversion to *Black* gayness and, by extension, a reification of the "proper" scripts of and for Black masculinity. Thus Black gayness exists within these Black-cast sitcoms to teach viewers what Black masculinity is not.

Black gayness can temporarily exist in these Black-cast sitcoms because it can teach viewers something about the characters who inhabit their homes each week. These Black-cast sitcoms, from *Moesha* to *Let's Stay Together*, are happy to welcome Black gayness into their worlds to demonstrate how cool and progressive they are. But Black gayness can be only a temporary interloper within these narrative worlds. While writers cited a number of different reasons to explain why Black gay characters are not frequently included within Black-cast sitcoms, ultimately the reason can be reduced to this: Black gayness, no matter how positively it is treated within the few episodes in which the topic is broached, is an unwelcome and unwanted visitor and must remain firmly within the generic closet.

NOTES

1. Darnell Hunt, Ana-Christina Ramon, and Zachary Price, *2014 Hollywood Diversity Report: Making Sense of the Discontent* (Los Angeles: Ralph Bunche Center for African American Studies at UCLA, 2014), 5.

2. Gross, "Out of the Mainstream," 131.

3. Ron Becker, "Prime-Time Television in the Gay Nineties: Network Television, Quality Audiences, and Gay Politics," *Velvet Light Trap* 42, no. 42 (1998): 38.

4. Alfred L. Martin Jr., "Notes from *Underground*: WGN's Black-Cast Quality TV Experiment," *Los Angeles Review of Books*, May 31, 2018, https://lareviewofbooks.org/article/notes-from-underground-wgns-black-cast-quality-tv-experiment/.

5. Yesha Callahan, "Oprah Winfrey Can't Save *Underground* Because It's Too Expensive," *Root*, June 7, 2017, https://thegrapevine.theroot.com/oprah-winfrey-cant-save-underground-because-its-too-exp-1795896808.

6. Ibid.

7. Martin, "Notes from *Underground*."

8. Robert J. Thompson, *Televisions Second Golden Age: From* Hill Street Blues *to* ER (Syracuse, NY: Syracuse University Press, 1997), 14.

9. Fuller, "Branding Blackness," 287.

10. Martin, "Generic Closets," 225.

11. Weinberger, interview.

12. Scott, *Extravagant Abjection*, 16.

13. Weinberger, interview.
14. Bady, interview.
15. March, interview.
16. Martin, "Queer Business of Casting," 283.
17. March, interview.
18. Martin, "Queer Business of Casting," 283.
19. Edmonds Cofer, interview.
20. Foucault, *Discipline and Punish*, 200.
21. Sedgwick, *Epistemology of the Closet*, 1.
22. Weinberger, interview.

APPENDIX A

List of Black-Cast Sitcoms with Black Gay Characters

These Black-cast sitcoms featured Black gay characters between 1977 and 2014. There were a number of representations of Black gay men on television more broadly, but this list focuses solely on those in Black-cast sitcoms, as these characters are the focus of this book.

1977–1978

Sanford Arms (NBC)—The series, a spin-off from the popular series *Sanford and Son*, ran for four episodes. The episode "Phil's Assertion School" featured Travis, a civil rights attorney. He is a friend of series costar Angie, who ultimately tells her father that Travis is gay. The episode originally aired September 30, 1977.

1991–1992

Roc (Fox)—In its first season, *Roc* included the first of four episodes that featured a Black gay character. Russell, played by Richard Roundtree, was the uncle to the axial family. In the episode, "Can't Help Loving That Man," Russell visits the Emerson family and gets married to his partner Chris in the Emerson's living room. The episode aired October 20, 1991.

1993–1994

Roc (Fox)—In its second and third seasons, Richard Roundtree's Russell returned to *Roc* in three episodes. In the second-season episode "Second Time Around," which aired January 17, 1993, Russell attends the vow renewal of Roc and Eleanor Emerson. On November 23, 1993, Russell awaits the arrival of

Roc and Eleanor's first-born child with other family and friends in the episode "God Bless the Child." Last, the April 5, 1994, episode "Brother" concerns Russell announcing his intention to move to Paris because of the allegedly more progressive stance toward gayness and gay rights.

1996–1997

Moesha (UPN)—The "Labels" episode, which aired October 1, 1996, concerns Moesha meeting and briefly dating Hakeem's cousin Omar. After meeting Omar's flamboyant friend, Moesha begins to spread the rumor that Omar is gay.

Good News (UPN)—On the "Pilot" episode of the series, which broadly concerns the trials and tribulations of a church attempting to rebuild its membership after the departure of a beloved pastor, the new pastor is confronted with a parishioner who seeks help in coming out to his mother. The episode originally aired August 25, 1997.

2000–2001

The Parkers (UPN)—Series star Nikki Parker seeks a new roommate in this September 18, 2000, episode. Instead of seeking a roommate who is most capable of paying the rent, Nikki chooses a male roommate who is the most handsome. Her new roommate, who Nikki sees as a potential romantic partner, turns out to be gay.

2002–2003

Girlfriends (UPN)—The first episode on which Peaches and Ronnie appear, "Sister, Sistah," aired February 4, 2002. The episode does not narratively concern Peaches or Ronnie; rather, they are present (and have dialogue) in the beauty salon in which they work. The characters return on the episode "Handling Baggage," which airs November 11, 2002. In the episode, Peaches and Ronnie tell series star Maya that they suspect her husband may be cheating on her with another woman. Peaches (without Ronnie) appears on the September 22, 2003, episode "If It's Broke, Fix It." On the episode, Peaches is now working as series star Joan's assistant. His primary narrative purpose on the episode is to provide relationship advice to his boss, Joan.

2004–2005

Girlfriends (UPN)—On March 29, 2004, the *Girlfriends* episode "Love, Peace and Hair Grease" does not narratively concern Peaches or Ronnie. However, much of the episode's action takes place in Ronnie's beauty salon. In "New York Bound," which originally aired May 24, 2004, Ronnie works as something similar to his cousin Maya's book publicist. He brings her a five-figure offer to publish her book *Oh, Hell Yes!* In the last episode on which Ronnie appears before the series moved to The CW, he is offended when his cousin Maya hires an agent to represent her in attempting to sell her book to a major publisher.

2006–2007

All of Us (UPN)—On the two-part episode of *All of Us*, series star Robert discovers that his biological father is gay. The episodes "Like Father, Like Son, Like Hell" and "My Two Dads" aired November 13 and 20, 2006.

Girlfriends (The CW)—In the seventh-season finale (its first on The CW), "It's Been Determined," which originally aired May 7, 2007, neither Peaches nor Ronnie serve a narrative purpose on the episode.

2009–2010

The Game (The CW)—On the January 23 and 30, 2009, two-part episode of *The Game*, the fictional San Diego Sabers are confronted with having a Black gay player on their team. The episodes, "Stay Fierce, Malik" and "Do the Wright Thing," featured the Black gay character Clay Smith.

2011–2012

Are We There Yet? (TBS)—"The Boy Has Style" aired January 19, 2011. The episode concerned Lindsey Kingston's high school crush and her parents' suspicion (and ultimate confirmation) that he is gay. The Black gay character Cedric is a player on the high school football team.

Let's Stay Together (BET)—The first episode on which Darkanian first appears is "Leave Me Alone." The episode aired April 24, 2012, and featured Darkanian, a closeted Black gay man and professional football player. In the episode, Darkanian begins to woo Crystal. The Darkanian story line continues in the May 22, 2012, episode, "No Wedding and a Funeral," which finds Crystal moving into one of Darkanian's "extra" apartments in downtown Atlanta. In the season 2 finale, "Wait . . . What?," Crystal discovers that Darkanian is gay when his long-term boyfriend visits the apartment in which Crystal lives. The episode aired June 5, 2012.

2013–2014

Let's Stay Together (BET)—On the March 26, 2013, season 3 premiere, "See, What Had Happened Was . . ." Darkanian asks Crystal to be his "beard"—an offer she accepts. In the episode "Buyer Beware," Darkanian and Crystal continue their public relationship, although Crystal begins to have sexual needs that Darkanian cannot fulfill. The episode aired May 14, 2013. In the season 3 finale, "Babies, Blindness and Bling," Crystal is caught kissing a man who is not Darkanian, leading to a media brouhaha. She is required to hold a press conference where she apologizes for her adulterous relationship. At the press conference, Darkanian proposes marriage. The last episode on which Darkanian appears is "Game Over," in which Darkanian comes out as gay. The episode aired April 1, 2014.

APPENDIX B

Interview Script for Black-Cast Sitcom Viewers

1. In what year were you born?
2. How do you racially identify yourself?
3. Do you identify yourself as heterosexual, bisexual, gay, or something else?
4. Annual personal income bracket (excluding income of a partner or boyfriend)
   a. Less than $10,000
   b. More than $10,000 but less than $24,999
   c. More than $25,000 but less than $39,999
   d. More than $40,000 but less than $59,999
   e. More than $60,000 but less than $74,999
   f. More than $75,000 but less than $99,999
   g. More than $100,000
5. What is your highest level of education completed?
6. With which political party do you most closely identify?

COMING OUT

7. How old were you when you first realized you were gay?
8. What age were you when you first told someone else that you were gay?
   a. Who was that person?

       b. Do you still have a relationship with that person?
          i. If not, why not?

9. Have you acknowledged your homosexuality to all of your family members?
    a. If not, have you acknowledged your homosexuality to any of your family members?
       i. If so, how many?

10. Have you acknowledged your homosexuality to all of your friends?
    a. If not, have you acknowledged your homosexuality to any of your friends?
       i. If so, how many?

11. Did you lose friendships or familial relationships as a result of your acknowledgement of your homosexuality?

12. What fears did you have related to your coming out?

13. Who and what helped you to come out?

BLACK GAY CHARACTERS IN BLACK SITCOMS

14. How do you define a Black sitcom?

15. What are some of the shows you classify as a Black sitcom?
    a. Probe: *The Cosby Show? Amos 'n' Andy? Everybody Hates Chris? A Different World?*
       i. If any of these shows are not Black sitcoms, why not?

16. Overall, how do you think Black gay men are represented in Black sitcoms?
    a. Are they represented differently in sitcoms generally?
    b. Are they represented differently in dramas?

17. Of the episodes from the series I gave you for this project, which of the series did you regularly watch?
    a. If you watched the series beforehand, do you remember the episodes with Black gay characters?
    b. Did you watch these shows in their original run or as reruns?

18. Prior to viewing the episodes I gave you for this project, did you recall having seen Black gay men on television?
    a. If yes, who were those characters?
    b. How would you characterize those image(s)?
    c. How did those characters make you feel?

19. Which episodes did you watch?
20. What are your initial thoughts on the episode?
21. How do you feel about that representation?
22. Did any of the Black gay characters seem like real people to you?
    a. If so, which ones?
    b. If not, why not?
23. What do you think that representation says about [the era] in which [show] was produced?
    a. What do you think the representation says historically about gay representation on television?
24. How important is it for you to see Black gay men on television?
25. How, if at all, do you think seeing or not seeing Black gay men on television influenced your coming-out process?
26. Do or did you look to television characters to teach you what it meant to be gay?
27. Did television shows or television characters help to teach you what it meant to be gay?
    a. If so, what show(s) and character(s)
28. Did television shows or television characters help to teach you how to "act" gay?
    a. If so, what show(s) and character(s)
29. Do you see yourself depicted on television shows?
    a. If so, which ones?
    b. If so, are there specific characters with whom you identify?
30. Do you see yourself depicted in Black sitcoms?
    a. If so, which ones? Describe them.
    b. If so, are there specific characters with whom you identify?
31. Are the representations of Black gay men in Black similar to or different from your experiences and knowledge as a Black gay man?
32. What do you think these images of Black gay men say about this group to Black communities?
33. What qualities or characteristics would you like to see in Black gay characters in the Black sitcom?
34. Were there characters on television who were not explicitly gay whom you thought might be gay?
    a. Who were these characters?
    b. Why did you think they were gay?

35. In the absence of gay characters, were there other characters you gravitated toward?
    a. Who were those characters?
    b. Why do you think you gravitated toward that character?
36. Were there Black sitcoms you watched that had what one might call a "gay sensibility" that you liked to watch?
    a. What were those shows?
    b. Why did you think the show had a gay sensibility?

APPENDIX C

Interview Script for Industry Professionals

1. How long have you worked in the television industry?
2. With what race or ethnicity do you identify?
3. How would you define the Black sitcom?
   a. What are some of the shows that you define as Black?
   b. Probe: *The Cosby Show*? *Amos n Andy*? *Everybody Hates Chris*? *A Different World*?
      i. If you do not consider any of these shows Black sitcoms, why not?
4. On how many Black sitcoms have you worked?
5. What are some of the other shows on which you have worked?
6. Are you aware of any Black gay characters on Black sitcoms?
   a. If so, which ones?
   b. What do you think generally about the Black gay characters you can recall?
7. Why do you think there are so few Black gay male characters in Black sitcoms?
8. Have any of the shows on which you've worked featured gay characters?
   a. If yes, what were the conversations like to include these characters?
   b. If no, why do you think there have been no gay characters?
9. If your show included gay characters (or considered including gay characters), what race were these characters?
   a. Why do you think the character was that race?

10. In the script you wrote that included a gay character, what was the impetus for creating the character?
11. What was the discussion like in the writer's room?
12. Was the idea for the script workshopped before you went off to write?
13. How did the script change from the time you wrote it to the time it was recorded?
14. Was there any pushback from other writers? Actors? Productions staff? The network?
15. What were some of your concerns writing the script?
16. To what extent do you think gay watchdog groups make writers afraid to include Black gay characters?
17. Overall, how do you think Black gay men are represented in Black sitcoms?
    a. Are they represented differently in sitcoms generally?
    b. Are they represented differently in dramas?
18. What do you think would need to happen in order to get more Black gay characters into the Black sitcom?

BIBLIOGRAPHY

Acham, Christine. *Revolution Televised: Prime Time and the Struggle for Black Power.* Minneapolis: University of Minnesota Press, 2004.

Ahmed, Sara. *On Being Included: Racism and Diversity in Institutional Life.* Durham, NC: Duke University Press, 2012.

Althusser, Louis. *Lenin and Philosophy, and Other Essays.* New York: Monthly Review, 1972.

Altman, Rick. "Television/Sound." In *Studies in Entertainment: Critical Approaches to Mass Culture,* edited by Tania Modleski, 39–54. Bloomington: Indiana University Press, 1986.

Andreeva, Nellie. *"Are We There Yet?* Heads to TV." *Hollywood Reporter,* July 14, 2009. https://www.hollywoodreporter.com/news/heads-tv-86503.

———. "UPN All about *Eve, Us." Hollywood Reporter,* October 14, 2003, international edition.

Angelo, Megan. "At TBS, Diversity Pays Its Own Way." *New York Times,* May 28, 2010. https://www.nytimes.com/2010/05/30/arts/television/30tbs.html.

Baldwin, James. *Nobody Knows My Name.* New York: Vintage Books, 1992.

Barker, Andrew. "Are We There Yet?" *Variety,* June 1, 2010. https://variety.com/2010/tv/reviews/are-we-there-yet-1117942876/.

Barthes, Roland. *Mythologies.* Translated by Annette Lavers. New York: Farrar, Straus, and Giroux, 1972.

Battaglio, Stephen. "UPN Catches FOX." *Arizona Republic* (Phoenix, AZ), February 19, 1998.

BCST Staff. "Remaking BET with Originals." *Broadcasting and Cable,* June 27, 2011. http://www.broadcastingcable.com/news/news-articles/remaking-bet-originals/112163.

Becker, Ron. *Gay TV and Straight America*. New Brunswick, NJ: Rutgers University Press, 2006.

———. "Prime-Time Television in the Gay Nineties: Network Television, Quality Audiences, and Gay Politics." *Velvet Light Trap* 42, no. 1 (1998): 36–47.

Beltrán, Mary C. "Meaningful Diversity: Exploring Questions of Equitable Representation on Diverse Ensemble Shows." *Flow* 12, no. 7 (2010). http://flowtv .org/2010/08/meaningful-diversity/.

BET. "BET Presents *Let's Stay Together,* A New Original Series That Gives an Updated, Urban Perspective on Love and Marriage Premiering Tuesday, January 11 at 11:00 p.m." Press release. January 11, 2011. https://www .betpressroom.com/press-release/never-knew-love-like-this-beforebet-presents -lets-stay-together-a-new-original-series-that-gives-an-/.

BET.com. "Football Players Who Would Support Darkanian Coming Out." April 2013. https://www.bet.com/shows/lets-stay-together/photos1/photos-old/2013 /04/football-players-who-would-support-darkanian.html.

Bobo, Jacqueline. *Black Women as Cultural Readers*. New York: Columbia University Press, 1995.

Bogle, Donald. *Prime Time Blues*. New York: Farrar, Straus, and Giroux, 2001.

Boling, Patricia. *Privacy and the Politics of Intimate Life*. Ithaca, NY: Cornell University Press, 1996.

Brady, Stephen, and Wilma J. Busse. "The Gay Identity Questionnaire: A Brief Measure of Homosexual Identity Formation." *Journal of Homosexuality* 26, no. 4 (1994): 1–22.

Brock-Akil, Mara. "A Conversation with Mara Brock-Akil and Salim Akil." Interview at ATX TV Festival, season 6, Austin, TX, June 11, 2017.

Brown, Timothy J. "Welcome to the Terrordome: Exploring the Contradictions of a Hip Hop Masculinity." In *Progressive Black Masculinities*, edited by Athena D. Mutua, 191–214. New York: Routledge, 2006.

Browne, Nick. "The Political Economy of the Television (Super) Text." *Quarterly Review of Film and Video* 9, no. 3 (1984): 174–182.

Butler, Jeremy. *Television: Critical Methods and Applications*. New York: Routledge, 2012.

Caldwell, John T. *Production Culture: Industrial Reflexivity and Critical Practice in Film and Television*. Durham, NC: Duke University Press, 2008.

Callahan, Yesha. "Oprah Winfrey Can't Save *Underground* Because It's Too Expensive." *The Root*, June 7, 2017. https://thegrapevine.theroot.com /oprah-winfrey-cant-save-underground-because-its-too-exp-1795896808.

Capsuto, Steven. *Alternative Channels: The Uncensored Story of Gay and Lesbian Images on Radio and Television*. New York: Ballantine Books, 2000.

Cass, Vivienne C. "Homosexual Identity Formation: Testing a Theoretical Model." *Journal of Sex Research* 20, no. 2 (1984): 143–167.

Cerone, Daniel Howard. "Ellen May Be Telling Even though Not Asked." *TV Guide*, September 28, 1996.

Chambers, Samuel A. *The Queer Politics of Television*. New York: Tauris, 2009.

Chirrey, Deborah A. "'I Hereby Come Out': What Sort of Speech Act Is Coming Out?" *Journal of Sociolinguistics* 7, no. 1 (2003): 24–37.

Cillizza, Chris, and Sean Sullivan. "How Proposition 8 Passed in California—And Why it Wouldn't Today." *Washington Post*, March 26, 2013. https://www.washingtonpost.com/news/the-fix/wp/2013/03/26/how-proposition-8-passed-in-california-and-why-it-wouldnt-today/?noredirect=on&utm_term=.45b3f70508e0.

Cleaver, Eldridge. *Soul on Ice*. New York: Delta Books, 1991.

Coates, Ta-Nehisi. "Proposition 8 and Blaming the Blacks." *Atlantic*, January 7, 2009. https://www.theatlantic.com/entertainment/archive/2009/01/prop-8-and-blaming-the-blacks/6548/.

Cobb, Jasmine, and Robin R. Means Coleman. "Two Snaps and a Twist: Controlling Images of Gay Black Men on Television." *African American Research Perspectives* 13, no. 1 (2010): 82–98.

Coe, Steve. "UPN Beats . . . Everybody. Debuts at Number One for Its First Night with New *Star Trek* Show." *Broadcasting and Cable*, January 23, 1995, 4, 10.

Cole, Kelly. "From Homeboys to Girl Power: Media Mergers, Emerging Networks and 1990s Television." PhD diss., University of Wisconsin–Madison, 2005.

Coleman, Robin R. Means. *African American Viewers and the Black Situation Comedy*. New York: Garland Press, 2000.

Coleman, Robin R. Means, and Charlton D. McIlwain. "The Hidden Truths in Black Sitcoms." In *The Sitcom Reader: America Viewed and Skewed*, edited by Mary M. Dalton and Laura R. Linder, 125–138. Albany, NY: SUNY Press, 2005.

Collins, Patricia Hill. "Learning from the Outsider Within: The Sociological Significance of Black Feminist Thought." *Social Problems* 33, no. 6 (1986): s14–s32.

Colman, David. "A Night Out with: James Collard; The Corner of Straight and Gay." *New York Times*, July 19, 1998. http://www.nytimes.com/1998/07/19/style/a-night-out-with-james-collard-the-corner-of-straight-and-gay.html.

Conerly, Gregory. "Are You Black First or Are You Queer?" In *The Greatest Taboo: Homosexuality in Black Communities*, edited by Delroy Constantine-Simms, 7–23. Los Angeles: Alyson Books, 2001.

Crenshaw, Kimberlee. "Mapping the Margins: Intersectionality, Identity Politics, and Violence against Women of Color." *Stanford Law Review* 43, no. 6 (1991): 1241–1299.

Cripps, Thomas. *Making Movies Black: The Hollywood Message Movie from World War II to the Civil Rights Era*. New York: Oxford University Press, 1993.

Critchley, Simon. *On Humor*. New York: Routledge, 2002.

D'Acci, Julie. "Cultural Studies, Television Studies, and the Crisis in the Humanities." In *Television after TV: Essays on a Medium in Transition*, edited by Lynn Spiegel and Jan Olsson, 418–446. Durham, NC: Duke University Press, 2004.

Daniels, Susanne, and Cynthia Littleton. *Season Finale: The Unexpected Rise and Fall of The WB and UPN*. New York: Harper Books, 2007.

Dates, Jannette L. "Commercial Television." In *Split Image: African Americans in the Mass Media*, edited by Jannette L. Dates and William Barlow, 267–328. Washington, DC: Howard University Press, 1993.

Davies, Christine. *Ethnic Humor around the World*. Bloomington: Indiana University Press, 1996.

DeAngelis, Michael. *Gay Fandom and Crossover Stardom: James Dean, Mel Gibson, and Keanu Reeves*. Durham, NC: Duke University Press, 2001.

de Moraes, Lisa. "For Black Sitcom 'Love That Girl!,' TV One May Be the Network of Its Dreams." *Washington Post*, January 6, 2010. http://www.washingtonpost.com/wp-dyn/content/article/2010/01/05/AR2010010503534.html.

Dhaenens, Frederick. "Gay Representation, Queer Resistance, and the Small Screen: A Reception Study of Gay Representations among Flemish Fans of Contemporary Television Fiction." Working Papers Film and TV Studies WP2011/1 (2011). https://www.ugent.be/ps/communicatiewetenschappen/cims/en/publications/working-papers/gay-representation-queer-resistance.htm.

Doty, Alexander. *Making Things Perfectly Queer: Interpreting Mass Culture*. Minneapolis: University of Minnesota Press, 1993.

Doyle, Vincent. *Making Out in the Mainstream: GLAAD and the Politics of Respectability*. Montreal: McGill-Queen's University Press, 2016.

Dunning, Stephanie K. *Queer in Black and White: Interraciality, Same Sex Desire, and Contemporary African American Culture*. Bloomington: University of Indiana Press, 2009.

Dyer, Richard. *The Culture of Queers*. New York: Routledge, 2001.

———. *Heavenly Bodies: Film Stars and Society*. London: Routledge, 2003.

———. "Stereotyping." In *Media and Cultural Studies: Keyworks*, edited by Meenakshi Gigi Durham and Douglas M. Kellner, 275–282. New York: Wiley-Blackwell, 2012.

Elliot, Stuart. "TBS Puts Serious Money into Promoting Itself as a Place for Laughs." *New York Times*, April 22, 2004. https://www.nytimes.com/2004/04/22/business/media-business-advertising-tbs-puts-serious-money-into-promoting-itself-place.html.

Estes, Steve. *I Am a Man! Race, Manhood and the Civil Rights Movement*. Chapel Hill: University of North Carolina Press, 2005.

Fabrikant, Geraldine. "BET Holdings To Be Bought by Viacom for $2.34 Billion." *New York Times*, November 4, 2000. http://www.nytimes.com

/2000/11/04/business/bet-holdings-to-be-bought-by-viacom-for-2
.34-billion.html.

Fanon, Franz. *Black Skin, White Masks*. New York: Grove Press, 1952.

Farhi, Paul. "For BET, Some Static in the Picture; Bob Johnson Wanted People to
Turn on His Cable Network. He Got His Wish." *Washington Post*, November 22,
1999. https://www.washingtonpost.com/archive/lifestyle/1999/11/22/for-bet
-some-static-in-the-picture/a929a6c6-9f82-4f78-997f-9c4d2c85db49/.

Farmer, Brett. *Spectacular Passions: Cinema, Fantasy, Gay Male Spectatorship*.
Durham, NC: Duke University Press, 2000.

Ferguson, Roderick A. *Aberrations in Black: Toward a Queer of Color Critique*.
Minneapolis: University of Minnesota Press, 2004.

Fiske, John. *Television Culture*. New York: Routledge, 2006.

Flint, Joe. "UPN Adds 2 Affiliates, 2 Sitcoms to its Lineup." *Daily Variety*,
December 11, 1995, 4, 18.

Foster, Guy Mark. "Desire and the 'Big Black Sex Cop': Race and the Politics of
Intimacy on HBO's *Six Feet Under*." In *The New Queer Aesthetic on Television:
Essays on Recent Programming*, edited by James Keller and Leslie Stratyner,
99–112. Jefferson, NC: McFarland, 2006.

Foucault, Michel. *Discipline and Punish: The Birth of the Prison*. Translated by Alan
Sheridan. New York: Vintage Books 1995.

———. *The History of Sexuality: An Introduction*. Vol. 1. New York: Random
House, 1990.

———. "The Means of Correct Training." In *Blackwell Reader on Contemporary
Social Theory*, edited by Anthony Elliot, 97–106. Oxford: Blackwell, 1999.

———. *The Order of Things: The Archaeology of the Human Sciences*. New York:
Routledge, 2001.

Freud, Sigmund. "The Joke and Its Relation to the Unconscious." In vol. 8 of
Standard Edition of the Complete Works of Sigmund Freud, edited by James
Strachey, 3–249. London: Vintage, 2001.

Fuchs, Cynthia. "*All of Us/Eve*." *Pop Matters*, October 13, 2003. http://www
.popmatters.com/review/eve-2003/.

Fuller, Jennifer. "Branding Blackness on US Cable Television." *Media, Culture, and
Society* 32, no. 2 (2010): 285–305.

Gamson, Joshua. *Freaks Talk Back: Tabloid Talk Shows and Sexual Nonconformity*.
Chicago: University of Chicago Press, 1999.

Gates, Racquel. "Keepin' It Reality Television." In *Watching While Black: Centering
the Television of Black Audiences*, edited by Beretta E. Smith Shomade, 141–156.
New Brunswick, NJ: Rutgers University Press, 2013.

Geertz, Clifford. *The Interpretation of Cultures*. New York: Basic Books, 2000.

Gitlin, Todd. *Inside Prime Time*. Berkeley: University of California Press, 2000.

Gray, Herman. "Black Masculinity and Visual Culture." *Callaloo* 18, no. 2 (1995): 401–405.

———. "The Endless Slide of Difference." *Critical Studies in Mass Communication* 10, no. 2 (1993): 190–197.

———. *Watching Race: Television and the Struggle for Blackness.* Minneapolis: University of Minneapolis Press, 1995.

Gray, Jonathan. "When Is the Author?" In *A Companion to Media Authorship*, edited by Jonathan Gray and Derek Johnson, 88–111. New York: Wiley, 2013.

Griffin, Horace. "Their Own Received Them Not: African American Lesbians and Gays in Black Churches." *Theology and Sexuality* 12 (2000): 89.

Gross, Larry. "Out of the Mainstream: Sexual Minorities and the Mass Media." In *Remote Control: Television, Audiences and Cultural Power*, edited by Ellen Seiter, 130–149. New York: Routledge, 1991.

Hall, Stuart. "Encoding/Decoding." In *Culture, Media, Language: Working Papers in Cultural Studies, 1972–79*, edited by Stuart Hall, Dorothy Hobson, AnColin Lowe, and Paul Willis, 128–138. London: Routledge, 1991.

———. "The Spectacle of the Other." In *Representation: Cultural Representations and Signifying Practices*, edited by Stuart Hall, 223–291. London: Sage, 1997.

———. "What Is This 'Black' in Black Popular Culture." In *Popular Culture: A Reader*, edited by Raiford Guins and Omayra Zaragoza Cruz, 285–293. London: Sage, 2005.

Havens, Timothy. *Black Television Travels: African American Media across the Globe.* New York: New York University Press, 2013.

Hawkeswood, William G. *One of the Children.* Berkeley: University of California Press, 1997.

Hemphill, Essex. "In Living Color: Toms, Coons, Mammies, Faggots, and Bucks." In *Out in Culture: Gay, Lesbian, and Queer Essays on Popular Culture*, edited by Corey K. Creekmur and Alexander Doty, 389–402. Durham, NC: Duke University Press, 1995.

Henderson, Felicia. "The Culture behind Closed Doors: Issues of Gender and Race in the Writers' Room." *Cinema Journal* 50, no. 3 (2011): 145–152.

Hilmes, Michele. *Only Connect: A Cultural History of Broadcasting in the United States.* 4th ed. Boston: Wadsworth, 2014.

Hinckley, David. "Ice Cube's *Are We There Yet?* Feels Like a Trip Viewers Have Already Taken with Stale Humor." *New York Daily News*, June 1, 2010. http://www.nydailynews.com/entertainment/tv-movies/ice-cube-feels-trip-viewers-stale-humor-article-1.180480.

Hunt, Darnell. "Making Sense of Blackness on Television." In *Channeling Blackness: Studies on Television and Race in America*, edited by Darnell Hunt, 1–24. New York: Oxford University Press, 2005.

Hunt, Darnell, Ana-Christina Ramon, and Zachary Price. *2014 Hollywood Diversity Report: Making Sense of the Disconnect*. Los Angeles: Ralph Bunche Center for African American Studies at UCLA, 2014.

Jackson, Ronald L., and Celnisha L. Dangerfield. "Defining Black Masculinity as a Cultural Property: An Identity Negotiation Paradigm." In *Intercultural Communication: A Reader*, edited by Larry A. Samovar and Richard E. Porter, 120–131. Florence, KY: Wadsworth, 2002.

James, Caryn. "New Minister in Town, No Angels in Tow: 'Good News.' UPN, Tonight at 9." *New York Times*, August 25, 1997. https://www.nytimes.com/1997/08/25/arts/television-in-review-778885.html.

Jet. "*All of Us*: TV Show Explores the Lighter Side of Blended Families." November 3, 2003, 58–61.

———. Singer Brandy Turns Actress in New TV Series *Moesha*." *Jet*, February 26, 1996, 58–61.

Jhally, Sut, and Justin Lewis. *Enlightened Racism: The Cosby Show, Audiences, and the Myth of the American Dream*. New York: Routledge, 1992.

Johns, Donna J., and Tahira M. Probst. "Sexual Minority Identity Formation in an Adult Population." *Journal of Homosexuality* 47, no. 2 (2004): 81–90.

Johnson, E. Patrick. *Appropriating Blackness: Performance and the Politics of Authenticity*. Durham, NC: Duke University Press, 2003.

———. "The Specter of the Black Fag: Parody, Blackness, and Hetero/Homosexual B(r)others." *Queer Theory and Communication* 45, nos. 2–4 (2003): 217–234.

———. *Sweet Tea: Black Gay Men of the South*. Durham, NC: Duke University Press, 2008.

Joyrich, Lynne. "Epistemology of the Console." In *Queer TV: Theories, Historic, Politics*, edited by Glyn Davis and Gary Needham, 15–47. New York: Routledge, 2009.

Julien, Isaac. "Black Is, Black Ain't: Notes on De-essentializing Black Identities." In *Black Popular Culture*, edited by Gina Dent, 255–263. Seattle: Bay Press, 1992.

Julien, Isaac, and Kobena Mercer. "Introduction: De Margin and De Centre." *Screen* 29, no. 4 (1988): 2–11.

Kimball, Trevor. "*The Game*: Season Four Starts on BET in January 2011." *TV Series Finale*, October 12, 2010. https://tvseriesfinale.com/tv-show/the-game-season-four-bet-18759/.

Knight, Arthur. *Disintegrating the Musical: Black Performance and American Musical Film*. Durham, NC: Duke University Press, 2002.

Kohnen, Melanie E. S. *Queer Representation, Visibility, and Race in American Film and Television: Screening the Closet*. New York: Routledge, 2016.

Kompare, Derek. *Rerun Nation: How Repeats Invented American Television*. New York: Routledge, 2004.

Kubey, Robert. *Creating Television: Conversations with the People behind 50 Years of American TV*. New York: Routledge, 2009.

Kus, Robert J. "Stages of Coming Out: An Ethnographic Approach." *Western Journal of Nursing* 7, no. 2 (1985): 177–198.

LaSala, Michael C. "When Interviewing 'Family': Maximizing the Insider Advantage in the Qualitative Study of Lesbians and Gay Men." *Journal of Gay and Lesbian Social Services* 15, no. 1–2 (2003): 15–30.

Law, Jeannie. "Kirk Franklin Tackles Abortion, Homosexuality on 'Breakfast Club': 'Bible Is Not Homophobic." *Christian Post*, June 6, 2019. https://www.christianpost.com/news/kirk-franklin-tackles-abortion-homosexuality-on-breakfast-club-bible-is-not-homophobic.html.

Lewis, Justin. *The Ideological Octopus: Exploration of Television and Its Audience*. New York: Routledge, 1988.

Liang, A. C. "The Creation of Coherence in Coming-Out Stories." In *Queerly Phrased: Language, Gender, and Sexuality*, edited by Anna Livia and Kira Hall, 287–309. New York: Oxford University Press, 1997.

Littleton, Cynthia. "Fast-Tracked Sitcom May Be Way of Future." *Variety*, June 26, 2012. http://variety.com/2012/tv/columns/fast-tracked-sitcom-may-be-way-of-future-1118055951/.

———. "UPN Pulls First 'Desmond Pfeiffer' Seg." *Variety*, September 30, 1998. https://variety.com/1998/tv/news/upn-pulls-first-desmond-pfeiffer-seg-1117480928/.

Lotz, Amanda Dyanne. "Segregated Sitcoms: Institutional Causes of Disparity among Black and White Comedy Images and Audiences." In *The Sitcom Reader: America Viewed and Skewed*, edited by Mary M. Dalton and Laura R. Linder, 139–150. Albany, NY: SUNY Press, 2005.

Martin, Alfred L., Jr. "Blackbusting Hollywood: Racialized Media Reception, Failure and *The Wiz* as Black Blockbuster." *Journal of Cinema and Media Studies* 60, no. 2 (forthcoming).

———. "Fandom while Black: Misty Copeland, Black Panther, Tyler Perry, and the Contours of US Black Fandoms." *International Journal of Cultural Studies* 22, no. 6 (2019): 737–753.

———. "FOX Formula 3.0? TBS, *Cougar Town* and the Disappearing Televisual Black Body." *Antenna*, June 18, 2012. http://blog.commarts.wisc.edu/2012/06/18/fox-formula-3-0-tbs-cougar-town-and-the-disappearing-televisual-black-body/.

———. "Generic Closets: Sitcoms, Audiences and Black Male Gayness." In *The Comedy Studies Reader*, edited by Nick Marx and Matt Seinkwicz, 222–237. Austin: University of Texas Press, 2018.

———. "It's (Not) in His Kiss." *Popular Communication*, 12, no. 3 (2014): 153–165.

———. "Notes from *Underground*: WGN's Black-Cast Quality TV Experiment." *Los Angeles Review of Books*, May 31, 2018. https://lareviewofbooks.org/article/notes-from-underground-wgns-black-cast-quality-tv-experiment/.

————. "The Queer Business of Casting Gay Characters on US Television." *Communication, Culture, and Critique* 11, no. 2 (2018): 282–297.

————. "The Tweet Has Two Faces: Two-Faced Humor, Black Masculinity and RompHim." *Journal of Cinema and Media Studies* 58, no. 3 (2019): 160–165.

Martinez, Dorie Gilbert, and Stonie C. Sullivan. "African American Gay Men and Lesbians: Examining the Complexity of Gay Identity Development." *Journal of Human Behavior in the Social Environment* 1, nos. 2–3 (1998): 243–264.

McBride, Dwight A. "Can the Queer Speak? Racial Essentialism, Sexuality and the Problem of Authority." In *The Black Studies Reader*, edited by Jacqueline Bobo, Cynthia Hudley, and Claudine Michel, 343–358. New York: Routledge, 2004.

McCune, Jeffrey Q., Jr. *Black Masculinity and the Politics of Passing.* Chicago: University of Chicago Press, 2014.

McGruder, Aaron. *The Boondocks: Because I Know You Don't Read the Newspaper.* New York: Andrew Keel, 2000.

Medhurst, Andy, and Lucy Tuck. "Stereotyping and the Situation Comedy." In *Television Sitcom Comedy*, edited by Jim Cook, 49–52. London: British Film Institute, 1982.

Mercer, Kobena. *Welcome to the Jungle: New Positions in Black Cultural Studies.* London: Routledge, 1994.

Miller, Quinn. "*The Dick Van Dyke Show*: Queer Meanings." In *How to Watch Television*, edited by Ethan Thompson and Jason Mittell, 112–120. New York: New York University Press, 2013.

Mills, Brett. *The Sitcom.* Edinburgh: Edinburgh University Press, 2009.

————. *Television Sitcom.* London: British Film Institute, 2005.

Minton, Henry, and Gary McDonald, "Homosexual Identity Formation as a Development Process." *Journal of Homosexuality* 9, nos. 2–3 (1984): 91–104.

Mittell, Jason. *Genre and Television: From Cop Shows to Cartoons in American Culture.* New York: Routledge, 2004.

Morley, David. *Television, Audiences, and Cultural Studies.* New York: Routledge, 1992.

Morreall, John. *Comic Relief: A Comprehensive Philosophy of Humor.* New York: Wiley-Blackwell, 2009.

Mullen, Patrick R. *The Poor Bugger's Tool: Irish Modernism, Queer Labor, and Postcolonial History.* New York: Oxford University Press, 2012.

Neal, Mark Anthony. *Soul Babies: Black Popular Culture and the Post-Soul Aesthetic.* New York: Routledge, 2002.

Newcomb, Horace, and Robert S. Alley. *The Producer's Medium: Conversations with Creators of American TV.* New York: Oxford University Press, 1983.

Ng, Philiana. "BET's 'The Game' Season Finale Draws 4.4. Million." *Hollywood Reporter*, March 30, 2011. http://www.hollywoodreporter.com /live-feed/bets-game-season-finale-draws-172832.

———. "*The Game* Series Premiere Huge for BET." *Hollywood Reporter,*
January 12, 2011. http://www.hollywoodreporter.com/blogs
/live-feed/game-season-premiere-huge-bet-70941.

Out. "The Big Gay TV Timeline." October 2012.

Owen, Rob. "Tuned In: TVOne, BET Debuts Sitcoms Slightly Used and New."
Pittsburgh Post-Gazette, January 7, 2011. http://www.post-gazette.com/ae
/tv-radio/2011/01/07/Tuned-In-TV-One-BET-debut-sitcoms-slightly
-used-and-new/stories/201101070169.

Palmer, Jerry. *The Logic of the Absurd.* London: British Film Institute, 1987.

Pearson, Roberta. "Cult Television as Digital Television's Cutting Edge." In
Console-ing Passions: Television as Digital Media, edited by James Bennett and
Niki Strange, 105–131. Durham, NC: Duke University Press, 2011.

Raley, Amber B., and Jennifer L. Lucas. "Stereotype or Success? Prime-Time
Television's Portrayals of Gay Male, Lesbian, and Bisexual Characters." *Journal
of Homosexuality* 51, no. 2 (2006): 19–38.

Rhimes, Shonda. "Shonda Rhimes Accepts Golden Gate Award at the
#glaadawards." Originally aired June 4, 2012. YouTube, 9:13. https://www
.youtube.com/watch?v=iHp2WvspFfs&t=331s.

Richardson, Valerie. "Gay Rights Left on Sidelines after Election." *Washington
Times,* November 18, 2008. https://www.washingtontimes.com/news/2008/nov
/18/gay-rights-abandoned-on-sidelines-after-election/.

Riggs, Marlon. "Black Macho Revisited: Reflections of a Snap! Queen." In *Out in
Culture: Gay, Lesbian, and Queer Essays on Popular Culture,* edited by Corey K.
Creekmur and Alexander Doty, 470–475. Durham, NC: Duke University Press,
1995.

———. "Unleash the Queen." In *Black Popular Culture,* edited by Gina Dent,
99–105. Seattle: Bay Press, 1992.

Romano, Allison. "Holding Its Own; BET Dismisses TV One as Serious
Competition." *Broadcasting and Cable,* April 14, 2004, 14.

Rose, Tricia. "Black Texts/Black Contexts." In *Black Popular Culture,* edited by
Gina Dent, 223–227. Seattle: Bay Press, 1992.

Rosenberg, Howard. "A Wobbly Start, That's for Sure." *Los Angeles Times,* August 25,
1997. http://articles.latimes.com/1997/aug/25/entertainment/ca-25696.

Ross, Marlon B. "Beyond the Closet as a Raceless Paradigm." In *Black Queer
Studies: A Critical Anthology,* edited by E. Patrick Johnson and Mae G.
Henderson, 161–189. Durham, NC: Duke University Press, 2005.

Rubin, Gayle S. "Thinking Sex: Notes for a Radical Theory of the Politics of
Sexuality." In *The Lesbian and Gay Studies Reader,* edited by Henry Ablove,
Michèle Aina Barale, and David M. Halperin, 3–44. New York: Routledge, 1993.

Ryan, Leslie. "Making Room for *All of Us.*" *Television Week,* May 5, 2003, 34.

Samuels, Allison, and Rick Marin. "Brandy: Keeping It Real." *Newsweek*, March 24, 1996. http://www.newsweek.com/brandy-keeping-it-real-175802.

San Filippo, Maria. *The B Word: Bisexuality in Contemporary Film and Television*. Bloomington: Indiana University Press, 2013.

Savorelli, Antonio. *Beyond Sitcom: New Directions in American Television*. Jefferson, NC: McFarland, 2010.

Scott, Darieck. *Extravagant Abjection: Blackness, Power, and Sexuality in the African American Literary Imagination*. New York: New York University Press, 2010.

———. "Jungle Fever: Black Identity Politics, White Dick and the Utopian Bedroom." *GLQ* 1, no. 3 (1994): 299–321.

Sedgwick, Eve Kosofsky. *Epistemology of the Closet*. Berkeley: University of California Press, 2008.

Seger, Linda. *Making a Good Script Great*. 2nd ed. Hollywood: Samuel French, 1994.

Mark Seliger. *TV's Gay Heat Wave*. December 2003. Photograph. *Vanity Fair*, cover, December 2003.

Sender, Katherine. "Dualcasting: Bravo's Gay Programming and the Quest for Women Audiences." In *Cable Visions: Television beyond Broadcasting*, edited by Sarah Banet-Weiser, Cynthia Chris, and Anthony Freitas, 302–318. New York: New York University Press, 2007.

Shomade, Beretta Smith. "'Don't Play with God!': Black Church, Play, and Possibilities." *Souls* 18, nos. 2–4 (2016): 321–337.

———. *Pimpin' Ain't Easy: Selling Black Entertainment Television*. New York: Routledge, 2008.

Simmel, Georg. "Fashion." *International Quarterly* 10, no. 1 (1904): 130–155.

Sinfield, Alan. *On Sexuality and Power*. New York: Columbia University Press, 2004.

Snorton, C. Riley. *Nobody Is Supposed to Know: Black Sexuality on the Down Low*. Minneapolis: University of Minnesota Press, 2014.

Squires, Catherine. "Rethinking the Black Public Sphere: An Alternative Vocabulary for Multiple Public Spheres." *Communication Theory* 12, no. 4 (2002): 446–468.

Staiger, Janet. "Authorship Approaches." In *Authorship and Film*, edited by David A. Gerstner and Janet Staiger, 27–60. New York: Routledge, 2003.

———. *Blockbuster TV: Must-See Sitcoms in the Network Era*. New York: New York University Press, 2000.

———. *Media Reception Studies*. New York: New York University Press, 2005.

Stanley, Alessandra. "A Rap Diva. A Painful Divorce. Cue the Laugh Track." *New York Times*, September 15, 2003. https://www.nytimes.com/2003/09/15/arts/television-review-a-rap-diva-a-painful-divorce-cue-the-laugh-track.html.

Stockton, Kathryn Bond. *Beautiful Bottom, Beautiful Shame: Where "Black" Meets "Queer."* Durham, NC: Duke University Press, 2006.

Sypher, Wylie. "The Meanings of Comedy." In *Comedy*, edited by Wylie Sypher, 193–255. New York: Doubleday, 1956.

Tartar, Andre. "XXL Magazine on Hip Hop Homophobia." *New York Magazine*, July 7, 2011. http://nymag.com/daily/entertainment/2011/07/xxl_magazine_on _hip hop_homoph.html.

Thompson, Robert J. *Television's Second Golden Age: From* Hill Street Blues *to* ER. Syracuse, NY: Syracuse University Press, 1997.

Tinkcom, Matthew. *Working Like a Homosexual: Camp, Capital, Cinema*. Durham, NC: Duke University Press, 2002.

Troiden, Richard. "Becoming Homosexual: A Model of Gay Identity Acquisition." *Psychiatry* 42, no. 4 (1979): 362–373.

Tropiano, Stephen. *The Prime Time Closet: A History of Gays and Lesbians on TV*. New York: Applause Books, 2002.

Turow, Joseph. "Casting for Television: The Anatomy of Social Typing." *Journal of Communication*, 28, no. 4, (1978): 18–24.

TV Guide. "Close-Up." August 23, 1997.

———. "Moesha." September 28, 1996.

UrbanDictionary.com. s.v. "Gay Ear." Last modified January 10, 2011. http://www .urbandictionary.com/define.php?term=Gay%20Ear.

———. s.v. "Right Earring Rule." Last modified May 1, 2011. http://www .urbandictionary.com/define.php?term=Right%20Earring%20Rule.

Walters, Suzanna Danuta. *All the Rage: The Story of Gay Visibility in America*. Chicago: University of Chicago Press, 2001.

———. *The Tolerance Trap: How God, Genes, and Good Intentions Are Sabotaging Gay Equality*. New York: New York University Press, 2014.

Wanzo, Rebecca. "African American Acafandom and Other Strangers: New Genealogies of Fan Studies." *Transformative Works and Cultures* 20 (2015). https://journal.transformativeworks.org/index.php/twc/article/view/699/538.

Warner, Kristen J. "ABC's *Scandal* and Black Women's Fandom." In *Cupcakes, Pinterest, and Ladyporn: Feminized Popular Culture in the Early Twenty-First Century*, edited by Elana Levine, 32–50. Champaign: University of Illinois Press, 2015.

Watkins, Mel. *On the Real Side: A History of African American Comedy from Slavery to Chris Rock*. Chicago: Lawrence Hill Books, 1999.

Wesling, Meg. "Queer Value." *GLQ* 18, no. 1 (2012): 107–125.

West, Candace, and Don H. Zimmerman. "Doing Gender." *Gender and Society* 1, no. 2 (1987): 125–151.

Williams, Raymond. "Base and Superstructure in Marxist Cultural Theory." In *Rethinking Popular Culture: Contemporary Perspectives in Cultural Studies*, edited by Chandra Mukerji and Michael Schudon, 407–423. Los Angeles: University of California Press, 1991.

———. *Television: Technology and Cultural Form*. New York: Routledge, 2008.

Wollenberg, Skip. "Viacom Acquires BET." ABC News. October 4, 2000. http://abcnews.go.com/Business/story?id=89100.

Wong, Curtis M. "This TV Sitcom Broke New Ground by Portraying a Same-Sex Wedding in 1991." *Huffington Post*, March 27, 2019. https://www.huffpost.com/entry/matt-baume-roc-gay-wedding-1991_n_5c9955afe4b0d42ce35fde67.

Yep, Gust A., and John P. Elia. "Queering/Quaring Blackness in *Noah's Arc*." In *Queer Popular Culture: Literature, Media, Film, and Television*, edited by Thomas Peele, 27–40. New York: Palgrave Macmillian, 2007.

Young, Alford A., Jr. "Coming Out from Under the Ethnographic Interview." In *Workshop on Interdisciplinary Standards for Systematic Qualitative Research*, edited by Michèle Lamont and Patricia White, 172–180. Washington, DC: National Science Foundation, 2008.

Zook, Kristal Brent. *Color by Fox: The Fox Network and the Revolution in Black Television*. New York: Oxford University Press, 1999.

INDEX

ALFRED L. MARTIN, JR., is Assistant Professor of media studies in the Department of Communication Studies and the program in African American Studies at the University of Iowa.

CPSIA information can be obtained
at www.ICGtesting.com
Printed in the USA
JSHW022012200521
14987JS00001B/15